D1015613

Mustache Shenanigans

Mustache Shenanigans

MAKING *SUPER TROOPERS* AND OTHER ADVENTURES IN COMEDY

Jay Chandrasekhar

DUTTON

DUTTON

An imprint of Penguin Random House LLC
375 Hudson Street
New York, New York 10014

LIBRARY OF CONGRESS CATALOGING-IN-PUBLICATION DATA
has been applied for.

ISBN 9781101985236

Printed in the United States of America
1   3   5   7   9   10   8   6   4   2

Set in Janson MT Std
Designed by Cassandra Garruzzo

*This book is dedicated to the many hilarious people
whom I've been lucky to call friends.*

CONTENTS

Mustache Shenanigans

INTRODUCTION

Every morning, at my small, private, suburban Chicago grade school, we all stood and said the Lord's Prayer. It didn't matter that I wasn't Christian. I loved it anyway. Afterward, we put our hands on our hearts and recited the Pledge of Allegiance. I loved that too. Saying those words, along with my 250 schoolmates, made me feel like I was part of a tribe. And I needed to be part of a tribe. Perhaps starting Broken Lizard (our own little tribe) is evidence of my continuing need.

They say that first-generation Americans are highly patriotic. For me, that was true, and it still is.

"We hold these truths to be self-evident, that all men are created equal."

As a kid, I loved those words. Those words meant that, though my sister and I were the only Indian kids around for miles, we were still equal. Eventually, I came to learn that Jefferson didn't mean for it to apply to *people who looked like me*, but thanks to Dr. King, President Johnson, and many others, equality became the law of the land—for everybody—and I intended to hold America to its word.

My parents were like propaganda specialists, instilling in me the idea that I could accomplish anything I set my mind to. *America was fair and rewarded hard work.* They drowned me in compliments, telling me how smart and good-looking I was, regardless of evidence that I was never much better than a B student and I was, objectively, an awkward-looking child. It's like their plan was to stuff me with confidence, hoping to stay ahead of the real (racist) world that was bound to break my heart. It worked, because if you looked at my grade-school notebooks, you'd find whole pages filled with the words "Jay the Great."

Even the name my parents gave me oozed confidence. My full name is Jayanth Jumbulingam Chandrasekhar, which literally translates to "Victorious Large-Penis Rising Moon." It's a family name. Though they never told me about the "large-penis" part. Instead, I found out at age twenty-five, from an Indian friend's mom, who saw "Jumbulingam" in the credits of our short film and burst into laughter. When my friend called to tell me the good news, I immediately called Mom.

"Does my middle name mean 'large penis'?" I asked pointedly.

She laughed. "Well, literally, sure, but it's really just a euphemism for power."

"You could have told me that earlier, Mom," I said, truly annoyed. "It might have been helpful."

When I was young, I didn't understand that my color might be a hindrance to my dreams. And like any kid, I had big dreams ... eventually. At age five, I wanted to be a garbage man so I could drive one of those *big red trucks.* Soon after, I decided I would follow my hero, Walter Payton, and be the starting running back for the Chicago Bears (yes, the first Indian in the NFL). Later, thanks to Muhammad Ali, I wanted to be the heavyweight boxing champion of the world (yes, the first Indian in professional boxing). President of the United States was a possibility (first Indian . . .). Heart surgeon was seriously considered (not the first Indian). My race didn't matter. In my mind, I was great, and if I worked hard, America would reward me.

Then I grew up and realized that life was more complicated. Inside, I was a red-blooded American, but that's not how I was perceived by strangers. For example, I was able to get girls, but only after months and months of a personality-driven long game. I had to use wit, charm, and friendship before lips ever touched, before I could get what my white friends just seemed to be handed. Racial reality didn't dissuade me from the idea that I could do great things, but it did teach me that I would likely have to work twice as hard as everyone else and would probably have to create my own path to get there.

Oddly, my being Indian is the very reason I made it in Hollywood—but not because there were racial quotas for Indians. No. In fact, it was just the opposite. When I was twenty-two, anyone with half a brain would tell you that my chances of making it as an actor, never mind a director, were less than zero. Because one had only to look at TV and movie screens to see that there wasn't a single Indian face on them. Well, there was one face: Ben Kingsley had played Gandhi and had won an Oscar for it. But Gandhi was also the *only* Indian Hollywood would ever make a movie about.

I had been acting in plays in high school and college, and I was playing leads. But the best I could hope for in *real show business* was playing the convenience store clerk, the cabdriver, or maybe a terrorist. Though, back in the eighties, Germans usually got those roles. *Ah, such an innocent time.* And I didn't want to play those characters. I wanted to play characters in movies that spoke like me, characters who had my own, *American,* accent. That, however, had never been done. All of the roles for Indians were small and/or accented and, frankly, played by white guys. When there *was* a major role for an Indian, Hollywood turned to a white actor and put him in *brownface.* Peter Sellers was great in *The Party*—"Birdie num num." Fisher Stevens played an Indian in *Short Circuit 2,* a film my dad counted among his favorites. When I asked him why, Dad said, "Because there's an Indian in it!"

When I told him that Fisher Stevens wasn't Indian, Dad shrugged. "Eh, it's as close as we'll get." Those words stuck with me. *This was America. Was that really the ceiling for me?*

Since Hollywood was never going to let me play with *their* ball, I made a decision to make my own ball. I started a comedy group and learned how to write and direct movies. My secret mantra became: *Oh, you don't think an Indian kid can do that? Watch me, motherfucker.* So I, along with my friends, wrote a script called *Puddle Cruiser.* We raised the money and shot it. I cast myself in the role of Zach, a college student, who spoke in my own voice. The film got into Sundance, as did our next film, *Super Troopers,* and the rest is history. Well, not exactly, but the rest—you're about to read the rest.

To be clear, being Indian isn't my whole story. Far from it. It's just something that informed my entry point into show business. Had I been white, I would have approached this business differently. I would have graduated from Colgate, moved out to Hollywood, auditioned as an actor, and hoped for the best. I never would have learned to write or direct, because I wouldn't have thought that I had to. Had I been white, I never would have made *Super Troopers, Beerfest,* or any of my other films, because I wouldn't have known how.

Look, I know I'm lucky—lucky to have this career, which pays me to write and direct movies and television shows, and sometimes to act in them. I've had enormous ups and some pretty big downs, but, on balance, I'm grateful—grateful, but not comfortable, because this business is not designed to make you comfortable.

Every week, someone asks me to talk to their son or daughter about their decision to pursue a career in show business. They want advice. "How did *you* do it? How did you get to make films with your college friends?" And while they're interested in *my* story, what they *really* want to know is, how can *they* do it? Here's what I tell them:

"Before you load your car for the drive to the left coast, let me warn you: At its core, this is a business of rejection. It's a massive ocean of 'no' surrounding tiny, almost invisible islands of 'yes.' Even *Super Troopers* endured seventy-five 'nos' before we got to 'yes.' And though Los Angeles is known for always being sunny, there's an unseen cloud of sadness hanging over it, filled with the dashed dreams of the millions of talented people who came out here and didn't get lucky. So if you can't handle rejection, *turn back now*. Give up while you still have the chance to do something else. Show business doesn't need you. We're doing just fine without you. Stop trying to take *my* job. There are enough writers, directors, and actors in Hollywood already. Go home. Your mama's calling! Fuck off!"

Still thinking about it? Okay, then read on. How one deals with the avalanche of rejection is the single most important determiner of who actually makes it and who doesn't. For some, hearing "no" is like blowing out their pilot light. For others, "no" is pouring gasoline onto a raging fire—a fire that won't go out until they finally beat the impossible odds and make something great (and financially successful) that they can shove up show business's ass.

Making films requires the creative skills you'd expect, but it also demands immense noncreative skills, like the ability to raise *all that money* and the savviness to work the studios' politics. Indeed, the most prolific filmmakers are also great wheeler-dealers who spend a thousand hours networking, negotiating, raising money, and arm-twisting for every hour spent writing, performing, and shooting. This career is a relentless hustle, because Hollywood is crowded, with too many smart, talented people pursuing the same dream and the same pool of entertainment investment dollars. And unlike in law or medicine, there are no college degrees required—no barriers to entry. Just ask the Kardashians, who are riding a wave of stardom on the back of a sex tape. That's who I'm competing with.

Filmmaking is the brutal intersection of art and commerce. When a painter messes up, he gets a new canvas and tries again. When a filmmaker messes up (loses money), he gets taken off the "hire list" and is relegated to "director jail." I've been there. It's not a nice place. Sustaining a career requires a combination of luck, persistence, talent, and more persistence. And when it all goes well, there's nothing quite like the connection you make with an appreciative audience who seem to be saying, "We get you!" Or in my case, "Who wants a mustache ride?!"

But when it goes poorly—and if you hang around long enough, *it will go poorly*—you have to be mentally tough to withstand the sometimes gleeful wave of negativity that is heaped upon you by the media and in the Internet chat rooms. You have to be able to look at yourself in the mirror and say, "I know why I made that film, and I'm comfortable with the decision."

What I'm talking about is *creative integrity*—something that is harder to come by today than ever before. And that's because the corporate beast that swallowed Hollywood whole seems willing to fund *only* superhero movies, vampire movies, remakes of classic films, and movies based on toys. So what do you do? Where's your *integrity* when you're convincing yourself that you always wanted to make *Monopoly, the Movie!* Maybe I'm being too cynical, but in the end, we'll be judged by the list of the films we made. And if you chase *potential* box office and forget what it was about your early films that made people pay attention, your audience will cry, "Sellout," and turn away.

I'm going to tell you the story of how I used a combination of persistence, luck, hard work, partying, charm, strategy, and (I suppose) talent to make it in show business.

The stories I tell as a writer/director are fiction. These stories are true. I am going to tell you about the test I gave myself, which would determine whether I would even attempt a *career in show business*. I'll tell you about how I met the members of Broken Lizard and about my early days as a stand-up. I'll tell you about the films I made, including *Puddle Cruiser, Club Dread, The Dukes of Hazzard,* and *Beerfest.* I'll tell you a lot about *Beerfest,* but more about . . . *Super Troopers.* I'll also tell you about *Super Troopers 2.* Spoiler alert! There won't be any spoilers!

I will also tell you what it was like to write, finance, shoot, edit, screen at Sundance, sell at Sundance, and have the film be released by a major studio. And I'll tell you lots of other stories, like about directing *Arrested Development,* and about the time I told the creators of *Entourage* that the first episode of their show was unrealistic, unfunny, and uninteresting. (It quickly became my favorite show.) You're not going to read a lot of gossip, but you will hear about my knock-down, drag-out, yelling fights with one of my childhood heroes, Burt Reynolds.

And I'll also tell you about smoking joints and hanging out with my other hero, Willie Nelson.

What follows is the story of a career that almost didn't happen, that by probability shouldn't have happened—an Indian kid trying to make it in Hollywood? *Ha! Good luck with that.* These are the stories of all of the nos I've heard, and how my pals in Broken Lizard and I hung around and turned them into yeses. It's a crazy business, but, man, do I love it.

When I started this book, I decided to write the stories exactly as I remembered them, regardless of how incriminating some of the details were. I figured I would go back later and "clean them up" for public consumption. But when I went back, I realized that the "clean" versions weren't actually . . . anything. So in the spirit of the great Richard Pryor and the great Howard Stern, I'm going to be honest. Aside from changing some names to protect the guilty, this is what really happened . . .

CHAPTER 1

Childhood

My life as an American was not guaranteed. In fact, my existence on this planet was the result of a cosmic fluke. My parents were both born and raised in the town of Chennai (Madras) in
South India. Both went to Madras Medical School, though they didn't
meet there.

My dad was the top student in medicine at the Madras Medical
School. Twenty to thirty students would show up each night to ob-
serve him in the obstetrics wards. He was so good that they nicknamed him "the Professor." His plan was to stay in India and become
a doctor, but during the practical portion of the exam, he answered a
single question wrong and, to the shock of his teachers, the external
examiner failed him. So now he had a year to kill before he could
retake the test. Or . . . Because of the Vietnam War, America had a
doctor shortage and was recruiting doctors from India. One of his
friends had an extra application for Queens General, so Dad applied
and got accepted. Off he went to New York City. A year later, he

moved on to the much more prestigious at the time Cook County Hospital in Chicago. My dad's friend Badri (short for Badrinath, *Beerfest* fans) followed him there. A year later, my mom graduated from Madras Medical School and chose Cook County because of *her* friendship with Badri.

My mom arrived at O'Hare Airport in the middle of the night, in the dead of winter, wearing only a sari (an Indian dress) and a light coat. As she waited for a cab in sub-zero weather, a homeless guy approached, begging for money for food. A soft touch, Mom gave him the only cash she had, a twenty-dollar bill. In a predicament of her own making, she called Badri collect to tell him that she had arrived and she needed cab fare. At two A.M., Badri and my father met my mom's cab outside the dorm and paid her fare. For my dad it was love/lust at first sight, because he whispered to Badri, "I'm going to marry that girl." Soon after, they started dating, and soon after that (months), my mom was pregnant. My parents got married in front of the justice of the peace, and then the fun started.

With my mom six months pregnant, my dad called back to India to tell his mother that he was "thinking" about getting married to a woman he had met in Chicago. My grandmother flipped. She had plans to *arrange* her doctor-son's marriage, so she told him that he was forbidden to marry my mother. Boxed in, my dad said he was going to marry her anyway and hung up. My grandmother was a wily woman who was used to getting her way, so she secretly called my mother and offered her $10,000 in diamonds to end her relationship with my father. My grandmother had a lot of diamonds. My mom was pissed and forced my father to tell his mom the truth. When he finally told Grandma not only that they were married, but that Mom was pregnant, my grandmother embraced reality, packed up, and booked a flight to America, where she would live for the rest of her life. She arrived in time for my sister's birth and became the full-time babysitter, which my parents needed because they were playing the real-life George Clooney and Julianna Margulies (yeah, I know Julianna M. played a nurse, but you get the point), treating gunshot wounds in Cook County's ER. Though my mother and grandmother made up, their relationship never quite got over its rocky start.

Two and a half years later, on April 9, 1968, my mom went into labor again. Dr. Martin Luther King Jr. had been shot five days earlier, and Chicago, or, more specifically, the area around Cook County Hospital, was on fire. My parents worried that they might not make it through the riots, but they did, and in a cosmic fluke, I was born. They'd been in America roughly five years at this point, and my father, likely at my grandmother's behest, suggested moving back to India to *raise the children properly*. But my mother balked, saying there was no way she was going back to a country where women were second-class citizens. I often wonder how different things would have been had Mom just gone along. I'm just guessing, but I imagine I would be skinnier and four inches shorter (because of Indian nutrition and pollution), I'd speak three languages (my parents both speak three), I'd have an Indian accent, I wouldn't eat beef, I might be vegetarian, and I'd probably be a doctor. Talk about a fuckin' fork in the road.

Three years later, we left our Oak Park apartment and moved to Willowbrook, Illinois. There was a lake in front of my house, along with a clubhouse, tennis courts, and a pool. I had a phenomenally active childhood and was part of a neighborhood pack of ten kids. In the summer, we'd fish, have raft fights, play baseball, and throw crab apples at one another. In the fall, we played a lot of tackle football. And in the winter, we played king of the hill on huge plowed snow piles, played broom hockey on the iced-up lake, and had snowball fights. In the summer we'd egg and toilet paper houses, and in the winter we'd hide in bushes and throw snowballs at passing cars. Punks.

The adults in the community ranged from late twenties to early forties, and, as it was the seventies, they partied. Everyone smoked cigarettes and drank a lot of martinis. My father was a lung disease doctor, and even he smoked half a pack a day. He eventually quit after my sister and I saw antismoking TV ads and bugged him into submission.

My best friend in the neighborhood, Jim, was a white kid with blond hair. We had been friends since we were three and used to walk around the neighborhood telling people we were twins. I was very close to Jim's family. His mom, a former flight attendant, treated me like one of her own, feeding me lunches of PB and J and Chef Boyardee ravioli.

My uncle was a neuroradiologist at Johns Hopkins in Baltimore and had a new baby, so my grandmother moved there to live with them. Meanwhile, Mom hired a Lithuanian woman, Irene, to look after us. Irene was friendly and strict, and she made us potato knishes. I still had a lot of freedom, including a house key, which I wore on a shoelace around my neck. After school, I came and went as I pleased, which was fine as long as I was home around the time my mom got back from work.

Mine weren't the typical hard-charging, grade-grinding Indian parents you hear about. They were warm, loving, philosophical people, and they were clearly influenced by the freedom vibe of their new country. It was a permissive environment and we took advantage of it. We dumpster-dived to collect knickknacks to decorate our basement forts. We played in an under-construction apartment building, leaping over the open fifth-floor elevator shaft. In the summer, we'd stop by our neighbor Mrs. Canfield's house for Popsicles. Afterward, Mr. Canfield would take us upstairs to show us his extensive handgun collection. Mr. Canfield was an ex–Chicago cop, and he'd let us hold guns while we peppered him with questions about how many guys he had killed. He never told us, though. He just smiled and laughed.

My friend Ted's dad took us skeet shooting, which was his family's obsession. His dad had huge bins of gunpowder and four shotgun-shell-making machines in his basement, and he put us to work making hundreds of shells for him. Ted's brothers were a few years older and introduced us to Monty Python, *Animal House,* Steve Martin's *Let's Get Small,* and Led Zeppelin. At my friend Mike's house, his older brothers taught us how to air-band and introduced us to the Beatles and the legend of Paul McCartney's death hoax. They showed us all of the *clues,* including how to play "Revolution Nine" backward to hear John Lennon say, "Turn me on, dead man, turn me on, dead man, turn me on, dead man . . ."

We watched *The Exorcist* and then held a séance using a Ouija board to raise the ghost of Ted's deceased sister. In the middle of the séance, Ted freaked out and started crying. And then my mom walked in and shut us down. Though Mom is a scientist, she felt strongly that we shouldn't mess around with the occult. She has a little of the Old World in her.

We played kick the can, spin the bottle, and truth or dare. And at age ten, we drank for the first time. A little context . . . Jim had a massive beer can collection in his basement. I'm talking floor-to-ceiling beer cans from all over the world. His father took us to beer can conventions, where he'd buy us rare cans. When we were ten, my friend Tom's parents took us on an overnight trip to Milwaukee to tour the Pabst Brewery. I got a red Pabst beer T-shirt, which I wore all the time.

I mention all of this to give you an idea of how much alcohol was part of the culture. *All* of the adults we knew drank, and no one ever spoke publicly about addiction. The funniest commercial on TV was for Miller Lite beer ("Taste great!" "Less filling!"). *Smokey and the Bandit*, a Burt Reynolds film about two guys who illegally drive Coors beer across state lines, was the biggest movie in America, and we loved it—lived for it. People drove drunk routinely and it was considered just fine.

We had tried sips of beer from stray cans at parents' parties, but what I proposed to my friends one day was about to take it to a whole new level. We had a full bar in the basement, and my idea was to take a plastic pitcher, fill it with ice, and then, to avoid detection, put a small amount of alcohol from each bottle into the pitcher. We poured in a little gin, vodka, whiskey, tequila, scotch, white wine, red wine, port, peach schnapps, and crème de menthe. Then we shook it up and walked around the neighborhood, drinking. Since it was from my basement, and I was out to impress, I drank the most, taking big guzzles. The next thing I remember, I was led, stumbling drunk, by my two pals to my doorstep. They rang the doorbell and left. They were ten and had curfews. I remember my mother opening the door. Then I remember being in the bathroom, throwing up as my mom comforted me. The next thing I remember, it was five P.M. the next day, and I woke up nursing my first, brutal hangover.

My parents filled in the rest the next day. Apparently, I threw up for about four hours. My mom was with me the whole time, taking care of me. She says I called her a "fucking bitch" a number of times. Yipes. My mom and I were close. We fought every morning, but only because she had to wake me up to go to school. I always woke up angry at being disturbed and lashed out. *What a prick.* That said, I loved my mom and respected her brain and was humiliated to have cursed her out.

My parents took me to dinner at an Italian restaurant that next night, where I assumed I would be hearing about my punishment: *Grounded for life* felt justified. I remember eyeing a glass of red wine on the next table and almost losing it. When I asked if I was being grounded, my dad said my hangover was punishment enough, and that based on my inability to even look at alcohol, it was clear that I wouldn't be doing it again. And I didn't, for another two years.

Ten was a transition age. I was playing a lot of sports, but also Dungeons & Dragons. My friends and I started using the word "boner," but I had no idea what it meant. When I asked my friend Mike, he scoffed, "You know, when your, uh ... thingy is like a stick ... in your pants."

"Ohhh yeah, stick, boner, sure, that," I murmured, but *wait—stick?* I figured it out soon after, when I had my first (and only) wet dream. I was starting to think about girls, but I wouldn't admit it. I had two posters on my wall—one was of Chicago Bears great Walter Payton, and the second was of Daisy Duke, in her tiny short-shorts. After the wet dream, I went about trying to accomplish *that feeling* again and stumbled onto masturbation. I hadn't yet discovered lotion, so I spent my days hammering away, dry handed and open eyed, staring at Daisy Duke's shorts. I wanted more of a connection, so I stood near the poster, jerking and kissing Daisy's lips. But even that wasn't enough, so I pressed myself up against the wall and humped the poster. It was a race between arousal and friction-generated heat, and arousal won when I finished onto the poster. I would have been ashamed if someone had walked in on me in the act, but it felt right at the time.

My father was a great tennis player, and he and I played a lot. I had a temper on the court, throwing my racket around like John McEnroe. It was bratty. Dad let it slide for a while, but then he told me he was embarrassed, so I changed my role model to Bjorn Borg. My game became calm, stoic, emotionless. During the summer between sixth and seventh grades, I went to John Newcombe's tennis camp in New Braunfels, Texas, where we bunked in group cabins and played eight hours of tennis a day. While I loved tennis, I was twelve, so I also loved masturbating. I considered myself a professional, finding time to work my root five to six times a day. I was jerking off so much, my dick looked like an hourglass. But the group cabins were cramping my schedule, so on the fifth day, I told the counselors I was sick and made a plan to spend the day making love to myself. I had since discovered lotion, and when everyone left for the courts, I searched the bathroom for some. But I couldn't find any. *Shit.* This was a problem. I couldn't exactly go to the camp store for lotion. They'd see right through that. And then I found it—a plump tube of Bengay. I was twelve. I had never had a muscle pain in my life. I didn't know any better. I squeezed a dollop into my left hand (I do everything else righty, but I jerk off goofy handed), lay back on my cot, closed my eyes, and started to disappear into my fantasy. You know, the one where my hot, blond tennis instructor in the too-short skirt keeps me after for special overhead lessons? *Ahhh.* All was good in the world, but then it wasn't. It started slow, like the frog in the slow-boiling pot of water. I cocked my head—*What's this?* Within thirty seconds, my dick was on fire. I leapt up, buck naked, with a hard-on, sprinting for the bathroom. I turned on the cold shower and used an entire bar of soap as I scrubbed the satanic cream off of my favorite stick. Relieved, I got out of the shower, toweled down, lay back down, spat in my hand, and went back to work . . . Nope—shooting, brutal, all-encompassing pain! Back in the shower, more soap. I got in and out of that shower all morning. After shower six, the pain wasn't gone, but it was tolerable. I still hadn't accomplished my goal, but I was too sore to touch it, so I just put on my tennis clothes and trotted out to the courts, claiming a miraculous recovery. To this day, I won't go near Bengay.

We played a lot of capture the flag in school. Since speed was currency among guys, and since I was the fastest kid in the class, I had a lot of guy friends. Girls, though, were another story. In fifth grade, I was the only kid not to be invited to a roller-skating party. That hurt. In sixth grade, my popularity with girls started to show signs of life. I talked to girls (friends) for hours on the phone, making my way with my wit. In seventh grade, I brought a large bag of Jolly Rancher watermelon candy to school, and magic happened. Like a Chicago politician, I passed the candy out at school, and my popularity spiked. So I kept bringing it. I brought two to three bags of candy a week for a couple of months. *Thanks, Mom.*

In eighth grade, I brought bags of balloons to school, which started *the water balloon wars.* I was the sole supplier, the Tony Stark of the eighth grade, and my popularity surged. I even got a girlfriend, Shannon, who I made out with in the school basement, during afternoon breaks—felt her up, outside the clothes, above the belt, all of that. Shannon was a cute, funny blonde with braces, and she was a fantastic first girlfriend.

I ran for president of the school and lost by six votes. Eighth grade was also the year when I started drinking again. This time, I drank in moderation, and just on sleepovers. Twelve is young to start drinking, but we were within the range of normal for suburban Chicago kids, so it didn't feel out-of-bounds. And drinking was as bad as it got. No one smoked cigarettes or even thought of smoking grass. We were deeply, morally opposed to both.

When it came time to apply to high schools, I took my B-plus average and my overinflated view of self and applied to the top high schools in the country—Exeter, Andover, Hotchkiss, and Choate. My father and I flew back east for the interviews, but my grades weren't good enough, and I was rejected by all of them. I decided I'd go to Hinsdale Central, a great public school a couple of miles from home, but my parents felt differently. My sister was already at a boarding school an hour north called Lake Forest Academy (LFA). I had applied there and was accepted, but I was reluctant because I loved the idea of going to school with my neighborhood friends. But my parents were insistent. They had both gone away to school young, and they assured me that I would love the freedom. Plus, they said, if I didn't like it, I could transfer sophomore year.

Going off to boarding school was a big unknown. On the night before I left, I drank with some of my neighborhood friends and eventually found myself alone with a girl from tennis camp who I had had a lifelong crush on. I was in love with her. She and I fooled around for the first (and only) time, and I ended up going down on her on a blacktop driveway. I don't know where the impulse to do that came from, since I had only been to second base up to that point. What can I say? I was a little animal. Thirteen was a messy, weird, nutty, and great year, and I was piling up new experiences and loving every minute of it. But I was leaving my neighborhood cocoon and things were about to get difficult.

CHAPTER 2

———

High School: A Narc's Tale

The most beloved sports team in the city of Chicago is the mighty Chicago Bears. Chicago is a tribal town, and being a Bears fan made me part of that tribe. For an Indian kid trying to belong, that was important. In the mid-eighties, the Chicago Bears were the roughest, toughest, most charismatic motherfuckers in football. My friends and I *all* wanted to be Walter Payton. I played a ton of tackle football in the yard, but when I joined a Pop Warner team in third grade, I quit after a week because the impact with pads felt different. Regardless, I still held on to the fantasy that I would one day be the starting running back for the Chicago Bears. So when high school started, I signed up again.

Football camp started in mid-August, two weeks before school began, so my best friend Van and I packed all of our stuff up and moved into the Warner dorm. Van's parents and my parents were close friends from medical school in India, so we had known each other from the time we were babies.

On the first day of practice, I ran the forty-yard dash in 4.5 seconds, which made me the fastest guy on the team—thank you very much. Our head coach was excited and put me in with the running backs. *Maybe my Chicago Bears dream wasn't so crazy after all.* Van, whose foot speed was a little slower, worked out with the linemen.

Practices were brutal—two-a-days in ninety-five-degree heat. We'd lose seven pounds of water weight in the morning practice, and another three in the afternoon. The ground was hard and crusty, which made tackling more painful. Our defensive coordinator, Coach Delaurentis (Delo), carried around a yellow whiffle ball bat, which he used to hit his linemen in their helmets when they made mistakes.

At night, our coach gathered us together to talk about the school's zero-tolerance policy. If you were caught with alcohol, drugs, or a girl in your room, you'd be kicked out—no second chances. If your roommate had alcohol or drugs and you didn't say anything, you'd be kicked out. Guilt by association.

On the first night, the freshmen gathered together in the TV room. When sophomore middle linebacker / co-captain Scott Jessman walked in, we all went silent. Jessman was an intimidating presence. He walked in, glowering, and grunted to signal that he wanted the prime seat in front of the TV. We moved.

On day two, while running with the ball, I was lifted off the ground and slammed hard onto my back. It was a clean tackle, but I jumped up, pissed, and shoved the tackler. He wasn't ready for it, so he fell over backward. He leapt up and ripped off his helmet to fight. It was Scott Jessman. Though other teammates restrained him, he stared at me, hard.

Back at the dorms, we wondered about when exactly he would come to kick my ass. But when I saw him in line at dinner, he just gave me a tough-guy nod, as though I'd earned his respect.

Every muscle hurt. We half-jokingly prayed for injury to avoid practice. *My kingdom for a broken arm.* We wondered how hard it would be to actually do it, so we laid our arms across a desk and karate chopped each other until we were bruised. Nothing cracked, so it was back to practice the next day.

On the third day, when the temperature was crawling up to one hundred degrees, Coach called for a water break. As we lined up at the garden hose, Coach Delaurentis held his linemen back: "*My linemen don't need water!*" Van smiled, though he was feeling anything but happy.

When our head coach went into his office, I followed.

As he sat at his desk, I walked in, offering my helmet. "Coach, I'm done."

He seemed ready for this. "Sit down, son." And then he gave "the speech." It was actually a pretty good speech, designed to stop quitters. It culminated with the words "Football will make you a better friend, a better student, and a better man."

I waited a second or two out of respect, and then exhaled. "Yeah, I'm gonna quit anyway." And I walked out.

Back at the dorm, I called Mom to come get me.

As I finished packing, Van walked in. He looked down the hall nervously and then shut the door. "We've gotta get out of here." He had quit too, though no one on the team knew it yet. But they did know about me, and he'd heard talk about guys kicking my ass. They were also talking about putting Bengay in my jockstrap. The last threat felt nonsensical, because why would I be wearing a jockstrap? I had *quit*! We didn't wait to clear it up.

We dragged our suitcases out to the woods and hid. Ninety minutes later, my mom rolled up in her pink Lincoln Continental Mark V. Relieved, we jumped into the air-conditioning and sped away.

On the ride home, I told my mom that it might be wiser if I just went to public school, but she wasn't having it. When I told my sister, Sandy, that the football team wanted to beat me up, she smiled. "Don't worry. I'll take care of it." And she did. She called her friend Maurice, who was a captain on the offensive line, and made it clear that I was not to be touched. And I wasn't.

A week later, I was back at LFA, ready to restart my freshman year. Van and I were assigned to a small dorm called New Hall, which housed eight guys, seven of whom were members of a minority group. Yep, we were in the minority dorm, a "safe space" for kids who might have trouble adjusting to life among the white majority. *Is that how they saw me?* Van and I had already assimilated, and putting us in New Hall was a form of "benevolent segregation" that I found humiliating. I wanted a John Hughes experience, but one where I felt like Ferris Bueller, not Long Duk Dong.

The racial makeup was as follows: a half-Asian, half-white-American kid, a Venezuelan, a Spaniard, two Indian American kids (me and Van), my Japanese roommate, Shinobu Takemura, a Greek American kid named Freddy Christophorus, and our resident adviser, Willie Wong.

Shinobu was a foreign-language student who spoke less than thirty words of English and couldn't have been nicer. But the poor kid was having trouble communicating, and I wasn't being very helpful. I didn't learn a single word of Japanese, and while I wasn't an overt dick to him, I didn't go out of my way to be friendly either. I had a different vision of high school. I wanted to make friends, drink beer, and hook up with girls, not teach English to a Japanese exchange student in the minority dorm. (I want to be clear: I wasn't anti-Japanese. I had had an eight-year crush on a Japanese American girl in grade school.) I was just homesick, and the girls weren't paying much attention to me. I'd gone from being a popular eighth grader to being a lost freshman *quitter*. And poor Shinobu was a stranger in a strange land who, as you'll see, drew a bad card when he got me as a roommate.

One day after school, I locked my door to jerk off. I won't tell you what fantasy I was working back then, but if they made a porno out of it, I'd be the thirteen-year-old Indian kid with the feathered hair, braces, and a hard-on.

Midjerk, the doorknob jiggled and a voice said, "Helloooooooo!?"

I stayed quiet. If it was Shinobu, he'd use his key to open the door and I would pretend that I was taking a nap. But no one came in, so after a frozen minute clutching my cock, I started back up again. Then I heard two voices snickering. It was Martin and Freddy, two guys from down the hall, who were also Van's roommates. "You're jerking off! We can hear the bedsprings!" I froze. *Slam! Slam! Slam!* They hit the door hard. I stayed silent, and when they eventually got bored and left, I finished up.

At thirteen, masturbating was *one of those things*. We were *all* doing it, but we didn't know that we were all doing it. When the topic came up, everyone just denied it. These guys had crossed a line for me, because the last thing I needed was them walking around school telling people that I was masturbating.

"Did you enjoy jerking your dick this afternoon?" Those were the words that greeted me when I walked into Van's room at study hall that night. Martin and Freddy sat at their desks smiling like fucking pricks.

"I don't know what you're talking about." I shrugged as Van smiled. (News was spreading.)

"We saw you through the keyhole!" they cackled as they mock

jerked off. I denied it, but it was a lost cause. If I had been capable of blushing, I would have. I headed back to my room, embarrassed and fuming.

The next week, Shinobu developed a nickel-size erupting boil on his cheek. I eyed it with trepidation, worried that it might be contagious. *Chicks would really dig me then, right?* Of course it wasn't, but I was thirteen.

A few days later, after school, I went back to my room, but the door was locked. I slid my key in, but when I tried to push open the door, I could feel a body against it. I heard whispered laughter and then noticed the towel that had been shoved in the crack under the door. I smelled smoke—not cigarette smoke. *Could it be pot? I had never smelled it before, so maybe . . . ?*

Not sure what to do, I wandered down the hall to Van's room. Fifteen minutes later, my door opened and a very stoned Shinobu, Martin, and Freddy tumbled out.

This is a hard story to tell, because I'm decidedly not the hero of it. And sure, I drank alcohol, but I was very anti-drug at the time. All of us freshmen were. On top of that, LFA had a guilt-by-association policy. Now, I don't want to make too much of that, since I was smart enough to know that that rule was probably bogus and that I would never be kicked out for my roommate smoking pot. But it was just more ammunition. I was pissed about being in the minority dorm, I was pissed about having a Japanese roommate with a boil, and I was pissed about getting busted jerking off. Now all three of my nemeses had smoked pot together . . . in my room.

I wanted those guys gone, so I went to my resident adviser Willie Wong's room to knock over the first domino. Willie was a cool guy from Taiwan, with glasses and a Taiwanese accent. I told him what had happened and that I was there only because I was worried about getting kicked out. *I didn't want to tell on them. I had to because of, you know, guilt by association.* I laid it on thick—probably deserved an Oscar. (No, I know they don't give Oscars to guys who look like me. I know.)

Willie listened, nodding. He was taking this seriously. Then he said, "Don't worry. I'll take care of it."

I paused. Something about that answer didn't sound right. "So they're really getting kicked out?" I asked, sounding like I didn't want them to get kicked out.

Willie shook his head. "Don't worry. I'll give them a warning."

I left Willie's room in a panic. *If Willie only gave them a warning, not only would I not be rid of Shinobu, but they'd all know that it was me who had ratted them out. That would make me a quitting, masturbating narc.* I was in too deep, so I went over Willie's head.

In the morning, before school started, I slipped into Vice Principal Andrews's office, sat down across from him, and told him everything.

Half an hour later, I left Adviser Period and walked down the hall, where a crowd had formed outside Mr. Andrews's office. Through the glass windows, I could see Shinobu, Martin, and Freddy sitting in chairs and looking worried. Mr. Andrews motioned to his secretary, who closed the drapes on the gathered crowd.

"What's going on?" I asked a sophomore I kind of knew.

"Martin, Freddy, and that Japanese guy are getting kicked out . . . for something," he said.

"How do you know?" I asked.

"Because the secretary closed the drapes. When the drapes close, you're gone."

They were gone. After school, I wandered back to New Hall to witness the carnage. Not a trace of Martin, Freddy, or Shinobu was left. I felt guilty, though by now I had actually convinced myself that I had done the right thing. *What choice did I have? How unfair would it have been for me to get kicked out?* There were rumors around school that I was the narc, but I denied it. And though a few people pressed the case, most let it drop. And with time, everyone moved on.

One night that winter, I woke up covered in a thick, pungent-smelling liquid. I came to the quick realization that someone had *thrown up on me*—all over my hair and face. I leapt out of bed, reeling, as vomit shot out of my mouth. Then I stumbled, through my own puke, into the hallway, where I threw up into a garbage can. Doors opened, and I saw people confused and smiling. When I went to the bathroom to shower, I realized that I hadn't been thrown up on at all. In fact, the thick liquid was just gel toothpaste. As a prank, someone had squeezed a bottle of toothpaste on me, and my brain had turned it into vomit. I never found out who did it, but I knew in my gut that it was payback for my narc job, and I knew I deserved it. (To this day, gel toothpaste still smells like vomit to me.)

That spring, in response to my grousing about school, my sister suggested that I audition for the school musical. She had been in the chorus of the fall show and said it was fun. I had never imagined acting, but I showed up to the audition, because, why not? They didn't cast me—not even in the chorus.

The next year, Van and I roomed together in Bates dorm, which housed about fifty freshman and sophomore boys. Living in Bates with everyone else made a world of difference. Soon I met a beautiful junior named Leslie and we started dating. Leslie was a boarding student from Grand Rapids, and she spent a lot of weekends signed out to my house. (A boarding student could go to a classmate's house for the weekend if the host parents gave their permission.)

Leslie and I were wild about each other, and as teenagers with raging hormones, we were sometimes reckless. In biology class, I would pull up my chair directly behind hers and slide my hand into the pocket of her flowing skirt so I could finger her.

One Saturday, she came over to my dorm to chat. The campus was empty, so we started making out through my window, which quickly progressed to her giving me head. Recognizing our exposure, Leslie crawled into the window and then into my bed. We were so hopped up, we didn't care that we were risking expulsion. After about an hour, one of my teachers knocked on my door. Leslie hid in my tiny closet while the teacher and I chatted for thirty minutes. When he finally left, Leslie crawled out of the closet, no longer in the mood.

Those days were fun. Van started playing electric guitar and became so enamored with Jimi Hendrix that, in addition to buying a brown Fender Stratocaster, he also permed his hair into an Afro and started wearing loose psychedelic shirts and bell-bottoms. He used to sit on his twin bed, plug in, and jam for adoring freshmen.

He had also started smoking pot. One Saturday, Van told me that he and a guy named Phil were heading out to the woods to get high. *Did I want to come?*

I was curious, but how could I reconcile it with what I had done? I went.

Lake Forest Academy was located on 250 acres of forested land, so if you wanted to do something illicit, you only had to take a short walk before you were in deep woods.

As the school disappeared from view, Phil packed a bowl, lit it, and took a big hit. Van followed, and then it was my turn.

"What's gonna happen?" I asked.

Van smiled. "It's like getting drunk, but kinda less. But don't worry, most people don't even feel it the first time."

I lit the pipe and inhaled smoke for the first of what would be thousands of times—cough-cough-cough-cough!

"You've gotta cough to get off!" Phil laughed.

Van was right. I kind of acted spaced-out, trying to "make it happen," but nothing did.

The next day, after the Bears game, we went back out to try again. This time, it worked.

Now, I didn't turn into a pothead. I never got high and went to class. I never even got high on school grounds again. To me, it was too risky. I smoked occasionally, on weekends, and only if someone else had it.

I knew I was a hypocrite. I had destroyed three guys' lives over a joint, and now I loved it. Yeah, that weighed on me.

That fall, auditions for the musical *Brigadoon* were posted. I didn't have a burning desire to act, but I was pissed about being rejected the first time, so I went. *I'll show them.* This time, I landed a part as a Scottish clansman. I wore a kilt, sang in the chorus, and even had two lines. Holy shit, I fucking loved it. After that, I auditioned for every play that was offered.

Here's the thing. The best actors in Hollywood spent some years acting onstage, in plays and musicals. Period. End of story. No debate. I know that a lot of young people think that musicals are nerdy, or they feel that they're too cool for plays, but if you want to be a great actor, go audition. Not only will you learn how to really act, but you'll have a phenomenal time too. To give credit where it's due, if my sister hadn't pushed me to audition, there never would have been a Broken Lizard.

In my junior year, I auditioned for more plays, and my roles got steadily bigger. I played Gangster 2 in *Kiss Me Kate*, and then Biff in *Death of a Salesman.*

Leslie and I broke up, and I was now dating a thrill-seeking actress named Courtney, who I was in a couple of plays with.

Courtney lived on the sexual edge. With ten minutes to curtain, she would pull me into a private dressing room and insist on having sex. You could hear the crowd chattering away just on the other side of the wall. We used the withdrawal method, so when I pulled out, her dress bore the brunt of it. We tried to wash it, but there was no time, so she went onstage that way.

Courtney was turned on by the prospect of getting caught. I used to sleep over at her house, and she would sneak into my room and crawl into bed to have sex, with her parents sleeping just twenty feet away. One night, after sex, I turned on the light, and it looked like someone had slaughtered a deer on the bed. She had had her period, and there was a three-foot circle of red on the sheet. Panicked, I started stripping the sheets, while Courtney just laughed.

Ten minutes later I was standing in the laundry room downstairs, watching the evidence melt away in the suds, when Court walked in buck naked. I whispered for her to get her clothes on, but she said (at full volume) that the only way she would be quiet was if we had sex on the washing machine. *High school.*

Lake Forest Academy assigned a lot of homework, so we stayed up late. The next day, we'd be tired, so we'd take NoDoz to get through our nightly study hall. When someone said that snorting it would make your brain process it faster, we tried it. I don't know if it worked, but it was fun, and we were idiots, so we started snorting everything—aspirin, Pixy Stix; some fool even snorted foot powder. From there, we progressed to Kensington snuff (snortable tobacco), which burned the inside of our noses and caused tears to run down our faces. We loved it.

We didn't hide it. Our doors were open and we'd cut lines of NoDoz right on the desk. When our befuddled study hall monitor walked into our room and eyed three fat white lines sitting there, he looked startled. "Oh gosh."

"It's NoDoz," I said. "It works faster this way." But he just covered his eyes and moved on.

How did all of this lead to cocaine? Cocaine was a big part of the culture back then, with *Scarface, Miami Vice,* the New York Mets players Keith Hernandez and Darryl Strawberry, Studio 54, and so on. Here's the thing. Doing coke wasn't something we aspired to. Coke-heads were portrayed by Hollywood as losers. They wore flashy clothes, they talked on huge cell phones, they were insincere, and they were all addicts. Sure, we were snorting everything in sight, but no one had talked about doing cocaine.

Then, one night, our friend Jimmy walked into my room. We were cutting lines of NoDoz and offered Jimmy a bump. He just laughed. "What're you messin' around with that kids' shit for? I can get you the real stuff." I remember feeling the same way I did about marijuana: curious. We asked questions: *What was it like? Won't we get addicted? Won't we have heart attacks?* Jimmy assured us that all of that was bullshit. He had done it a couple of times and it was fun. The thing is, we liked Jimmy. He was a smart, small, Irish American kid, with a big fucking brain and a great sense of humor. If Jimmy said it was fun, it was fun.

A few weeks later, Jimmy and I and three other pals crowded into the bathroom at a motel party and had a mind-bending ball.

Before I go on, let me say that I'm not an advocate of teens doing drugs. I'm just talking about what it was like when I was a teen. The adult exaggerations about the dangers of drugs had the opposite of the intended effect on us. Most of us tried them anyway and realized that the claims were bogus, which made us disregard any future claims made by adults. If the goal is to prevent teens from trying drugs, scaring them with false info is not working. Maybe being honest about drugs could work. The real dangers are from heroin and legal pain-killers. I've known a number of comics, including Mitch Hedberg and Harris Wittels, who died young from heroin. That shit's real, and that's where the focus should be. Okay, I'm stepping off of my soapbox.

My roommate and good friend Franklin was a wealthy kid from Hong Kong whose parents owned a two-bedroom condo on the thirty-third floor of a high-rise on Lake Shore Drive. Franklin's parents lived in Hong Kong and Toronto and had only been to the apartment four or five times in the six years they owned it. There was almost no furniture in the place, but the view of Lake Michigan was breathtaking. I was part of a tight-knit group of five guys. On weekends, four friends would sign out to my house, even though we were really going to be spending the night at Franklin's. With my braces and fake ID, I'd buy eight cases of Michelob, which we would roll past the doorman on luggage dollies. The parties were massive, unsupervised, and glorious.

That spring, I played the part of Tony in *West Side Story*. Still, the idea of acting as a job hadn't entered my mind.

One day in acting class, our teacher, Carla Maria Sullwold, told us about an opportunity to be extras in a film in Chicago. Carla was the head of the theater department and is the person most responsible for encouraging me to act. She was passionate and believed in our little core group of LFA actors.

The next week, we all went down to Navy Pier to be extras in the film. The name of the film was *The Color of Money*, and the director was Martin Scorsese. I didn't know who he was at the time, but I did know who Paul Newman and Tom Cruise were. The film was a sequel to *The Hustler*, and we played spectators at an Atlantic City pool tournament.

I watched Scorsese, Cruise, and Newman standing in the center of the set, talking, joking, and laughing about shots and performance and whatever. They were in the most important conversation in the room, and I was dying to hear what they were saying. I wanted to be in that conversation. That was the moment when I finally thought about it—when I finally thought about a career in show business. And today, when I'm on set talking to an actor about his or her performance, I know that I'm there. I'm in that "most important" conversation.

I actually got to meet Paul Newman—sort of. When he went to the bathroom, I followed him, pretending like I had to go too. I caught up to him, and when he looked up, there I was. I introduced myself. He was cool, but our meeting ended when a production assistant intercepted me and told me not to talk to the actors.

In the end, I made the final cut. When Paul Newman quits the tournament, he walks by a crowd of people, and there I am, standing in front, in a coat and tie, with a look on my face that was supposed to say, "No, Fast Eddie! Why?"

It was my first professional job, for which I was paid a dollar.

That spring at prom, we rented a suite at the Hyatt, where we partied after the dance. We had a scare when our friend Jimmy had a seizure from what I imagine was too much coke. He was on his back, convulsing, with his eyes rolling back. My friend the future valedictorian was thinking quickly when he stuck his wallet between Jimmy's teeth to keep him from biting his tongue off. Later, the bite-marked wallet would become the hit of the weekend. That should have been the wake-up call, but since we were sixteen, it wasn't.

On the last day of junior year, I was getting ready to host the school talent show when my friend Mike from Little Rock, Arkansas, popped in. He said he had bought a couple of pills of this legal psychiatric drug called ecstasy, which he said they called "the love drug." *Did I want to do it at the party later?* (There was an off-campus rager at a kid's house in Lake Forest, so Mike and I planned to pack our rooms up after the show and head straight there.) I eyed the pills and said, "Sure, why not?"

Then Mike said, "No time like the present," and he swallowed one. I didn't like to do *anything* on campus, but since the school year was over, and it was *legal*, I swallowed mine. (Three weeks later, MDMA would be classified as a Schedule 1 drug).

The show started, and I was onstage cracking jokes, but I wasn't feeling anything. That would change. Thirty minutes in, as I was introducing a rock band, *whooosh!* It hit me. I stood in the wings, smiling my face off, as the band played the wildly inappropriate Eric Clapton (J.J. Cale) song "Cocaine." There were parents and teachers at that show. I don't know what the band was thinking. I don't know what any of us were thinking.

After the show, Mike and I headed back to the dorm to pack—it was a fun pack. Halfway through, one of our teachers stuck his head in to tell us that it was too late to leave and that we should just stay there for the night. I assured him that we were signed out to my house and that we'd be done soon.

He disappeared, and ten minutes later, the headmaster walked in. "Sorry, fellas, I'm shutting you down. You're staying in your rooms tonight."

I politely explained the situation, but he said he didn't care. *His decision was made.*

Mike lost it, throwing down a towel and screaming, "This is fucking bullshit!" before disappearing down the hall. Now, you have to understand: We were seventeen, school was over, and the biggest party of the year was happening less than five miles away. *We really wanted to go.* But I could tell we had a losing hand, so I calmly told the headmaster that we were sorry and we'd be fine to stay there for the night. Though we didn't know it at the time, this was the beginning of a cascading series of events that would rock our senior years.

That summer I worked for a couple of weeks valeting cars at an antiques show. Flush with a few hundred in cash, my new girlfriend, Lyssa, and I went downtown to the Hard Rock Cafe to have lunch. Afterward, on our way to my car, a guy approached.

"Hey, wanna buy a video camera?" You know, I actually did. Watching Scorsese work had put a bug in my head. Did I know that I wanted to be a filmmaker? *An Indian kid from the Chicago suburbs? Naw. That wasn't realistic. But still, it might be fun to shoot stuff.*

The guy introduced himself as Leon, and he told me that his friend worked in a camera store that had stocked too many of last year's model of Sony cameras. He needed to get rid of them to make room for the new ones, so he could get me a great deal—$300 for a $1,000 camera.

I negotiated. "How about two hundred?"

Leon rubbed his chin. "That's a thousand-dollar camera! Two seventy-five!"

"Two twenty. Take it or leave it." Hardball.

Leon's finale: "Shit, I'm barely makin' a profit, but okay, fine. Meet me here tomorrow at one P.M. and we'll do the deal." We shook hands and exchanged numbers.

The next morning, my mom woke me up, nervous. "Jay! There's a ... *Leon* on the phone for you? He says you're buying a ... video camera?"

I jumped off the couch and grabbed the phone as Mom looked on, worried. Leon was all business. "We on for one o'clock?"

"I'll be there," I said, and I hung up.

Mom jumped right in. "Don't buy a stolen camera! I'll buy you a camera if you want one."

"Mom, I'm not! I earned this money. I want to buy my own camera. It's totally legal."

Since arguing with a seventeen-year-old when he's made up his mind is a waste of time, she gave up.

When I got downtown, I parked on the street, where Leon was already waiting. "You got the money?"

I patted my pocket. "Where's the camera?"

He motioned me over to his car, where he popped his trunk. There it was—a brand-new Sony video camera in a box. I handed him the money, but as I reached for the camera he stopped me. "Pop your trunk. Let's make this fast." Leon grabbed the camera, quick walked to my car, and put it into my trunk. As he slammed it shut, a siren wailed off in the distance. Leon looked up as though the siren was for us. "We better move."

I headed straight to Van's house, where we laid the box on his bed and started tearing away the packaging. The images of the camera that were on the box fell away. They were just *cutout* pictures. The box was blank.

"That's weird," Van said.

"Eh, it might just be how they . . . Maybe they rebox it when they put it in the store," I said, as though that made sense.

We opened the blank box and started scooping out packing peanuts. Then Van pulled out a brick. "What the hell?"

I held on. "They probably just do that to keep everything weighted correctly on the truck."

He kept digging, and then he pulled out another brick—and then two more.

I sat there on the bed with the empty box, the packing peanuts, and four bricks, dumbfounded. It felt like the scene in *The Sting,* after Redford and Newman "shoot" each other and then pop up alive, signaling the con no one saw coming. In this case, *I* had been the mark. My first attempt at becoming a filmmaker had not gone well.

When I told my dad what had happened, he shook his head. "If it's too good to be true, it's not true."

In the summer before my senior year, I swung by school to say hi to my history teacher, Mr. Turansky. Turansky was a phenomenal teacher, certainly the best I've ever had. When teaching about the French Revolution, he delighted in telling us that since we were children of the elite, our heads would have been on pikes in 1789 France. While we were talking, my headmaster walked by, and then, a few seconds later, he doubled back. "Hey, can we have a chat? My office?"

Sitting across the desk from me, my headmaster dropped the bomb. "I know that you and your friends are snorting cocaine."

Whoa! What the hell? He had no proof of that! "I've never done cocaine in my life!" I said, defensively.

"That's not what I hear."

"Well, that's an unbelievable accusation. What proof do you have?"

He shrugged. "Perception is reality." That steamed me. *Was this America?* "Your friends are gone."

I looked at him, not comprehending. "Mike McGuire?" (Mike from Little Rock.)

"I didn't invite him back."

Measured, but angry. "Why not?"

"Because he had bad grades . . . and he's doing cocaine."

"He's never done cocaine in his life!" I lied.

"And your friend Van, he's got a decision to make. It's either rehab or he's gone." I was in shock. Van really had never done cocaine. Sure, he had bad grades, but it was because he spent study hall socializing.

The headmaster nodded. "Your grades saved you this time, but trust me, we're watching and we're going to catch you." I walked out.

I immediately drove to Van's house, where he told me that he was leaving LFA and enrolling in Catholic school. Just like that, our gang of five, who were so ready to have the best senior year ever, had been reduced to three.

When school started in the fall, I was more careful, but not much more. One weekend, we signed out to my house but stayed downtown at my roommate Aaron's, where we threw a party. On the train back to Lake Forest, I headed to the snack car to grab a coffee. At the other end of the car, walking toward me, three years after I had narc'd on him, was none other than Shinobu Takemura. He had a crew cut from the military school that I had made him go to. We approached. As we stood there, face-to-face, in the aisle of the speeding train, my first thought was: *Does he know martial arts?*

I spoke first. "Shinobu, I am *so* sorry—"

Shinobu interrupted. "No, I sorry. I so sorry." Then, in a crushing moment, he *Japanesed* it, going down to his knees and touching my feet in a gesture of apology and respect.

I needed to stop this. "No, man, I was wrong. I smoke pot now."

Shinobu stood up, strong. "No pot. Never pot!"

He wasn't getting it, so I mimed smoking a joint. "Me. I smoke pot."

His denial was intense. "No! Never! Never!" He still didn't get it. Did he think I was mocking him? I needed to explain to him that I now liked drugs, so I pretended to snort a line of coke. "Me! Cocaine!"

Shinobu almost exploded. "Me! No cocaine! No pot! No! No!"

This was going nowhere, so I just said, "I'm sorry, man, sorry." But I knew that my apology was lost in translation.

In October 1985, the Chicago Bears, in the cockiest move in American sports history, released their video, *The Super Bowl Shuffle,* three months before the Super Bowl was to be played. The Bears practiced in Lake Forest, but the media attention was so overwhelming that they needed to hide out. So they came to LFA and practiced on our field. The entire student body showed up to watch. The Bears were cockiness personified, and we loved it.

Some of that cockiness must have rubbed off on me when I chose which colleges to apply to, because my list was preposterous: Harvard, Yale, Dartmouth, Columbia, Stanford, Northwestern, and Brown. No safety schools. None.

A feeling of worry was oozing through my brain when I ran into my girlfriend, Lyssa, in the hallway. *What if I didn't get into any schools?* I asked her if she had any extra applications to . . . *any schools at all.*

At her locker, she pulled out five clean applications. For two, the deadlines had passed, but for three others, Boston College, Boston University, and Colgate, I had until the next day. I filled them out, repurposed my Brown college essay, ran around begging for last-minute recommendations, and sent them off before the deadline.

The *only* three schools I got into were Boston College, Boston University, and Colgate. Loaded with plenty of "good" Indians, the Ivy League had completely rejected this junky old B+ Indian.

I had seen only the brochures for the three schools, so I was having a hard time making a decision. When Lyssa committed to Boston College, I started to lean toward there, but I put a pin in it for a few weeks to think.

In March, I signed out three friends to my house, though we spent Friday night at Aaron's place, downtown. Thanks to an inside source, Dean Rosen caught wind of our weekend sign-out scheme and tried to bust us. She called my parents at two A.M., waking them up and asking if we were, in fact, home.

"Of course, and they're sleeping," my mother said. "Like I was before you woke me up." Like Burt Reynolds, my mother has an anti-authority streak a mile wide.

A week later, the school announced a room search. The routine went as follows: A room search was announced for the next evening. Next, whoever had anything illegal in their room waited for lights-out and then marched their beer or pot out to the woods, where they'd stow it under a pile of leaves. After the search, everyone would go back to the woods to gather up their stuff. You had to be an idiot to get caught. And yet it happened. A guy across the hall got busted with six empty Pabst beer cans under his bed.

I never kept *anything* illegal in my room, because it just wasn't worth the risk. During study hall, Aaron and I evacuated our room while two deans performed their search. When we got back to our room, everything looked undisturbed, except for a framed picture of an Indian god that my grandmother had given me when I was a baby. It lay there on my desk, with the glass, the picture, and the frame taken apart.

Aaron looked at me. "Wow, kinda rude not to reassemble your picture of *God!*"

The next morning, I arrived at Adviser Period to find the rest of the advisees filing out. Assuming it was canceled, I waved to Turansky and said, "See ya."

But he stopped me. "We have to go see Mr. Andrews."

"About what?" I asked.

"I can't tell you."

As we walked through the empty school hallway, my mind raced. *What could they possibly have on me? Did one of the rehab narcs rat me out? That would be fitting.*

Outside Mr. Andrews's office, Turansky nodded, sadly, and said, "We'll talk later."

As I entered Mr. Andrews's office, I looked up to see the secretary closing the drapes to the large glass windows. *What the . . . ? Nobody survives the closing of the drapes.* "Why are you closing the drapes?!" I blurted out, but she didn't answer. Realizing I was in some major fucking trouble, I said, "What's going on?"

Like a Bond villain, Mr. Andrews swiveled his chair toward me, dramatically slapping a small folded piece of paper onto the desk. "Would you mind telling me what *this* is?!" I examined the folded paper. It was a small, handmade envelope, about two inches wide by an inch and a half high, and it was folded in *exactly* the same way as a snow seal (cocaine envelope) is. On the envelope was some Sanskrit writing. I looked up at him and smiled. Andrews didn't know it yet, but I was about to checkmate him. "It's vibhuti."

"What?!" he said, annoyed by my smirk. I opened the envelope. Inside was some whitish gray powder. To his shock, I dipped my pinky finger into the powder and licked it.

Nearly jumping out of his chair, he yelped, "Don't do that!" *Did this kid really just taste cocaine in front of him?*

"What?" I said, innocently. "It's Indian religious ash. It's called *vibhuti.* You put it on your forehead during Hindu religious ceremonies. What did you think it was?"

He was flustered and didn't want to answer.

I leaned back in my chair, cocky. "Where'd you find it? In the frame of that picture my grandmother gave me when I was a baby? The picture of Lakshmi, the Hindu god of prosperity?" I was getting pious now. *Sure, I was a big-time Hindu.* This was like game one of the

1995 basketball playoffs, when the New York Knicks were celebrating their six-point win over the Indiana Pacers before the game had actually ended. And then the assassin, Reggie Miller, scored eight points in the final nine seconds to pull off one of the most shocking comebacks in sports history. I was Reggie Miller. Mr. Andrews was the Knicks.

He stammered, "We're going to send that to the lab!"

"Great! Send it!" I said gleefully. "Can't wait to see the results." It must have infuriated him to sit across from this glib little bastard in a coat and tie, so he tried to retake the advantage. "Well, you're going to be suspended until we get the results back."

That was his second mistake. In history class, I had learned about a little something called the US Constitution, and I had a hunch that it was probably illegal to suspend me without evidence. *Innocent until proven guilty, right?* That said, it was a private school, and they had thrown out my friends without proof. I left his office, indignant. "This is bullshit!"

I went straight back to Turansky's classroom. He had a surprised look on his face. When they close the drapes and kick you out, they don't let you walk around to say good-bye.

I told him what had happened and that they were suspending me while they waited for the lab results.

He shook his head. "They can't do that."

What happened next was surreal. Turansky enlisted a group of sympathetic teachers to preemptively protest the constitutional violation Mr. Andrews was about to perpetrate. That the ash was associated with Hinduism made the situation even more radioactive. *Did the school really want to mess with this?*

It turned out they didn't. In the end, they backed down—way

down. I received a written apology letter from Mr. Andrews and Ms. Rosen stating, unequivocally, that they were wrong. They also called my parents, expressing remorse and asking forgiveness.

From then on, I was untouchable at that school. And, believe me, I took advantage of it.

When I entered high school, I came in as a cool eighth grader. But when my freshman fall started, it felt like I had regressed back to fifth grade, back to the kid who wasn't invited to the roller-skating party. Quitting the football team didn't help. And then, telling on my roommate sunk me deeper. But by spring semester, I came out of it and thrived again. If you really examine it, I just had one really bad semester, and three unsuspecting fourteen-year-olds paid the price. And for that, I'm sorry.

As graduation approached, it was time to make a decision. Still having only ever seen a brochure, I chose the highest-ranked college of the three. I chose Colgate.

CHAPTER 3

Race in America: A Case of Mistaken Identity

Before I go on, let me talk a little bit about race. I wouldn't describe my life as being defined by racism. In fact, it's just the opposite. Mine has mostly been a life of racial acceptance. That said, to truly understand my story, it's important to have a little perspective about where I stand in the racial body politic.

Indians (real Indians) have always occupied an odd position in America, thanks to Christopher Columbus's enormous screw-up. When Columbus was looking for a shortcut to India, he sailed west and landed in the Bahamas. Rather than admit that he was horribly lost, Columbus doubled down. Despite finding neither elephants nor spices, he declared victory to his crew! *Welcome to India, motherfuckers!* This mistake set in motion one of the longest-running cases of mistaken identity the world has ever known, one that endures to this day. Because if you're going to claim that you found India, you've naturally got to call the people there "Indians." And though Columbus would never set foot in North America, like a virus, his mistake spread north, where all of the natives there would come to be known as *"American* Indians." Interestingly, his mistake was almost a whole lot worse, because when Columbus landed in Cuba, he thought he had found China. Had Columbus's name for *those* people stuck, Fidel Castro would have been the father of the Chinese revolution.

As a kid, when I told people I was Indian, one out of ten would sincerely ask me, "What tribe?" I always said Cherokee since they seemed the most badass. When my friends and I played the game cowboys and Indians, guess who *always* played the Indian? I would have liked to have played the cowboy once in a while, but being the Indian just sort of made more sense.

I was always jealous that they were called "American Indians" because I truly felt that that name more accurately described me than the name "Indian American." I've been to India three times and I identify with it, but I was born and raised here, so I'm American first.

Indians in America had a good thing going. We were doctors, computer programmers, lawyers, diamond brokers, deli owners, motel owners, and cabdrivers. Indians studied hard, worked hard, and reaped the benefits. To me, being Indian was cool. India is the world's largest democracy, and it has a thriving film business. Our ancestors invented meditation, chess, yoga, peaceful resistance, and sitting cross-legged. Oh, and we invented Tantric sex. We'll hump you for days but never come. (I never understood that one.) Sure, we were portrayed as asexual nerds on TV, but that always set the bar low, so you only had to be *half* cool to outperform expectations.

And then 9/11 happened. After that, Indians were stuck in another case of mistaken identity, though this one was nightmarish. It began on September 15, 2001, when some dipshit in Arizona, in an attempt at revenge for 9/11, mistook a Sikh Indian gas station owner for a Muslim and shot him dead. Oops. (I'll tell you more about that fun post-9/11 time later.)

Before 9/11, Indians were defined by the peaceful legacy of Mahatma Gandhi. After, because of our appearance, we were stuck in between. We kind of looked like the bad guys, and yet the bad guys also hated our guts—as evidenced by the 2008 Mumbai Massacre, in which Pakistani terrorists mowed down 164 Indian civilians. Before 9/11, no one was afraid of Indians. After, some of our less sophisticated citizens looked at Indians and wondered, *Are those guys dangerous too?* We're like the koala bears that get slaughtered because some grizzlies killed a kid in town. *Maybe it's just safer to kill all of the bears.*

Sometimes, racism is just the natural expression of tribalism. Humans are more comfortable spending time with people who look like them. That's what makes the American race experiment so challenging. By accepting minorities from all over the planet, America is swimming against deep, ancient tribal currents. Some of us are attempting to make a new tribe—a multiracial, American tribe. But when a small minority of one group of immigrants starts shooting and blowing the rest of us up, we all revert to ancient, darker instincts.

During college, I brought my (white) girlfriend home for Thanksgiving. In a private moment, my lovely, sweet, amazing grandma pulled me aside and said, "How come you never date Indian girls?" I told Grandma that I *would* date an Indian girl if I met one that I liked. She just sighed and said, "Well, it's okay to marry a white girl; just don't marry a black girl." Was my dark-skinned grandmother racist? It's the only racist thing I ever heard her say, but yes, that's the definition of racism. But look, there are almost no black people in India, so . . . We excuse that generation, don't we? The point I'm trying to make by selling out my grandma is that racism in America is far more complex than the picture that the media paints, where all white people are racists and all minorities are innocent angels. Sure, there's plenty of racism coming from white America, but there's also lots of racism in minority communities. So none of us should get a free pass.

Let me be superclear. All racism is not alike, and Indians don't have to deal with the same challenges that African Americans do. When I was in high school, I took the Calculus 2 Advanced Placement class but only got a 3 (out of 5) on the final test, which meant I didn't get college credit and had to retake it at Colgate. Since I had *just* taken the class, the redo was easy—so easy that I stopped going to class and would only show up for quizzes and tests, which I aced—100 percent. The math teacher was convinced that I was a prodigy and apologized for how easy his class was for me. One day, he asked me to accompany him to a math conference in New York City. He wanted to show off my mind. I demurred, telling him that I loved math, but only as a hobby. *All Indians are good at math?* Racism!

In 1964, a year after my dad arrived in New York, he and his (Indian) buddy took a cross-country road trip from NYC to California, along the southern route. When they went into a Georgia diner, the waitress told them that they didn't serve blacks there. When Dad informed her that they were Indian, the waitress apologized, profusely, and brought them dinner. *Fucking nuts!*

Indians are not discriminated against when it comes to housing or education, and we're not being shot by the police at routine traffic stops. And that's a bit unfair, considering that African Americans (and Jews and whites) paid with their blood in the civil rights movement. *They* fought hard and won critical rights for all minorities, including the right to marry whomever we wanted, to vote, and to be educated alongside everyone else. *That's* important to remember when you think it's okay to be antiblack, all of you new immigrants.

CHAPTER 4

Colgate to Chicago: Making Strangers Laugh

Okay. Back to the story. As my parents and I drove to Colgate, they ribbed me about the number of cows we'd seen on the way. *Those weren't in the brochure.* Since I was going there no matter what, I hadn't bothered to visit after accepting. When we pulled onto campus . . . Wow. Colgate is located in hilly Hamilton, New York, a small town three hours north of New York City. Founded in 1890, Colgate's got stone buildings, a beautiful quad, and ivy-covered walls, and it's built on a huge hill. In 2010, *The Princeton Review* ranked Colgate the most beautiful campus in America. I agree.

A small school of around 2,750 students, Colgate is the epitome of *having it both ways.* Academically, it ranks in the top twenty schools in the country, but it is also a famous party school. As the legend goes, in the seventies, *Playboy* ranked the top party schools in America. Florida State was ranked number one. Next to it was listed Colgate,* with the asterisk explaining, "Colgate is the real number one, but it's a professional drinking school, so it can't officially top our list." I say that not to brag, but to give you some sense of the environment that Broken Lizard was born in.

As beautiful as Colgate was, I arrived hell-bent on leaving it. In my mind, Colgate was merely a way station. I was going to get good grades and transfer to Brown, where I thought I belonged. In addition to being in the Ivy League, Brown was also in Providence, a good two hours closer to Boston, where my high school girlfriend, Lyssa, was in school. Freshman fall was fun, but I didn't really engage. Weekends were spent in Boston with Lyssa, or with her visiting me. Still, I fell in with a group of freshmen and formed some cool friendships. When all of my friends decided to head down the hill to fraternity rush, I tagged along for the fun of it. Truthfully, I was anti-fraternity at the time. The way fraternities had been portrayed in the culture had made them seem elitist and dorky to me. And when my pals all put in bids at the same house, Beta Theta Pi (or Beta), I put in a bid too, as an insurance policy. When my first-semester grades averaged a B-, Brown let me know that my brown magic act wasn't Ivy League material, and they rejected me a second time. Beta Theta Pi, however, accepted me, so I was now a fraternity pledge and about to be part of a new tribe.

The American fraternity experience in the eighties and nineties was highly influenced by the hilariously subversive John Landis film *Animal House.* Whether it was chugging entire bottles of whiskey, toga parties, road trips, or Blutarsky's grade point average of 0.0, the film was a pushed-for-comedy view of the American Greek system. Our fraternity had about a hundred guys and was devoted to a philosophy of relentless, hilarious personal comedic insult. We called it "the House of Pain." We did all of the things you would think. We drank competitively, smoked tons of grass, and had lots of parties—cocktail parties, beach parties, toga parties, and parties without themes. We had a dinner called "Beef and Blow," where we prepared funny, insulting limericks about one another and delivered them as we gobbled roast beef and pounded immense amounts of cheap red wine. It was creative, silly, and often brilliant. That sense of humor, specifically as it relates to rhythm, the willingness to go dark, and the evolution of jokes over weeks, months, and even years, had the most influence on Broken Lizard's collective style of humor.

Hollywood portrays fraternities as all-white, wealthy, racist, raping gangs of alcoholics. Movies need villains. And while it's probably true that fraternities *used* to be like that, so, too, were a lot of America's institutions. Our house had five Indians, three African Americans, five Asians, and multiple Jewish guys, Catholic guys, and WASPs. After we graduated, four guys came out as gay. The first one to come out was an enormously popular guy named Andy, who remained enormously popular afterward. At the time, the word "faggot" was used liberally both in our house and everywhere else in America. On the night he came out, I asked Andy how much *I* had used the word. He said I had used it some but not as much as others. By the time the other three guys came out, we had all transitioned away from that word, entirely. Does that fit the "fraternity stereotype"?

I spent my first two years at Colgate splitting time between majoring in pre–World War II German history, minoring in philosophy, smoking grass, drinking Milwaukee's Best, hitting on beautiful preppy girls, and acting in plays. I fell hard for the place.

Because of race-blind casting in the theater, I was often (enough) cast in the lead, and like a lot of young, egocentric fools, I started to actually consider a career as an actor. Up until then, I had planned to be a heart surgeon, like the wisecracking Hawkeye Pierce from *M*A*S*H*, but that dream went up in smoke when I got a C- in organic chemistry my freshman year. My physician parents weren't terribly surprised.

"If you are going to be a doctor, you have to want it with every fiber of your being. And getting a C- in organic chemistry suggests you probably don't," my father said dryly.

Then my mother jumped in with some life philosophy. "One-third of your life is spent sleeping, one-third working, and one-third with friends and family. You better love your job if you're going to spend that much time doing it."

I've since talked to my parents about the moment I told them I was going to try to be an actor. My dad said that he and Mom thought it was a terrible idea, but they pretended to be supportive because they had decided that I was going to be an experiment. They were just going to let me do what I wanted, and then we'd all see what happened. They had the instincts of Indian tiger parents, but they suppressed them. I made it slightly easier by telling them that if it didn't work out in a couple of years, I'd apply to law school.

But was a career in acting a real possibility? I felt like I had some talent, but getting laughs from friends in a school play wasn't enough to justify making such an enormously high-risk career bet. So I decided to give myself a test. Most Colgate juniors spend a semester studying overseas. I decided to head to Chicago, where I planned to perform improv comedy on real stages, in front of real audiences. Only if I could get strangers to laugh would I be willing to give acting a try. And if I couldn't, then my plan would be to follow in my sister's footsteps and go to law school.

So, the fall of junior year, I enrolled at Loyola University Chicago, where I took classes during the day. Now all I had to do was figure out how to break into the Chicago comedy scene. I had a small in, through my high school friend James. Before I go on, I should tell you that James didn't owe me shit. In high school, James and I had been in tons of plays together and had formed an incredibly close friendship. When he started dating a charming, ridiculously beautiful girl named Lahna, the three of us hung out all the time, including going to Prince's film *Purple Rain*. Lahna and I were boarding students, so we hung out in the evening, without James, which then turned into a months-long affair. Terrible, I know, but we were sixteen and we fell for each other. Since Lahna and James were in love, you can imagine how humiliating and awful it was for James when he inevitably found out. I apologized and apologized, and after about a year, he amazingly started to forgive me. The trauma of this event burned into me *the most important* lesson of my life: Don't mess around with friends' girlfriends (or wives). What can I say? High school was a time of intense learning for me. *You don't come out of the womb fully baked.*

James was taking classes and performing at the Improv Olympic (the iO), a theater started by Del Close, one of the early members of Second City. Del was a legend in comedy circles, known for being one of the early shapers of the style of sketch and improv comedy that would go on to dominate in shows like *Saturday Night Live* and *SCTV.* Just glancing at a list of his students tells the whole story: John Belushi, Dan Aykroyd, Bill Murray, John Candy, Tina Fey, Shelley Long, Bob Odenkirk, Tim Meadows, Jon Favreau, Andy Dick, Jeff Garlin, Stephen Colbert, Dave Koechner, Chris Farley, and many, many more.

If you want to see Del, watch the film *The Untouchables,* where he plays a crooked city alderman who tries to bribe Kevin Costner. Del was brilliant, odd, and intimidating. When he died, legend has it that he bequeathed his skull to the Goodman Theatre to be used in future productions of *Hamlet.*

Del taught a mixed class, which included rookie improvisers like myself, as well as top-level guys like James Grace, Dave Koechner, and Chris Farley. Farley was a brilliant improviser and was always the funniest, most talented person in a room full of funny and talented people. Watching Chris perform night after night was truly something special. The Chris Farley I knew in Chicago played it super-smart, combining his immense physical gifts with a razor-sharp brain that always seemed to be one step ahead. Chris played leading men, detectives, teachers, and scientists, not just the big men. This is only my opinion, but the true scope of Farley's brilliance wasn't used enough on *SNL*. Yes, he was amazing on the show, but he was pushed, too often, toward jokes about his weight. (*Only my opinion; don't kill me.*) And the reason is because of the difference between stage and screen. The stage has embraced non-type casting, so actors of different races and weights can play any role. On-screen, the worlds we create are so real that it feels strange to cast against physical type. And so, in the movies, the handsome white guy gets the girl, the black guy is street-smart, the Arab guy is a terrorist, the Italian guy is mobbed up, and the Indian drives the cab. Kevin Heffernan, who shares Farley's gift of girth, told me that one of his reps once told him never to lose weight because "fat is funny and funny is money." Types.

Del Close taught a long-form improvisation style called the Harold, in which a five- to ten-person team gets a suggestion from the audience and then performs a thirty-minute, entirely improvised show inspired by the suggestion. For example, if the suggestion was "hot dog," you might see sketches where the actors played hot dogs in a package or were hot-dog vendors at a Cubs game. When performed by an experienced team, the Harold is an almost religious experience, where the players form a "group mind" and communicate wordlessly, anticipating where the joke is going. But when performed by rank beginners, like my team, the results were usually thirty minutes of grinding hell for the audience.

My time in Chicago was fun. We drank a lot, smoked a ton of grass, and occasionally went harder. I was twenty years old and I was a bit of a wild animal, taking real pride in the volume of my substance intake. One night, I dropped acid with some guys from one of the top improv teams, which included Farley. We were flying, barhopping, and nearly breaking ribs from laughter. Eventually, we stopped in to *At the Tracks*, the bar where our performance stage was, to have a drink. We were parked at the bar, drinking it dry, when I noticed some of the guys making their way toward the stage. Soon enough, they were all onstage, tripping their faces off, asking for a suggestion. A suggestion was thrown out, and Farley and the rest of the team performed a forty-five-minute, fully improvised show that was one of the funniest I've ever seen.

The relationship between drugs, alcohol, and comedy is complicated. Certainly, the great unlocking agent is marijuana and some of the funniest stuff ever was written in that altered state of mind. Broken Lizard has written our fair share of jokes that way, including the "meow" joke and the resurrection of Landfill as his twin brother, Landfill 2. Yes, the vast majority of writing is done sober, but smoke with the right group of people who are all vibing on the same idea, and magic can happen. But let me be clear. Smoking pot every day won't get you my job. The heavy lifting in scriptwriting requires an immense amount of structural outlining—work you simply can't do in anything but a clear state of mind.

When I listen to old-timers lecture us on how it was okay for *them* to smoke grass and do coke and write comedy, but no one else should,

I cringe. So I'm not going to judge my twenty-year-old self. He was fun and loved the nightlife.

And certainly there are people, like Chris, who went off the rails with alcohol, coke, and the harder stuff. And while it's sad to have lost him, it doesn't diminish how fun it was to party with him. Chris, in a bar, was a blazing ball of fun who was so full of life. I remember, fondly, spending a Saturday afternoon doing lines, drinking beers, and cracking hours and hours of jokes with him. We actually videotaped the whole thing. I have no idea where that tape is—it's probably in some dusty box in a basement in the Midwest. On reflection, while Chris's death was not entirely shocking, it was quite sad.

It's a complicated topic. I've been close to some people who have had serious substance abuse issues, people who seemed to be wired that way by their genes. But if I'm being honest, the vast majority of people have no trouble with alcohol and drugs at all, which is hard to tell because the public conversation seems to be *only* about addiction.

I heard a *Saturday Night Live* original cast member talk about cocaine use at the show, and he said, "We didn't know that cocaine was addictive. Addiction wasn't a thing back then. We just knew it was fun, it helped you stay up late, and you wanted more."

Eventually people did get addicted, though, and the eighties addiction/recovery culture was born. When my friends and I first got into it, we had heard about addiction, so we looked at alcohol and drugs with a wary eye—we knew the dangers of overdoing it.

Look, if you're young and reading this, me telling you not to try alcohol and drugs is fine and responsible, but you're probably gonna do what you want to do anyway. So what I will say to you that you should listen to is: Take these substances very seriously, because if you have the addictive gene(s), recognizing it early may save you from a life of hardship, seclusion, and possibly early death. And listen to your body. If your body is telling you that something doesn't agree with you, don't do it. Your friends may give you shit, but trust me, they'll move on when they realize you don't care. Don't drive, fight, or go to work or school high. Go to school, learn, do your homework, and become as smart as you can. The most successful comedians and writers are well-read and *learned* how to write. Acting like a stoned goofball is fun and sometimes funny, but it won't help you make it in show business long term.

Okay, enough of the lectures. Back in Chicago . . . My experience performing improv with my newbie team wasn't paying off. We weren't getting laughs, and it didn't look like they'd come before I had to head back to Colgate. I decided sketch might be a better idea for me, so I went to Second City to see if I could take classes there. But Second City required an audition to take classes, and since I was in town for only a few more months, they wouldn't grant me an audition. It became clear that if I was going to pass my "career test," which was to get laughs from strangers, I was going to have to go it alone. I was going to have to do stand-up.

Damn it.

The first stand-up I remember seeing was Bill Cosby on *The Tonight Show*. (Sigh.) After that, I became obsessed with Steve Martin's album *Let's Get Small,* which I listened to on repeat. When I saw the film *Richard Pryor: Live in Concert,* a show he did in Long Beach, California, I remember thinking, *This feels real.* That one performance is the best recorded stand-up act of all time, because it captured Pryor's immense charisma, his crackling brainpower, his perfect timing, and his courage to be dead honest about topics no one else was willing to tackle. That Pryor was black meant something to me, even if it was in a subconscious way. Sure, there were no Indians doing this job, but Pryor and I shared the same skin color, so maybe . . . ?

His riff on taking acid manages to simultaneously be honest, emotional, bizarre, and hilarious. Later, Pryor talks about being so high on coke that he went outside to his driveway and pulled a gun on his car. He shot the engine and the car said, "Fuck it." When the cops came, Pryor went inside because, as he said, "They don't kill cars. They kill nig-gars!" If you aspire to be a stand-up, watch that film.

In 1980, Eddie Murphy joined *Saturday Night Live* and broke the country's mental chains to the original cast. In 1982, I saw the tough and hilarious film *48 Hrs.* The film starred Eddie Murphy and Nick Nolte and is still my favorite film of all time. When I heard Eddie Murphy was coming to Chicago with his *Delirious* tour, I begged my dad to take me. We sat in the back row of the balcony of the Chicago Theater, and it was otherworldly. That show had a massive impact on my young brain. *Was this really a job?*

What makes someone think they can step onto a stage and make a room full of strangers laugh? I'd always gotten laughs from my pals, so I *thought* I was funny, but standing on a stage with a microphone and a light in my face sounded like a nightmare. But my test was my test, so I had to either make strangers laugh, or start applying to law school.

I looked through my journals, which Del had asked us to keep, and found a couple of ideas I thought I could turn into a stand-up act. After a week of writing, I grabbed a copy of the *Chicago Reader* and found an open mic at a dive bar in Lincoln Park called the Matchstick. I had ten minutes of material, which I rehearsed until it was rote.

On Tuesday, I drove to the club and put my name on the list. The MC told me I was going up fifth, and my stomach started to churn. I went to the bar and ordered a Tom Collins, which inexplicably was my drink at the time. I downed that and hit the bathroom, where I took a liquid nerve shit. For the next fifteen years, I would take one of those before *every* stand-up show I'd ever perform.

Afterward, I went back to the bar, drank another Tom Collins, and lit a Camel Light—bars were fun back then! I rolled through my act one more time as the fourth comic wrapped up his set. It was time for my stand-up debut. I pressed record on my cassette player and exhaled as the MC grabbed the mic. "Ladies and gentlemen, please welcome to the stage . . . Jake Chandler!"

Okay. I admit it. I had a stage name—actually I had a couple of stage names. After I'd gone up a couple of times as Jake Chandler, a woman in the audience approached me and told me she thought I should just be myself. So I changed my stage name to Jay Chandras. I was convinced that I wouldn't make it in show business with my thirteen-letter *Indian* name. Sure, Schwarzenegger had fourteen letters, but he was already famous from weight lifting when he started acting, so he had no choice. Krishna Pandit Bhanji changed *his* name to Ben Kingsley. Even Fisher Stevens's name isn't Fisher Stevens—it's Steven Fisher. Not a big revelation, but vaguely interesting, right?

That night, when I took the stage, I was so nervous that I raced through all ten minutes of my material in five minutes. The jokes weren't brilliant—I did something about how you could tell what car someone drove by their race. Meh. The performance wasn't brilliant either, but it wasn't bad, and I didn't bomb. There were silences, but there were also laughs—strangers' laughs. Enough that I became hungry for more. Over the next four months, I went up several more times, which resulted in a mix of great shows, good shows, and some outright bombs. The strange thing was that the act was exactly the same each time. It was the same jokes, but with wildly different responses. *What the hell?* How could I eliminate the crushing bombs, where an audience stared at you with seeming hatred, refusing to make any noise beyond a bored sigh? I looked for patterns. And then I found one.

Open mics usually have about ten comics, with each performing for about five to seven minutes. The MC makes a list and tells you exactly when in the night you're going to go up. If he told me I was going up ninth, I'd hit the bar, and when the sixth comic would take the stage, I'd go outside and start pacing around, running through my jokes, looking like a madman. Then I would slip back in, with my set fully memorized, and take the stage. When I did this, the result would usually be either an average show or an outright bomb. However, when the MC told me I was going up ninth but then accidentally called me up fourth, I had to scramble. I knew my act, but I hadn't had time to fully memorize it. I'd take the stage and perform my jokes, but because my jokes weren't fully memorized, my performance had a fly-by-the-seat-of-your-pants spontaneity to it, which usually resulted in big, constant laughs.

So wait. The better prepared I was, the worse I did? And the less prepared I was, the better I did? What kind of fucking business was this?

When I told my mother about my discovery, she had some advice.

"Stop memorizing your act. Just be confident in your jokes and let 'em fly!" I told her that felt like skydiving without a chute and she said, "What's the worst that can happen? They don't laugh? Embrace it. You need to love the good and the bad equally, because life is full of both. If you can love standing onstage with a mic in your hand and a light in your face, in front of an audience of people who hate you, then you'll be bulletproof." This from the woman who forbade the use of umbrellas in our family because "the rain is as good as the sun." (To this day, I still don't use them.)

The next time I went up, I was bombing. Desperate, I tried to create some fake excitement by telling the crowd that I would improvise some jokes on any topic they threw out. "Any topic that begins with the letter *A*." I already had three minutes on automobiles, so when someone said something like, "Armadillo," I planned to say, "Okay, 'armadillo' begins with *A* and so does 'automobile,' so here are some jokes about automobiles." It was lame, I know. When I asked the crowd for an *A* word, a woman yelled out, "Asshole!" It was the first laugh of the night, and it was at me—only seven more minutes of this nightmare to go. With nowhere else to turn, I decided to try out Mom's advice. I smiled, acknowledging the heckler's line.

"That was the best joke we've heard tonight." The crowd laughed again, this time at least partly *with* me. From there, I pulled out of the nosedive and salvaged the rest of my act with more of a loose, spontaneous feel.

Stand-up, done right, should feel like you're in a bar telling funny stories to your friends. Over-memorizing doesn't work because it makes the story feel canned, which the audience can sense. A skilled storyteller can take a good story and make it great with a relaxed attitude. A bad storyteller can tell the same story, word for word, but if it's over-rehearsed or if the storyteller seems nervous, the story will fall flat. In other words, it's great to rehearse, but it's just as important to make it seem like it's the first time you've ever told this story. Today, one of my favorite things to do is to go on a stage with newly written, untested material. *Are these jokes funny? We're about to find out.* It's an adrenaline-soaked high-wire act—it's a feeling you can only get from walking onstage without an *exact* plan.

After seven months in Chicago, I had made a decision. I was going to try this. Not as a stand-up, necessarily. I would continue to do some of that, but I wanted to try to make it as a comic actor. Maybe I'd try to get on . . . *Saturday Night Live?* I didn't know, but that could be figured out later, because it was time to go back to my favorite place on earth—Colgate.

CHAPTER 5

_____

Colgate Part 2: The Seeds of Broken Lizard

In the spring of 1989, I was back at Colgate, excited to see my old pals and finish my junior year. While I was gone, a sophomore named Jonathan Glatzer founded the Kinetic Theater Group, a student-run outfit devoted to staging avant-garde plays. Glatzer adapted an edgy version of the biblical story *The Book of Job* and cast me as Job. During rehearsals, Jon and I talked about my experiences in the *real world* of the Chicago comedy scene, and I'm sure I exaggerated my improv prowess. I know I did. I also lamented the fact that Colgate had no improv group. *It would be so nice to introduce Colgate to improv.* Chicago was 720 miles away. Who was gonna call me on my bullshit?

In June of that year, Glatzer was invited to study at the British American Drama Academy (BADA) in London, which would take him away from Colgate for the fall semester. He wanted to go, but he was afraid that leaving would doom his fledgling theater group. So he decided to ask four people to direct one-act plays under the Kinetic Theater banner. When he called me he dove right in.

"Hey, bud, how about starting that improv group you're always talking about?"

Look, I was flattered. But what I knew that Jon did not was that I was not qualified to start an improv group. I was a beginner and I sucked at improv. But Jon said that he needed me, and since everyone is a sucker for being needed, I was willing to consider going against my gut and just winging it.

There was another problem. Having earned four AP college credits in high school, I was in a position where I needed only two more credits to graduate. So I signed up for two history seminars, one of which met on Tuesday at seven thirty P.M. and the other on Thursday at seven thirty P.M. I was free the rest of the time—free to go out every night and drink, smoke, and joke my way through a fucking epic senior year. Frankly, I wasn't sure how starting an improv group fit into this schedule.

I was also worried about the embarrassment factor. Colgate is a phenomenal school, but it didn't have the richest tradition of support for the school's theater program. If we went to the trouble of creating an improv group, would anyone even come? And if they did, and we sucked, wouldn't that just be humiliating? I had a great thing going at Colgate, so why take the risk? So, I told Jon no and forgot about it.

In July, a couple of friends and I camped out in the parking lot of Alpine Valley, where we saw four Grateful Dead shows. We dropped acid, danced in circles, and had a lot of good fun . . . in relative moderation. When I returned home, a message was waiting. It was Glatzer. "I've got three directors doing one-act plays for me this fall. I need a fourth. Will you reconsider and do the improv show?"

Since I was feeling a little jelly headed, I told him I'd think about it. So, after we hung up, I called my pal Kevin Heffernan, who was at his house in Connecticut.

KEVIN HEFFERNAN

I first met Kevin in the foyer of the Beta Theta Pi fraternity house at Colgate, in the fall of our freshman year. We were eighteen and part of the new pledge class. At that moment, we were standing in a semicircle, being yelled at by our pledge masters, who were informing us that we were certainly the worst pledge class in the history of the house. It was all good fun and it was meant to bond us, which it did. In case you're wondering, we never got hazed at Beta. I was never punched, I never sat in urine, I was never branded, I never grabbed anyone's dick, nor did I fuck a sheep. As I've said, our house was devoted to drinking, telling jokes, and insulting one another, and I couldn't have had a better time.

Heffernan was funny and smart and had a ton of charisma, and we hit it off. We spent a lot of hours together, cracking jokes and watching the three VHS tapes that had been randomly left in my room—*Fletch; Vernon, Florida;* and *Bill & Ted's Excellent Adventure.* I also gave him his nickname, "Queen." It was in the winter of our junior year. Kevin had just showered and was coming out of the bathroom as I was going in. His hair was tousled, his skin was winter white, and he was wearing his royal blue towel, above his nipples, which made him look like the queen of England might look if she came out of our bathroom. I started calling him "Queen," and since he didn't love the nickname, it stuck. There are probably a hundred people who call him "Queen," or derivations of, like, "Queeno" or "Queen Bee." For a while, his mother called him "Queenie." At his parents' barbecue, his father took me aside. "You know there's a certain connotation to the name 'Queen,' right?"

I laughed. "Yeah, but this is royal."

If I was going to start an improv group, Heffernan had to be part of it—the dude just oozed funny. The problem was that, aside from playing Captain Hook in his fifth-grade play, Kevin wasn't an actor and didn't aspire to be one.

When Queen picked up the phone, we bullshat awhile before I got to the point. "Hey, how would you feel about starting an improv group? You know, like I did in Chicago?"

Silence. Then: "What?"

"It's for the Kinetic Theater. I was thinking we could gather up some funny people and put on a show."

"Put on a show?" He couldn't have sounded any snider. "Yeah, I don't think I'm gonna be 'puttin' on any show.'" That's all it took for my own insecurity to flame up. My gut was screaming loudly: *Don't do this!*

So I said, "Yeah, you're right. Fuck it. See you back at school, big man." He was right. Why would we do this? What if it didn't work? Why expose ourselves to failure? Relieved, I called Glatzer and for the second time said it just wasn't gonna happen.

That fall, I was back at school and all was good in the world. I had my two night classes, and I was basically drinking, smoking, and playing poker the rest of the time. Then I got a phone call. It was fuckin' Glatzer calling from London, trying one more time. I tried to stall. "Hey, buddy! How's jolly old?"

He wasn't having it. "Look, I'm not taking no for an answer. You have to do an improv show for me. You just have to."

I exhaled. My response would radically change the course of my life: "Okay, fine. Fuck it."

After I hung up, I went down the hall and walked into Kevin's room. We didn't knock. Kevin looked up. "What up, home girl?"

"We're doin' the improv show. It's a done deal."

"What do you mean?" He looked as angry as he did confused.

"I told Glatzer we're doin' it, so we're doin' it. Done deal."

Here's the thing. Heffernan and I both *thought* we were funny, but the fact that I had actually gone to Chicago and performed onstage was intriguing to him, because, like me, he loved *SNL* and Monty Python and all of the John Landis movies. And now I was going to start an improv group at Colgate with or without him. So as much as he really didn't want to do it, because he would be exposed and it would be a hassle, he also didn't want to be left behind. He exhaled.

"Fine. Fuck it. Whatever."

HOW TO MAKE A COMEDY GROUP

Since the three other one-acts were holding auditions, I decided we'd do the same. *Let's see who's out there.* We made signs: "Auditions for comedy group! Come one, come all!" and we put them up around school. Though this had stirred some interest from the theater community, the true comic giants at Colgate weren't actors at all. I needed *them.* Pulling a page from *The Magnificent Seven,* I made a list of the funniest people on campus and paid each one a visit. Here was my pitch:

"Hey, you're really funny, and I know you're not an actor, but I'm starting a comedy group and I need you to join." After they got over the surprise and confusion about what I was proposing, most of them were flattered enough to come to the audition. Most. This guy Riley turned me down flat. "No! Fuck no. I'm not an actor!"

I countered, "Most of the people I'm talking to aren't. That's what'll make this cool."

He shook his head. "Seriously? You want me to go up onstage and perform ... comedy, for the first time in my fucking life, in front of all of our cynical friends? Yeah, right."

As I left Riley's apartment, my original fear started creeping back up. *What if we did suck?* We were starting something new. This wasn't Harvard, where they had the long history with the legendary *Lampoon.* This was Colgate—a place full of cynical, funny people who did three things really well: drink cheap beer, smoke bad grass, and crack great jokes. If we weren't funny, it was going to be humiliating. I buried that thought and drove over to meet the next funniest person on my list.

The audition included a series of improv games. Borrowing from the Improv Olympic, I had the auditioners play pencils in a case, with the twist being that one of them was used to cheat on a test. The audition was effective, but more than that, it was nice to finally sit on the other side.

STEVE LEMME

Steve was a year younger than me. He was a junior in our fraternity and was always good to stay up late, drinking, smoking, and trading insults. He was also one of the great storytellers at Colgate, and when he found out I was interested in show business, he regaled me with the tale of his one acting experience.

Steve grew up on Manhattan's Upper East Side and went to Dalton, a ritzy private school. Steve was a faculty kid there—his mother taught French. On his way home from school one day, he stopped to watch some African American kids break-dance on the street corner, and he was spellbound. When he asked the two teens if they would teach him how to break-dance, he became their protégé. One day, while the three guys were roboting on a corner, a casting director approached, saying she was looking for break-dancers for a Colombian jeans commercial. Excited, the guys immediately started popping and locking, trying to out-peacock one another. By Steve's own admission, he was the worst of the three, but she hired him anyway, saying his look would play best in Colombia. (His white look.) Heartbroken by the injustice of show business, Steve's dance teachers cut off his lessons.

In the commercial, Steve and another white break-dancer are wearing Bobby Brooks jeans while freestyling on a street corner. Soon, two hot female cops walk up to arrest them (I assume break-dancing is illegal in Colombia). As they're about to be cuffed, Steve and his pal pull some sick dance moves, which charms the cops. Before you know it, the cops and the break-dancers are walking off, hand in hand, for a fun date. Without any irony, I'll admit that Steve Lemme is a good break-dancer.

On the Saturday morning of our auditions, Steve and his girlfriend, Kathy, were tailgating before a football game. Steve had always told Kathy that he wanted to be an actor when he graduated, which she found odd, since he had never auditioned for a play at Colgate. Kathy told Steve about our auditions and said if he wanted to be an actor, he should show up. Steve said that he had already had a few beers and he

wasn't in the right mind-set. Kathy called him a chickenshit, so an annoyed Steve Lemme downed his beer and trudged off to our audition.

The junior class (Lemme's) and senior class (Kevin's and mine) had
a silly rivalry going over who was cooler and who could party more.
Ah, the good old days. Lemme and five of his classmates lived in a downtown apartment above a place called the Eagle Mall. This led to us
nicknaming their apartments "the Ego Mall." The joke was that
Lemme and his vain, pretty-boy friends preferred to spend their time
looking in the mirror and masturbating, rather than drinking. (I think
that's still true of Steve today.)

As much as we made fun of each other, Lemme had a special place
in my heart, because on my twenty-first birthday, someone joked that
I should walk through our packed, four-hundred-person party in my
birthday suit. I was vaguely considering it, and then my girlfriend,
Denise, egged me on. So it was now happening. It was at this critical
point that Lemme stepped up. He knew I needed a wingman more
than anything else in the world, so he offered to join me in my birthday suit walkabout. The two of us marched through the party, buck
naked, which meant that I owed the little dude a favor.

So when Lemme walked into the audition, I wanted him to succeed. But could he act? Because, favor or not, if he couldn't, this wasn't
going to happen. Luckily Lemme nailed his audition. There was one
problem, though. Queen didn't like him. When I suggested to Heffernan that we cast Lemme, he shook his head. "Nah. No way. He's a
thief." *I had a feeling he would say that.*

When Steve was a freshman, rushing our fraternity, he … well, he
stole Kevin's jacket. According to Heffernan: It was the dead of winter, and we had an after-hours party at our house. A lot of people left
their jackets on the benches in the foyer, near the front door, includ-

ing Kevin Heffernan. The morning after the party, Kevin went looking for his jacket, but it was gone. Stolen! A week later, a bunch of freshmen who were rushing our fraternity came down to the house for dinner. After dinner, Heffernan wandered through the foyer, where he miraculously found his missing jacket. When he rifled through the pockets, he found the college ID of none other than Steve Lemme. When Kevin confronted freshman Lemme about the stolen jacket, Lemme denied it. So Heffernan pulled out Lemme's college ID and said, "Then why the hell is your ID in my pocket?"

Not missing a beat, Lemme said, "Ahh! That's where it is! Whoever stole your jacket must have also stolen my college ID!"

Lemme tells the story a little differently: It was a snowy, freezing February night. After the party, when it was time to go back to his dorm, Lemme checked the benches for *his* jacket, but it was gone. (This wasn't uncommon. There were a lot of drunks around and the weather was brutal, so jackets disappeared and reappeared all the time.) Faced with the prospect of walking a mile up Cardiac Hill, back to his dorm, in heavy winter weather, Lemme just grabbed a jacket off the bench and headed off into the night.

When he woke up the next day, Steve noticed a jacket balled up in the corner of his room. But since he had been hammered, he had no recollection of where the jacket had come from. And now it was the only jacket he had, so he started wearing Heffernan's ridiculously oversized jacket around campus, including when he went back down to Beta for dinner that next week. When Heffernan confronted him, Lemme admits he lied. And when Heffernan produced Lemme's college ID, Steve knew he was fucked and he was likely not going to get into our fraternity now.

He was almost right. Heffernan did tell the story of the stolen jacket at our fraternity bid meeting as evidence of why Lemme shouldn't be allowed into the house. After Heff spoke, I stood up and vouched for Lemme, because he really was a funny guy, and jackets did disappear all the time. Lucky for him, I prevailed and he got in.

But back in the audition room, Heffernan was a dog with a bone. "Fuck that guy."

I smiled. "Let the jacket go. Lemme is funny."

Eventually, Heffernan gave in, but not before firing one last sneering shot. "I guess we *do* need someone to play the scumbag roles."

CHARRED GOOSEBEAK

Rounding out the cast were a number of really funny people, including Alison Clapp, Ursula Hanson, John Cooke, and three freshmen, Ted Griffin, Zach Chapman, and Francis Johnson.

With the improv group assembled, I set out to teach them all the Harold, the long-form improv style I had learned in Chicago. Unfortunately, I was unqualified, so it was the blind leading the blind. While I understood the basic rules of improv, when people asked questions about why we should do one thing over another, I didn't have the answers. Our rehearsals went poorly. We were all funny people, but this improv thing was shaking our collective confidence, which, in turn, was making people question the whole venture. *Should we quit now before we embarrass ourselves in front of the whole school?*

So I decided to shift gears. We had signed up for this because we loved *SNL* and Monty Python; we loved sketch. So at the next rehearsal, I told everyone about my struggles on the improv stage in Chicago. I told them that we were going to abandon improv and perform a sketch show instead. Though the relief was palpable, we did have one problem: We didn't know how to write sketches.

Aside from English and history papers, the only writing I had done was my ten-minute stand-up set. Now we had to write an eighty-minute sketch show. I told everyone to carry around notebooks to jot down ideas for sketches and jokes. At our writing meetings, we pitched ideas, which we would riff on like a jazz band figuring out a song. Sometimes we'd smoke joints and the riffs would get nutty. Ideas would get stretched, bent, and turned inside out. We were learning how to write sketches, and it was feeling right. I remember bringing in ideas I thought were funny and then watching them bloom into something far funnier once the group got ahold of them. The group mind was funnier than the individual mind. Yes, there were individuals who were funnier, more prolific writers, but everyone was contributing. The idea of being a team was important, so I told everyone that we needed to share credit. If someone asked who wrote a joke, the response should be, "We all did."

To take this idea further, I held off on casting until all of the sketches were written. This way, the funniest writers couldn't write all of the best parts for themselves, because writing a sketch didn't necessarily mean you were going to be in the sketch. These rules continue in Broken Lizard today. If you ask us who wrote the "meow" joke, you'll hear, "We all did," and that's true. And our film roles are not cast until at least draft fifteen, which ensures that everyone keeps writing jokes for *all* of the different characters, because they don't know which one they're going to play.

We organized the structure of the show to be sort of a hybrid between *SNL* and *Python*. Some sketches would be stand-alone, like in

SNL, while others would have second and third parts like *Python:* "Nobody expects the Spanish Inquisition!"

The sketches included a healthy mix of political humor, historical humor, Colgate humor, and just plain bizarre humor. We did a sketch where Plato is a freshman wrestling recruit at Athens University, but he's failing his Basic Thought class. So the school hires a hotshot senior philosophy major, Socrates, to tutor him. The two go to a party, where Socrates teaches Plato the meaning of life by teaching him how to hit on girls. Two of the girls Plato meets are Medusa and Anorexia.

We did a political sketch where we played a group of Republican superheroes called Team America. We basically burst into places where liberals were doing typically liberal things and berated them for not being American enough. I played Captain Nationalism, Zach Chapman played Kid Liberty, and Fran Johnson played Fanny Freedom. No relation to the great *South Park* film.

Borrowing from *SNL,* we decided to make video shorts, which would play in between our sketches. My directorial debut was a sitcom parody called *My Wacky Grandma.* In it, we played a family with a nutty grandmother who plays pranks on us. In the sketch, we're all hanging out on the couch, when Grandma gets up and walks off screen. Then we hear the sound of Grandma falling down the stairs. After a worried beat, we hear her yell, "Just kidding!" Then we all fake laugh, and freeze.

I set up the camera on a tripod and pointed it at the couch. Then I pressed record and slid into my place on the couch. "Action!" After shooting the wide shot five times, I wasn't sure what else to do, so I said, "I guess we got it."

My first time in the edit room was thrilling. I thought it was un-believably cool to see how videos were cut together. The student editor and I watched the raw footage for *My Wacky Grandma*, and he laughed. "This is funny." I smiled proudly. Then he said, "Where's the coverage?"

"Coverage? What's that?" I asked.

"You know, the close-ups?"

When I told him I hadn't shot any close-ups, he looked nervous. "But we can't just show the wide shot."

"Um, why not?" I asked. "Can't we just show the best take?"

The editor played our "best take" and I immediately saw the problem. Everything is going along great, until Fran forgets her line. We sit in silence for a moment and then I nudge her, after which Fran says, "Oh," and then says her scripted line.

The editor said we had two choices. "You can either go back and shoot a close-up, so I can cut out you nudging Fran, or you can just play it as is." We didn't have time for a reshoot, so we played the take as is. The crowd laughed, as though maybe we had intended it, but it was personally embarrassing, and the pain burned grooves into my future filmmaker brain. I hated myself for missing the close-up and I never made that mistake again. Not *that* mistake. I made plenty of others, and each time I got into the edit room and realized what I'd done wrong, whether it was a missed shot or slow pacing, I cursed out the fucking director (me) for his mistake. But next time, I'd be sure not to make the same mistake. I didn't go to film school, where I would have been exposed to shot lists, pacing, and blocking. I learned filmmaking through experience—I learned through pain.

We shot two other videos, both of which were directed by a freshman from Los Angeles named Ted Griffin. Ted was an aspiring filmmaker who knew about shot selection and editing, and his work showed it. Ted directed a great parody of the Brian De Palma film *The Untouchables*, which poked fun at Colgate's Greek system. When Ted graduated, he moved back to LA and become a successful screenwriter, writing such major studio films as *Ocean's Eleven, Matchstick Men,* and *Tower Heist.* If you want to see Ted, he plays the owner of Rick Johnson's Pizzeria in our first film, *Puddle Cruiser.*

As the show approached, I realized we needed a poster, so I went to see my artist friend Chris Chaudruc, who owed me a favor. Chris and I had gone to high school together at Lake Forest Academy, and we had a complicated history. Our junior year, Chris asked me if he could drive my car the short ride from the gym to my dorm. He was sixteen and had no license, but since it was the middle of the day and the drive was only a third of a mile, I figured it'd be okay. The road was windy and lined with trees, and the speed limit was ten miles per hour.

I put my seat belt on as a joke. *Ha-ha-ha, why did we need seat belts if we were just driving to my dorm?* He laughed and put his on too. Then he put the car in reverse and floored it.

I laughed. "Slow down."

He put the car in drive and floored it. The wheels spun in the gravel.

I laughed. "Seriously, slow down."

He kept the gas floored. We screeched around a tree-lined corner. "Slow down!" He kept it floored, screeching around another tree-lined bend. And there it was—dead center to the windshield and coming fast: a mature, fat oak tree that . . . *Wham!* I blacked out for a brief second and woke up covered in tempered glass. Chris had driven straight into a tree at forty-five miles an hour.

Chris looked at me and screamed, *"I crashed your car! I crashed your car!"* Why did he do it? I never quite got a good answer from him. I don't think *he* even knows. He wasn't drunk. He was just a sixteen-year-old doing what sixteen-year-olds sometimes do. They fuck up. The car was totaled and the fireman who arrived first was looking for bodies. We were lucky to be alive and, aside from some small cuts, unharmed.

Five years later, at Colgate, I was cashing in my chit by making him design our poster. He looked up from his sketchbook. "What's the name of the group?"

I shrugged. "Um, we haven't come up with one yet. We want to avoid the cliché college sketch group names like 'Strictly Giggles' or 'Funny Business' or 'The Kidders.' We want something unique."

Chris was an odd dude in the best way. On his sketch pad were drawings of birds of prey ripping flesh with their beaks. After a beat, he looked up. "What about 'Charred Goosebeak'?"

Charred Goosebeak's first show (the first of four) was on a snowy Wednesday night in November. We were scared, excited, and wondering what the hell was going to happen. Would we remember our lines? Would the audience laugh? Would there even be an audience? Wednesday was a big party night at Colgate, so we were concerned that people might just hit the bars instead. We built a stage and lined up three hundred folding chairs, hoping for the best. Forty people showed up, which was depressing, but it was showtime, so we put our hands in the middle and chanted, "Uno, dos, tres, no problemos!" (This is our pre-show chant to this day.) And we started the show.

Copying *SNL,* I opened with a monologue, which we followed up with our sketches and videos. And you know what? It went well. The forty people who came laughed, and laughed often. When it was over, our relief was palpable. While it would have been great if more people had come, at least we knew that we weren't going to be an embarrassment.

On Thursday, as we were getting ready backstage, our producer, Ira Liss, stuck his head in. "There's a huge line out there! Huge! I'm gonna have to add more chairs!" We peered out to see that every seat was filled. *Holy shit! Word of mouth from those forty people had gotten around.* When I came out for the monologue, there was an air of expectation in the crowd—it was electric. The monologue and the first sketch killed, and we rolled from there, with big peals of constant laughter. After the show, the cast was giddy. *We were on to something here.*

Friday brought another sold-out show, with wall-to-wall laughs, where we actually had to turn people away.

We kept our run up, selling out the Saturday finale. Charred Goosebeak had planted a flag at Colgate. We had created something funny, unique, and risky, and we'd done it all on our own. Everyone in that cast felt it—this was going to continue.

We didn't know it at the time, but two decisions we made that semester led directly to Broken Lizard's eventual future in film: The switch from improv to sketch taught us how to write jokes, character, and story. Without that ability, we would have never had the confidence to try writing film scripts. Second, our decision to shoot videos allowed us to learn this very specific and technical art out of the broader public eye. And when I graduated, I had a bed of knowledge that made our videos that much more complex, interesting, funny, and technically sound.

In the spring, Charred Goosebeak added four new members: Jay Ward, Lauren Bright, Erik Stolhanske, and Paul Soter.

PAUL SOTER

Paul was a junior whom Heffernan and I first saw in the play *Noises Off*, and he stood out. We'd also seen Paul perform stand-up on a night when Erik and I also performed. Paul's act was hilarious and inventive. The highlight was a bit on an Amish UPS service, where Amish guys lined up and passed a package hand to hand until it got to its destination. Paul turned out to be not only a great actor, but also a phenomenal writer. He has a great understanding of both big-picture story progression and minute joke structure. He always knows where the joke is. We also tend to be on the same side of the argument when it comes to rhythm and tone. To borrow a metaphor, we make good music together.

ERIK STOLHANSKE

The story of how I first met Erik Stolhanske is, well, it's kind of crazy. During my sophomore fall, I was in the Arthur Miller play *A Memory of Two Mondays*. The theater department required actors to help build sets, so I woke up early on Saturday to do my part. Before I went to the shop, I popped into the kitchen for a little breakfast. While I was buttering an English muffin, our rush chairman, John, walked in. A rush chairman's job is to recruit freshmen to join our fraternity, a job I didn't envy. As much as I loved the house, it felt awkward coaxing freshman dudes to join. When John found out where I was going, he asked me to look out for a freshman from

Minnesota named Erik Stolhanske. He was an actor and, apparently, cool. I told John okay, but I wasn't really planning to come through.

In the shop, I was assigned a job staple gunning fabric onto a stage flat. After a while, a lanky, blond kid walked up out of a J.Crew catalog and introduced himself as "Erik Stolhanske from Minneapolis."

I said, "I'm Jay from Chicago," and he sat down next to me with his hammer, and we got to work. Erik and I hit it off, cracking jokes that veered quickly toward insult. Wanting to test his mettle a bit, I said, "John said you were cool, but I don't really see it." He smiled and then insulted the entire city of Chicago and all of its residents. The back-and-forth quickly devolved into which city was tougher, Chicago or Minneapolis. We traded barbs on the Bears and the Vikings, the Bulls and the Timberwolves, and so on. After I insulted Prince (whom I love), he'd had enough.

"Oh, you think you're tough, huh? Okay, tough guy, if you're so tough, can you do this?" And then he lifted his hammer and swung down hard, *thwocking* himself directly on his right anklebone. "*Ahhhh!*" Down he went, rolling around on the floor in pain, but smiling through tears.

I had to pause. This wasn't where I had expected this to go. But I wasn't going to let Chicago down, so I smirked at him, picked up the hammer, and short-swung down, popping my own right ankle. *Ahhh! Holy shit did that hurt!* I rolled around on the ground, knowing in my heart that I hadn't hit myself as hard as he had. But still, ouch!

Erik was just getting started. "Okay, Chicago, let's see what you've got." Erik ran full speed at a cement wall and kicked it with the tip of his toe, in a way that can only be described as—*as hard as you can.* The sound was sickening. And down he went—"*Ahhhhh!!*" He was rolling around on the ground, grabbing his toe in clear agony, and through gritted teeth, he said, "Care to give up?"

Who was this fucking guy? That thought passed, because there was no way I was going to let this freshman from Minneapolis show me up. So I ran toward the same wall and kicked it really hard. Rather than sacrifice my toes, I kicked it with the ball of my foot. It hurt, and I went down holding my foot, again, knowing that his toe kick had been harder.

Erik nodded as if to say, *Not bad.* But he was already scanning the room . . . looking. Then, he smiled and picked up . . . a power staple gun, its cord snaking menacingly toward the socket.

Now, in your typical game of chicken, this would be your clucking point. Erik had overplayed his hand. *Hitting yourself with a hammer? It hurt, but fine. Kicking a wall? Painful, but manageable. But a power staple gun? What the hell was he going to do with that? I didn't need to call chicken because I knew he would.* Erik whipped the cord for dramatic effect and then put the gun to his right calf. "Last chance?" he offered.

"Go for it." I laughed cockily, knowing he was about to give.

Then Erik widened his eyes and yelled, "*How now, Brown Cow!?*" *Boom!* He fired a staple into his leg. "*Ahhhhhh!*" He dropped to the floor, rolling around in deep agony. I went to my knees to examine where the staple went in, hoping to see that he had pulled away at the last second and that it had only gone through his pants. But, sure enough, not only had the staple gone through his pants, but it was clearly anchored into his flesh beneath. This fucking maniac had just shot a staple into his leg with a power staple gun to prove that he was tougher than me. He hopped around, wincing. "Ouch. Ouch. Ouch. Don't do it, don't do it, don't do it."

I was full of dread. *I could chicken out now, but if I did, it would say something primal about me that could never be unsaid. Before this, I would have said that the human body couldn't handle getting a staple blown into its flesh. And yet . . . Erik wasn't a superhero. If he could handle it, so could I. What was the worst that could happen? It would hurt like hell going in and twice as bad coming out, but then it'd be a great story, right?*

I slowly picked up the staple gun, looking at him. "How bad is it?"

He smiled with seriousness. "I think I fucked up. I might need to go to the hospital."

Not seeing a way out, I decided to cheat (again). Instead of shooting the staple into my calf, I would shoot it into the back of my meaty thigh. *That had to be less painful, right?* I exhaled and pressed the staple gun against my thigh. Looking straight at him, I started to squeeze . . . But then . . .

Erik threw his hands up. "Don't! Don't! I have a fake leg! I have a fake leg!" And he grabbed his pants and ripped them up, popping the staple out and revealing his skin-colored polyurethane leg.

Erik was born without a right fibula, so his leg was amputated below his right knee when he was eighteen months old. Clearly, none of that affected his comic mind.

When I went back to our fraternity, I immediately found John. "We've gotta get this guy in the house."

The spring shows were great, and our videos were both funnier and more technically sophisticated. We were quickly realizing how many different, and subtle, jokes you could tell with a camera.

Graduation was looming, which was, frankly, sad. I loved Colgate and knew that life would never again be this dreamy. Where you could drop into one of two bars in town and know a hundred people. Where you could walk down the hall, listening for music, and then smoke bongs and crack jokes with good friends until four in the morning. The four years I spent there were the funniest and most joyful of my life, and the friendships I made have endured well beyond graduation. I often wonder what would have happened if I had taken a different hallway that afternoon back in high school and not run into Lyssa. I wouldn't have gone to Colgate. I would have never met the guys in Broken Lizard, and I would have never become a filmmaker. And *Puddle Cruiser, Super Troopers, Club Dread, Beerfest,* and *The Slammin' Salmon* would have never happened. Life—is—fucking—random.

Leaving the cocoon of Colgate meant some big decisions were looming. I willed control of the group to Steve and Paul, whose job it would be to keep Charred Goosebeak running. I had decided to give show business a try, but I wasn't sure from where to start. I could go to Chicago, where I could fall back into the Improv Olympic scene, but I was now such a devotee of sketch that improv no longer felt right.

I could go to Los Angeles, where most of show business was, but where I knew no one. I could move to San Francisco, where my girlfriend, Denise, was moving. There was a good stand-up scene there, and it was close to LA, so maybe I could have the best of both worlds. Or I could go to New York City. Alison, Ursula, and Heffernan had decided to move to New York, where they were all going to pursue non–show business careers. In their minds, performing comedy was over . . . unless I moved there and put a new group together. New York had another benefit. It was the primary destination for Colgate grads. If I went there, I would know literally hundreds of people.

In the end, though my heart was in San Francisco, we had made magic at Colgate, and I wanted to see if we could do it again, in Manhattan.

CHAPTER 6

New York City: Hacking Our Own Path
into Show Business

The summer after we graduated, six friends and I rented a van and drove across the country. We went to baseball games; we hit bars; we camped wherever possible. We even had a beard-growing contest. Used to smoking pot every day, we were flummoxed by the countrywide marijuana shortage that summer. We tried to buy in every town we stopped in, but it was all junk. In Minneapolis, we bought a green pot-like substance that bubbled and smelled of dish soap when we smoked it. We were staying at a friend's lake house in northern Minnesota when one of my premed pals said he read that nutmeg could *get you high*. So we headed to the grocery store, where we bought eight tins of . . . nutmeg.

Back at the house, we drank beer and played hearts. Then, at around eleven P.M., we each poured a tin of powdered nutmeg into a glass of water and chugged it. Heffernan immediately threw up, but not wanting to be left behind, he poured another tin into more water and downed that. After a while, nothing happened. So we tried to smoke it, but it wouldn't light. So we just kept drinking. At four A.M. it was time for bed, and still, no one was feeling anything. So we went to sleep.

When we woke in the morning, no one could move. We were all overcome with intense body fatigue, coupled with an overwhelming thirst. The fatigue was so debilitating that it was hard to even get up to go to the bathroom. Occasionally, someone would muscle up and crawl to the kitchen for a cup of thirst-quenching juice, while the rest looked on jealously. The new catchphrase of the trip became (British accent) "Bring me the juice! I desire the juice!" Fuckin' nutmeg. Never again.

We kept heading west, taking turns reading the best sellers *Bonfire of the Vanities* and *Silence of the Lambs*. We played seemingly endless card games: hearts or deuces. We also never stopped arm-wrestling.

After seeing Mount Rushmore in South Dakota, we took a helicopter ride, flying over the area's wildlife, which ended up being just a single goat.

Outside Aspen, we went to a place called Devil's Punchbowl and jumped off forty-foot cliffs into the freezing river below.

In Wyoming, we were camping in the woods near Jackson Hole, drinking beer around a fire, not smoking pot, and arm-wrestling, when two cowboys walked out of the dark woods. One was eighteen and the other twenty, and they asked if they could have a couple of beers. After a couple of nervous minutes of us wondering whether they were two psychos coming to kill and eat us (*Silence of the Lambs* style), they admitted that they were in the woods stealing trees on protected land. We hit it off with these guys, and when the conversation turned to arm-wrestling, as all of our conversations did, the scrawny eighteen-year-old claimed to be the Wyoming State arm-wrestling champ. *Yeah, right!* Nobody believed him, so, we each challenged him, and he made quick work of all of us. We got drunk and he said that if we wanted to have some fun, we should ride a bucking bronco tomorrow in the rodeo. I swore that I would, but the next day we opted to go to the Schwarzenegger film *Total Recall* instead. Cluck, cluck, cluck.

We heard that the Grateful Dead were playing in Eugene, Oregon, in two days, so we drove fifteen hours and camped in the parking lot. We tried to buy pot and again struck out. Yeah, at a fucking Dead show. We did find a guy who had pot brownies, and we all ate one. When nothing happened, I assumed we'd been tricked again, so I ate another. Big mistake. I spent the next twelve hours in a nauseatingly uncomfortable high. I hate edibles. Like nutmeg, never again. The next day, we bought some Dead tickets, dropped some acid, and played a crazy six-hour game of tag during the show. After four great shows, we headed south to San Francisco, to see my girlfriend, Denise.

It was a magical road trip, and also a great way to transition out of Colgate. Afterward, I went back home to Chicago, where I spent the rest of the summer. The big news out of Chicago was that Chris Farley had joined the cast of *SNL*. That someone I knew had made it through to the Promised Land was cool, and proof that this dream might just be possible.

In the fall, I drove my packed car to New York City, where five friends and I rented a West Village duplex on Bleecker Street between Eleventh and Perry. I got a job at an art gallery as, essentially, muscle. I wore a suit and just kind of hung around, occasionally answering the phones. Kevin got a job as a paralegal at a place where two of our Colgate friends were lawyers. We went out every night until four A.M., usually in the East Village, or sometimes to a bar called Richter's, where Colgate grads congregated. If you were a Colgate alum and you walked into Richter's, you might know between ten and fifty people at any time. Sometimes we'd go dancing with these hot Trinity College girls at Delia's, a downtown spot. No matter what, we always ended our night either buying gyros at Karavas Place, or at the Corner Bistro, where we'd eat bacon cheeseburgers, smoke Camel Lights, and drink $2 McSorley's or vodka gimlets. Afterward, we'd go back to our place, smoke grass, drink Bud tallboys, and laugh into the night. In the morning, an exhausted Kevin would go to work at his paralegal job and sometimes nap under the desk of his boss, who, lucky for him, was also a Colgate grad. Sometimes, Kevin would put his back to the door and the phone up to his ear and sleep. His colleagues would walk in with business and say, "Oops, sorry—you're on the phone?" And they'd leave.

We weren't doing any sketch because we didn't have enough people. I was doing stand-up at open mic nights at a place called the Boston Comedy Club. I won an open mic contest one night when Dave Attell was hosting. On any night, you could see Attell, Louis C.K., Marc Maron, or Chris Rock perform. I knew none of them, but it was cool to watch.

That January, Steve Lemme was drunk up at Colgate and put his foot through a window, severing a tendon in his leg. He was on crutches, and that made getting to class, which was up a mile-long hill through the snow, impossible. Steve's grades plunged and he dropped out and moved back to New York City. His parents were giving him grief, so he moved onto our couch.

Soon we started talking about re-forming the comedy group, with the core being me, Kevin, Steve, and Alison Clapp. Ursula Hanson bowed out, saying her performing days were over. We added the Colgate actress Lauren Bright and an actor/performance artist named Josh Gladstone. I booked us a show on Monday nights at the Duplex, a cabaret theater on Christopher Street and Seventh Ave.

We wrote a show, shot some videos, and then hung out in our apartment for three days, smoking grass and pitching ideas for a name for the group. We decided on the Chocolate Speedo Team, but then abandoned that for Five Whiteys and an Injun. But when I went to the poster store I unilaterally changed it to Broken Lizard. I didn't tell anyone why, but it was because I was hoping that the name would remind people of who I wanted us to become: Monty Python. *Python begets Lizard.* We made cards advertising the show that said, "Broken Lizard in Jolly Joe Triphammer Hits It Big!" Our first Monday night show sold out, which shocked the club. It was filled with Colgate grads, and they drank a ton, which also made the club happy. When they moved us to Wednesdays, more Colgate sellouts followed. When that crowd almost drank the place dry, we were moved into the Friday and Saturday night slots. The nightclub business is about selling booze, and Broken Lizard floated on the thirsty tongues of that Colgate crowd. Our New York shows were the same mix of monologue, sketch, and video shorts. After one show, a young guy who had run a sketch festival at Skidmore College approached us. His name was Dave Miner and he said he loved the show and wanted to manage us. There was one issue: Dave wasn't a manager; he was only an assistant to a manager. But we were flattered, so we hired him anyway.

In June, Erik Stolhanske and Paul Soter moved to town and joined the group. Erik moved in with us on Bleecker Street, though the end of that apartment was nigh. After a year at Bleecker, we were told that our numerous noise complaints had made us "not a good fit" for the apartment. Not only would our lease not be renewed, but we were also expected to allow prospective renters into the apartment for viewings. When a Frenchwoman came to see the apartment, Erik and I decided to walk around with our shirts off to try to make her think we were crazy. Our goal was to spook her out of wanting to rent the place. She wasn't fazed, and when we struck up a conversation with her, we found out that she owned a production company that made commercials and music videos. We quickly asked her for jobs, and she hired us as production assistants.

The first music video we worked on was for the band C+C Music Factory for their song "Gonna Make You Sweat (Everybody Dance Now)." My job was to pick up the models and dancers in the van, and then make sure they were happy all day. I hit on most of them, but none of them went for my bottom-of-the-show-business-ladder pitch. Still, I enjoyed that job.

We worked on a lot of commercials and videos, but our favorite project was a Japanese miniseries called *Banana Chips Love*. It was a story about a couple of Japanese teenagers who come to New York and get into a bunch of crazy misadventures. Both Timothy Leary and Allen Ginsberg were in the cast, though we were instructed not to tell either of them that the other one was in the show. I guess they were enemies. Erik's and my job was to sit in the van and guard parking spots. It was a February night and the temperature was close to zero. Erik was in one van and I was in the other. We were bored and started cracking jokes on the walkie-talkies, but the assistant director broke in to tell us to shut the fuck up. So we sat in the vans and quietly froze in the dark while listening to AM radio.

New York City in the nineties was the center of the indie film revolution. Writers, directors, and producers scraped together small amounts of money, recruited skeleton crews, and shot films they hoped to use to bash their way into the film business. This was a time when you could make a movie for as little as $40,000, starring total unknowns, and Miramax might buy it and release it—not only in thousands of US theaters, but also worldwide. Before that could happen, though, your film had to get into either the Sundance Film Festival or the Toronto International Film Festival, the only two North American festivals that had proven to be reliable film sales markets for comedies. If Sundance accepted you, it was a signal to acquisition execs that the film was good and that they might have to compete for distribution rights. But getting into these festivals is not easy. Every year about 3,800 feature films are submitted to Sundance, with only 118 making the cut. That's a 3 percent chance of success. By comparison, applicants to Harvard have a 6 percent chance of getting in.

There are two ways to get into Sundance or Toronto. You can send your film in and hope one of the programmers takes a liking to it. Or you can hire a sales rep to advocate on your film's behalf. If your film gets in and is deemed commercially viable, the sales rep's job is to negotiate offers from distributors. Sales reps and filmmakers are in it together, because no one gets paid unless the film sells.

At the time, there were four highly influential film sales reps: John Sloss, John Pierson, Bob Hawk, and Cassian Elwes. Savvy filmmakers sent these guys rough cuts of their films before sending them to festivals, because if one of them championed your film, you stood a much better chance of getting in. That said, sales reps can't make a festival program a film it doesn't want to.

Indie film is high-stakes gambling, and only a few make it all the way through to the big prize. The landscape is riddled with the bones of films and filmmakers who racked up huge debts, only to be rejected by the major festivals and then forgotten. If you don't get into Sundance or Toronto (or, maybe, Cannes), your chances of selling your film drop precipitously.

In 1989, Steven Soderbergh took his indie film *Sex, Lies, and Videotape* to Sundance and sold it to Miramax for $1 million. The film grossed $25 million domestically and started a DIY indie film gold rush. Distributors now looked to Sundance to find the next big thing, and filmmakers jockeyed with one another to *be* that next big thing.

In 1991, Richard Linklater shot *Slacker* on 16 mm film for $23,000 and sold it to Orion pictures. Kevin Heffernan and I saw the film at the Angelika Theater on Houston Street in Manhattan and left excited. The movie had a structure and rhythm all its own. It was cool, smart, funny, and really entertaining. And what was this place? Austin, Texas? Could you really make a film for $23,000 ($65,000 after the 35 mm blowup) and get it released in theaters? *Slacker* showed us that someone close to our age was in the game and nailing it. *If Linklater could do it, maybe we could too.*

Heffernan and I saw *Clerks* in 1994 (again at the Angelika), a film shot on 16 mm black and white for $27,000 and acquired by Miramax at Sundance. More evidence that people our age were doing this.

The Brothers McMullen was next, shot on 16 mm for $28,000. It was acquired at Sundance in 1995, this time not by Miramax, but by 20th Century Fox, which released the film through its newly created indie label, Fox Searchlight. When the film grossed over $10 million at the box office, Hollywood took notice. There was real money in this low-budget game.

Robert Rodriguez bested everyone in the "how low can you go" contest with his film *El Mariachi,* which he made for a reported $7,000. He shot the film in Mexico and sold his blood to buy raw film stock.

Kevin and I loved the film, but you couldn't make a feature for that in the US. No way. Regardless, how much these films cost or, more specifically, how little, had become a key part of the press's story. The lower you went, the more press you got.

The last film I'll mention is Quentin Tarantino's million-dollar debut, *Reservoir Dogs* (1992). We loved that film. Loved. The dialogue was tough and funny and weird and specific. The action was visceral and everyone was a badass. We still imitate Joe, the crime boss: "How about a little . . . Rémy Martin?" We went to see it again the next day, and then bought it on laser disc. To this day, *Reservoir Dogs, This Is Spinal Tap,* and *48 Hrs.* are my three favorite films.

Caught up in the thrill of the independent film movement, Broken Lizard soon started talking about making our own film. The problem was that the technical gap between video and film was huge, and we didn't have any idea how to bridge it. Then, luck intervened. My friend Karan Chopra was at a restaurant in the Village when he saw a stack of brochures for a summer film class at NYU. The next night, he handed me the brochure.

"You should do this." It was a six-week class called Sight and Sound, where you learned how to make silent black-and-white 16 mm films.

Here's the thing. Karan and I were close friends, but this is not how we interacted. We were too cool to ever be this thoughtful. So I just shrugged and said, "Naw. No, thanks. I'm good."

But Karan wouldn't give up. "If you want to do this for a career, you've got to learn how it's really done." That landed. This was one of those seemingly random moments in life upon which everything hinged. If Karan hadn't gone to that restaurant and found that brochure, I never would have taken that class, and I never would have learned how to make movies. I might have still tried to make it as a comedian, but I never would have dared try to direct a film. The technical side of filmmaking was too intimidating. I'd been on movie sets before and was mystified. *What were all those people doing? What was all that equipment for?* That NYU class demystified it for me, and the reason Broken Lizard was able to make its first movie was because of the technical knowledge I began to learn in that class. I learned how to load a camera, how to use three-point lighting, and, most importantly, how to edit. I made five silent black-and-white films. One was about a couple that meets in Washington Square Park, and then they get old together. Another was about a wizard. All were meant to be funny and they got good laughs. I loved that film class and I earned an A-. Energized, I applied to graduate film school at NYU, USC, UCLA, and the American Film Institute, or AFI. I was rejected everywhere. People laugh when I tell them that, but I feel for admissions staffs. How're they supposed to know who is going to go on to be a successful filmmaker and who is not? I thought my work with Broken Lizard and in Sight and Sound made me a good fit, but they did not. In truth, half of the current, working directors went to film school and half did not. As a side note, I've lectured at many of these schools since, and I love being able to tell the students the tale of how I couldn't get in.

So now what? I had made friends at NYU with a guy named Kevin Cooper who was getting his film degree. Coop had served in a military intelligence unit as an interrogator and had been part of a group that went through Manuel Noriega's house during the invasion of Panama. I brought Coop to a Broken Lizard show, and he hit it off with the group. He started taping our live shows and eventually became our director of photography on our video shorts. This took a huge weight off my shoulders, since acting and directing is difficult, but acting, directing, and camera operating is impossible. With Coop aboard, the quality of our shorts made a huge jump. When Coop needed to make his thesis film, we collaborated on a half-hour Broken Lizard short called *The Tinfoil Monkey Agenda*. We shot the film in Florida, with Coop's future wife, Deanna, producing, and Coop and me codirecting—he chose the shots and I directed the actors. It was a fun shoot, and our first taste of having a real crew.

In the film, the United States sends a four-man military extraction unit into a Central American country called Palogna to capture and interrogate their dictator, General Manuel La La La Gamboa. A CNN news crew is embedded with the soldiers and reports live along the way. It was basically *Wag the Dog*, four years before that film came out. No, they didn't steal it. No one saw our film.

For the edit, we split time between rooms at NYU and the editing house where I was working, Film Video Arts (F/VA). Since we couldn't afford to hire an editor, Kevin and I did it ourselves. I'd work my manager's job from ten A.M. to nine P.M., and then we'd edit from ten P.M. to four A.M. When we ran into a problem, we brought in more experienced editors for advice. It was ad hoc film school, but it worked. Sometimes, we'd cut so late, we would just turn the machines off and sleep on the floor. More than once, we woke up to mice staring us in the face.

The finished film was pretty good, though not great. The jokes and performances hinted at our future, but its thirty-minute length prevented us from getting into festivals. Festivals want shorts that are eleven minutes long or less because they want to group a bunch together into ninety-minute blocks. They will make an exception for a longer short, but only if it's ridiculously good, and ours wasn't. Making things worse, no one in show business wanted to watch our film either, because thirty minutes was just too much time to commit to unknown filmmakers. If you want the most people to watch your short, make it between ninety seconds and two and a half minutes. Remember the Budweiser ads about the guy who buzzes his friend's intercom and says, "Whassup?" Before it was an ad, it was a two-minute short made by Charles Stone. This hugely popular short made its way around the executive suites of Hollywood and gave Charles a legitimate feature film career that continues to this day.

Ditto for the *South Park* guys. In 2000, we went to Los Angeles for meetings, and before each one, the executive would say, "Have you seen Clooney's Christmas card?" George Clooney had seen an animated short created by Trey Parker and Matt Stone and had commissioned them to make a raunchy video Christmas card inspired by their short. That ninety-second video was hilarious and turned into *South Park*, which launched Trey and Matt's careers. By contrast, our thirty-minute short was viewed by almost no one and failed to advance our careers at all. The one saving grace was that we learned a lot about filmmaking, so it wasn't a total loss. When I showed the film to my father, he said he thought it was sometimes funny but that it didn't look like a *real* movie. *Dad never lies.*

Meanwhile, our sketch show was killing it. We were selling out every show and got a big win when Comedy Central paid us to film one of our sketches for their interstitial programming. They hired an outside director, which we thought was smart, since we felt that I could never direct something that would go on real TV.

While the final result was solid and professional, and it was cool as hell to see ourselves on TV, the shot selection and timing didn't quite feel like us. That convinced me that we could never outsource direct-ing again.

Soon after, MTV called. They were making a sketch show, and rather than audition individuals like *SNL* did, they were going to hand over the reins to an already formed comedy group. Our man-ager, Dave Miner, learned that MTV was going to choose between Broken Lizard and the State. This is hard to believe, but at the time, we were the only two comedy groups of note working in New York City. (UCB hadn't formed yet.) The State was made up of eleven NYU grads, and though we'd never seen their act, we liked our odds. Our show was smart and we were getting huge laughs. Plus, we were the only comedy group that was making videos, so we thought that we were more TV ready.

MTV came to our sold-out Friday night show and we killed. There was raging, boisterous laughter throughout the whole show. I talked to the MTV execs after and they were glowing with enthusi-asm. Our careers were about to take a big leap forward. Though they didn't mention it, we knew that they were going to see the State the next night. On Saturday, we had another show, which went great, but our minds were across town, wondering—how was the State doing? *Couldn't be as good as us, right? It's not possible to do a show as good as the one we did.*

Sunday came and went, and we heard nothing. Monday was more of the same—silence. Finally, Dave Miner called with the bad news. MTV was moving forward with the State. *Wow. Okay. Wow.* We were crushed. The TV landscape was full to the brim with sketch shows. There was *SNL, The Kids in the Hall, In Living Color,* and now, *The State.* We could bang our heads against the wall, but it was pretty clear there wasn't need for *another* sketch show. With TV closed off to us, our only hope was to turn to feature film.

This was a critical moment for Broken Lizard because it changed our approach to show business from reactive to proactive. Instead of waiting for MTV to give us our break, we were going to make our own break. That attitude shift set the course for our careers. Our private reaction to MTV was crisp. *Fuck you. We're funny. You'll see.*

CHAPTER 7

———

Puddle Cruiser: How I Made a Film,
When I Wasn't Sure How to Make a Film

We were pissed off (about MTV) and convinced that we could make a film that could compete with the other DIY first features we were watching in theaters. But nothing quite prepares you for making your first feature. Sure, shooting shorts is helpful, but feature scripts are ninety-minute-plus stories, organized around the three-act structure. As a sketch group, we told stories lasting between ninety seconds and five minutes, so we had no idea how to expand to feature length. So we decided to follow in the footsteps of the Zucker brothers and Monty Python by making a sketch movie. We met for days, listing the various sketches we thought could be converted to the big screen. The problem was that we had sketches that took place in ancient Greece, in Hell, on a castle wall, on a fly strip, and so on. Each sketch would require a different set and would be very expensive to do well. When we examined the films *Clerks, The Brothers Mc-Mullen,* and *Slacker,* we found that the common denominator was simplicity of location—a mini-mart, apartments in New York, the town of Austin.

And then I remembered something I had been working on back at Colgate. It was sixty pages of a feature comedy script called *Felix and Suzanne,* which was based on my college relationship with my girl-friend, Denise. When everyone read it, the reaction was good. The whole story took place at Colgate, which felt very manageable. If we could add a few more characters, we thought that this could be our first feature. We wrote, rewrote, and rewrote again, and fifteen drafts later, we had the script, which we renamed *Puddle Cruiser.*

The story is about a college guy, Felix, who starts a casual rela-tionship with a girl, Suzanne. Suzanne is still in a long-distance rela-tionship with her high school boyfriend, Tracy Shannon, who attends a nearby college and plays rugby. Eventually, Suzanne breaks up with Tracy to date Felix full-time. While in bed, Suzanne jokes that Tracy wants to kill Felix.

Felix just laughs. "I'm not worried."

Suzanne is amused. "No offense, but he's huge. So . . . you know."

This bothers Felix enough that he joins his own school's rugby team to show Suzanne how tough *he* is. I actually did this in real life. I joined Colgate's rugby team (for a week) to prove to Denise that I was as tough as her ex. When he realizes that his rugby team is sched-uled to play a match against Tracy's team, the showdown is set. The-matically, *Puddle Cruiser* is about modern-day machismo. One of my favorite jokes in the film is when the guys realize that Tracy Shannon not only has two first names, but two *girls'* first names, which makes him a "firsty-firsty, girlie-girlie."

The name of the script wasn't great, but back then, we loved ran-dom names. We named one of our sketch shows "Jolly Joe Triphammer

Hits It Big" and another "The Return of the Biscuit Champion." We thought the words "Puddle Cruiser" would catch a film festival crowd's attention. When people asked what it meant, we made up something about Felix being a big fish in a small pond (puddle). There was no obvious connection to the film, and most people called it *Puddle Jumper.* A well-known, flamboyantly gay film rep lit up when he misheard the name. "Tunnel Cruiser?" Ah well.

Having a script we liked was great, but how the hell were we going to make it? Since Kevin Cooper and Deanna, who had helped us make *The Tinfoil Monkey Agenda,* had left New York, we needed help. We needed a producer—someone to budget the film, hire crew, and possibly raise money. I met with a couple of indie producers and quickly realized that I was out of my depth. I didn't know what the hell they were talking about—unions, insurance, blah-blah-blah.

Erik Stolhanske was temping at an investment bank and told me that his boss, Rich Perello, had overheard him talking about movies. Rich had *almost* produced a movie once and wanted to meet about becoming our producer. I was skeptical. *Were we really going to hire an investment banker who had only* almost *produced a movie?*

When I met Rich, he told me his story about being in the Arizona desert with a cast, crew, equipment, and trucks full of food, all of which he had secured with his charm, his hustle, and his verbal promise of future pay. But the check from the investor, which was supposed to be in the bank weeks earlier, still hadn't arrived. It never did. So when we sat down, Rich's first question was, "Do you have the money?"

"Not yet," I said, "but we're hell-bent on getting it." He smiled and rolled his eyes. *Great.*

Rich knew about unions, camera packages, insurance, and crew—all

of the things I had no idea about. He was smart, passionate, and straight-
forward, and he wanted the job badly. In the end, it was obvious that he
was our guy. Meeting Rich was critical to Broken Lizard's success. Sometimes, a filmmaker will hook up with the wrong producer and the money
will disappear, through either poor budgeting or graft. With Rich, the
money always ends up on the screen, and the budget before we start is
always the budget at the end. Rich doesn't go over. Period.

Back at Film Video Arts, one of the editors, Sooz Hewitt, was leaving
to go to her second job, where she worked as a paralegal. She mentioned
that her firm was hiring and asked if I was interested. Interested in being
a paralegal? I was trying to avoid law school. But then she told me that the
firm was the Sloss Law Office and her boss, John Sloss, repped a list of
filmmakers that included John Sayles, Steve James, Kevin Smith, Eddie
Burns, and Richard Linklater. My ears perked up. "Linklater?"

My job at Sloss Law Office was answering phones, revising con-
tracts, copying, and filing. Lots of copying and filing. I was part of a
team of assistants who worked for John and his associate, Jodi Peikoff.
The Sloss Law Office was the legal heart of the independent film
business. John had posters from seemingly every major indie film
from the past ten years, all of which had been touched by that office
in some way. When I'd "roll calls" for John, I'd get to listen in as he
spoke with financiers, directors, producers, actors, and studio heads
like Harvey Weinstein. It was fun to hear the two spar, negotiate,
manipulate, charm, and sometimes openly fight.

Filmmakers sent tapes of their finished and half-finished films to
John, hoping he'd sign on as their sales rep. One such tape was of a
ten-minute short called *Bottle Rocket* by an unknown filmmaker named
Wes Anderson. When Sooz and I marched into John's office telling
him he *needed* to see this filmmaker, he shrugged.

"You're too late. They already shot the feature at Columbia Pictures. It's coming out this fall."

I didn't meet Linklater, but I did talk to Whit Stillman, Kevin Smith, and Eddie Burns about their films and what I needed to look out for when I made mine.

Rich did a budget and we began our raise. The investor pool was composed of my parents, their doctor friends, some uncles and aunts, my sister, Lemme's parents, his aunt, and some of our friends. In total, we raised $125,000, which was a huge fucking sum. Look, film is an expensive art form, and investing in a first-time filmmaker requires having *extra* money. If you're worrying about rent and food, you're not investing five grand in your nephew's film. That's why there are so few films about the impoverished *by* the impoverished. The film business, like life, is unfair.

When we approached our alma mater, Colgate, to discuss our plan to shoot there, the dean was friendly but asked for a script, so we sent him one.

We put a casting notice in *Backstage* magazine and got stacks and stacks of headshots from aspiring New York actors. One day, while eating at a local dive, Milady's, I chatted up our waitress, who turned out to be an actress. When I asked her to come to our apartment to audition, she was understandably skeptical. Eventually, she got over her kidnapping fears and showed up. Her name was Kayren Butler, and she was hilarious and smart and the best actress by far, so we cast her in the role of Suzanne.

Then Colgate called back. The dean had read our script and said that it "just wasn't something they'd like to pursue." *Say what? Shooting at Colgate was emotionally important to us. What were we supposed to do? Just shoot it somewhere else?*

We started scouting other schools while simultaneously trying to change the dean's mind. We hit the phones, enlisting the hundreds of alums and current students we knew, to start a letter-writing, faxing, and phoning campaign. The gist of the message was, *Colgate claims to be a liberal arts school, but when alumni are trying to make it as liberal artists, Colgate is standing in the way. What a damning contradiction!*

Hundreds of letters later, the dean called.

"Call off your dogs. You can shoot here. And send me your list. We want to use it to raise money." Before the dean hung up, though, he added one last thing.

"I'm agreeing to this on three conditions: The film can have no sex, no drugs, and no drunkenness." *Aw, come on, man, this is a college movie.*

We went up to Colgate in the summer of '95 to make Broken Lizard's first feature film. Rich said we had enough money for only three out of four weeks of shooting, but I assured him that the rest would come. It was the classic wing and a prayer. We hired Tony Foresta, the same director of photography who shot *The Tinfoil Monkey Agenda*, and we rented two 35 mm Moviecam Compacts, lighting trucks, sound equipment—all of it. I was intimidated. What was I doing directing a feature film? I didn't know shit. Or at least it felt like that. Terry Gilliam had directed six years of television before directing *The Holy Grail*. I'd tell Tony to put the camera in a certain place and then I'd look around, half expecting the crew to laugh about my choice. They didn't because I was the director and they were there to execute my vision, whatever that was.

On the first day, I shot twelve takes of the master, which is the term used for the widest shot of the scene. In my mind, I needed to keep shooting until every line of the master was perfect. That took three hours. After the twelfth take, our Venezuelan sound guy, David (pronounced Dah-veed), mercifully came up to me and said, "Are you sure you need more takes of the master?" I nodded, unsure, but moved on. When we got into the edit, Kevin and I used only three seconds of the master. Meaning we spent 180 minutes shooting to capture three seconds of on-screen footage. It was an important lesson because, beyond the creative, filmmaking is very much about time management. The smartest filmmakers spend the most time on the shots that they believe are going to appear on-screen the most. Now when I shoot a scene, I shoot two takes of the master, using about twenty minutes of production time, and I spend way more time on two-shots and singles, which tend to take up more screen time in the final film.

I was under immense psychological pressure, which was amplified by the crew's watching me learn how to direct on the fly. The stress was so intense I lost fifteen pounds and developed back and knee pains so debilitating that I limped around for a week. The medicine my mom prescribed to combat the pain listed potential side effects like "vomiting a coffee ground–like substance." All of the Lizards hoped to have a ringside seat if that happened.

Stressful as it was, shooting *Puddle Cruiser* was also a dream come true. We were back at our school, living in our old fraternity house, and starring in our own movie. At night, we drank and smoked like the old days and savored our "bonus month" of college. Seeing our faces on-screen, beautifully lit, on 35 mm film for the first time was intoxicating. *This looked like a real movie.*

As Rich had predicted, we ran out of money three weeks into the shoot and had to stop production to dial for dollars. When I came up short, I laid out my secret weapon: four credit cards with the name "Dr. Chandrasekhar" on them. To be clear, I didn't set out to commit credit card fraud. In a bit of reverse racism (all Indians are *doctors*, right?), the credit card companies had accidentally sent me those cards, along with the corresponding doctor credit limits. I didn't correct the error, and I used those cards to keep the film rolling and the crew fed.

When we got back to New York City, Heffernan and I rented a nonlinear editing system called D/Vision from our soundman, David. We worked our day jobs and then came in to edit at night. To our great surprise and relief, the film cut together really nicely. *Maybe I knew more than I thought?* The first cut was two and a half hours, and though we were excited about it, when we showed it to Broken Lizard, their response was underwhelming. *It felt long. Where was the music? Why did it look so washed-out?* We were bummed, but Heffernan and I knew we had a good movie in there somewhere.

I then decided it was time to show my boss, John Sloss, hoping he'd agree to represent the film for sale. When I walked into John's office, he looked up from his papers.

"Are you sure you want me to see this now? You only get one chance to make a first impression." I thought about Broken Lizard's reaction to the cut and walked out. This piece of advice stuck with me, and it's a line I often repeat. Whether it's an early draft of a script or an early cut of a film, when you're showing it to someone you need help from, make sure what you're showing is great. Because if it's not, they're unlikely to watch draft two.

Kevin and I headed back to the edit room to find a tighter version of the film, when disaster struck. A computer bug had wiped out the entire edit—two months of work, just gone. We had to reconstruct the edit by eye, using a VHS tape we'd made as a guide. Having lost two term papers in my school career, you'd think I would have learned. Today they call me "the Backup Kid"—because I back up a lot. Well, they don't, but they should.

The Sundance deadline was quickly approaching, and we were bogged down in the reconstruction, so I just sent them the two-and-a-half-hour cut.

Thanksgiving weekend is when Sundance calls filmmakers with the good news that they got in. We heard nothing, because they don't call the rejects. So we continued to edit. Five months and $45,000 in credit card debt later, I got a call from Visa that said, "You're not a doctor, are you?"

"Not at the moment, no," I admitted. My credit was cut off, but it didn't matter, because *Puddle Cruiser* was done.

We had our premiere at the Gramercy Theatre on East Twenty-Third Street. The Gramercy was a beautiful old New York theater that perpetually smelled of Indian food, because they only showed Bollywood films now.

The place was packed with four hundred of our closest pals, who all made jokes about the Indian food smell. This was going to be the first time John Sloss saw the film, which we had trimmed down to a svelte 104 minutes. If he liked it and thought he could sell it, he'd sign on as our representative. If not, I'd go back to making copies. As the film started, he leaned in, driving the obvious home.

"This better be good."

The friends-and-family premiere screening was gangbusters, with big, constant laughs. I imagine some of the response was relief— *Oh thank God it doesn't suck.* As the credits rolled and the audience clapped, John leaned in again.

"You're fired."

I smiled. "You're hired."

After the screening, Samantha Mazer, the director of the Hamptons International Film Festival, approached. "We want your movie!"

When I told John, he groused about our Sundance rejection and said, "Let's find out what Toronto thinks first." Selling a film requires a careful strategy, starting with where the film premieres. Sundance and Toronto were the only two North American festivals where films had actually sold, so Toronto had become critical to our sales prospects. Truthfully, there's no better place to sell a comedy than at a film festival, where the crowds are smart and they get every joke. And since the majority of festival films are about heroin addicts, sex trafficking, incest, and genocide (kidding—well, I'm kinda kidding), watching a comedy can be a welcome respite. When selling a comedy, you're relying on the enthusiasm, energy, and laughter of the crowd to overwhelm the opinion of the acquisition executive. You want them to think, *Holy shit. People really like this film. We've got to buy it.*

For festival programmers, premieres are the ultimate prize, because they want to say that their festival was the first place that Film X was exposed to the world. Sundance took it a step further with their unwritten policy of not programming films that had already premiered at other US festivals. The big dog eats first. Only after Sundance made its intentions clear did anyone dare commit their film to another US festival. The one exception was Toronto. If your film got into Toronto, you went, and Sundance had no problem with that.

Film distribution companies each have a team of acquisition executives whose job it is to watch every independent film made in a given year. If the executives find a film they love, they'll tell their boss (the check writer), who will watch the film and make the final decision on whether to buy it.

When a film gets into a festival, acquisition execs immediately call up the filmmakers, hoping to sweet-talk them into showing their film early. For the filmmaker, it's a huge mistake because of how their film will be watched, which is on a computer screen, in an office. There'll be no hype, no word of mouth, and no laughing festival audience to influence the buyer. Saying no to the acquisition executive guarantees that they'll be at your first festival screening, because if they're not, and a competitor buys your film, they will miss out on a relationship that could be enormously lucrative to the company. The best example of this is when Miramax bought Quentin Tarantino's *Reservoir Dogs*. It started a relationship that gave Miramax (and eventually, the Weinstein Company) *Pulp Fiction, Jackie Brown,* and everything else Quentin has done since. But when you're a new filmmaker and have a film with unknown stars, you've got a problem. The execs who go to the first screenings are never the ones who can write the check. Why would the boss come to our screening when Gwyneth is in town and wants to have dinner? Shit, I'd choose that too.

But let's say you had a good premiere screening, and the first wave of execs (at, say, Miramax) love your film. They'll tell the film's rep, John Sloss, that Miramax is interested, but they need their boss, Harvey Weinstein, to see it. The problem is that Harvey isn't in Utah yet, so a print needs to be sent to him. This must be avoided at all costs because Harvey will watch the film alone in a screening room, where he'll be free to check email or roll calls (if he's bored). He may recognize that the film is funny, but he won't be swept away by the energy of the rowdy, sold-out Egyptian Theatre crowd, and the likely result will be that Miramax will pass on buying the film. So the key to selling a film at a festival is to get Harvey (or his equivalent) to watch the film in a theater, with a rowdy audience. That's the only way he'll buy it.

Because of this, John Sloss's job is to tell the acquisition executives that *if Miramax is serious about buying the film, they had better get Harvey to the screening tomorrow night, because check writers from the other distributors were there tonight and offers are starting to come in.* That's what you tell them even if it's not *strictly* true. John's goal is to get them worried. *What if another company makes an offer tonight and the film is sold before Harvey can see it? And what if the film goes on to become a hit and make tens of millions of dollars like* Napoleon Dynamite?

When Toronto let us know that they were not going to program *Puddle Cruiser*, it was off to the Hamptons Film Festival for us. Since the Hamptons was only three years old, it was considered an upstart and was unlikely to have check writers there. So our strategy was to build buzz and then follow up with distributor screenings in New York and Los Angeles, where we would pack the room with a crowd and invite check-writing acquisition executives to watch.

The Hamptons Film Festival couldn't have gone better. The screenings were packed, and the crowds loved the film so much that they gave us the Golden Starfish Award, the audience award for most popular film. This was the first time we'd shown the film to strangers, so the laughs told us that maybe we had appeal outside our own friends. The late, great actor Roy Scheider (*Jaws, All That Jazz*) and David O. Russell, the director of *Flirting with Disaster* (one of the great comedy films of all time), gave us the award. Afterward, Ken Hardy, from the Creative Artists Agency, said he wanted to sign us. *Wow. CAA. Surreal.*

When we got back to Manhattan, I talked to Sloss, who said that our plan had worked. *Puddle Cruiser* had great buzz, and check-writing company heads had requested film prints. Per the strategy, John told them that no prints were going out, and if they wanted to see the film, they had to come to our distributor screenings. The distributor screenings were crowded, great, and got big laughs, but the bosses, who assured us they were coming, each canceled at the last minute, leaving us with multiple $500 theater-booking bills. We just weren't a priority. Now what?

John had an idea. He called Geoff Gilmore, the head programmer of Sundance, to rib him about missing out on the discovery of *Puddle Cruiser.* Geoff was curious, so he went to one of our distributor screenings. Afterward, he called John, saying he agreed the film was really good and he wanted to talk to me. When I called Geoff, he said he really dug the film, but he had one question.

"Why didn't you send it to Sundance first? I would have definitely programmed it there, but I can't now, since it already premiered at the Hamptons."

When I told him I had sent a rough cut to Sundance a year ago, he said he never saw it. Ouch. My heart sank. I get it. Sundance gets thousands of films every year. How can the head programmer see every one? When I told Sloss, he said he'd work on him.

Meanwhile, we had been invited to the London International Film Festival, which took place the week of Thanksgiving. The film played well in London, except for one seventyish-year-old woman, who followed me for two blocks, chastising me for the foul language in the film. That night, I was spending a lonely pre-Thanksgiving night in my hotel room when the phone rang. It was Sloss.

"You got into Sundance."

This was a big moment for me. I had been to Sundance as a spectator three years in a row, lurking around the edges, unable to get into screenings or parties. Now we were going with our own film. It was really happening. Geoff Gilmore, bucking precedent, had made us the first-ever film to premiere at another US film festival and then be let into Sundance. It was a big give and it had a huge impact on our careers. So, thanks, Geoff.

When I got back, Broken Lizard took a trip out to Los Angeles, where we were wined and dined and then officially signed by CAA. CAA held a couple of screenings of the film at their agency screening room to "introduce us to the town." They connected us with one of our childhood heroes, David Zucker, codirector of *Airplane!, The Naked Gun,* and many others. Our agent, Ken Hardy, had come up with the idea of David putting his name on our film—something like: "Presented by David Zucker." It would be an old-guard comedy guy giving his seal of approval to the new guard. We spent a lot of time with David and his crew, talking about their films. David told us that *Airplane!* was written to be a black-and-white film set in a 1940s propeller plane, but Jeffrey Katzenberg said the studio would green-light it only if the Zuckers shot the film in color and set it on a jumbo jet. They reluctantly agreed, but in an act of rebellion, in the sound mix, they made the sound of the plane that of a 1940s propeller plane.

Going to Sundance with a film can be one of the great joys in life. The audiences are enthusiastic, the press is bountiful, and you are treated like a real artist. But Sundance is also a place of intense stress, because most filmmakers arrive in Park City in some form of debt, having rolled the dice on their dreams. The pressure is on to make a sale, erase the debt, and get the film into theaters. Accomplish that, and your chances of making a second film just went up. Sundance is also the first time a filmmaker is going to read reviews. When they're negative, as inevitably some will be, it can feel personal, embarrassing, and crushing. As the days drag on, it becomes painful to read about other films selling when your phone is quiet. *You beat the odds to make it to Sundance, but you didn't sell. Now what?*

Sundance scheduled four screenings for us, two in the six-hundred-seat Library screening room, one in the legendary four-hundred-seat Egyptian Theatre, and the last in the lobby of the Yarrow Hotel, which sat seventy.

Our job was simple: Get the check-writing bosses into one of the first three, big screenings, where they would be swept away by the enthusiasm of the crowd. If we could do this, we figured they'd make the obvious decision to buy our movie, which would put us in the company of other DIY films like *Slacker, Clerks, The Brothers McMullen, Reservoir Dogs,* and *Swingers* in getting a theatrical release deal.

The Hamptons had showed us that the film played great to audiences, but it also showed a potentially fatal flaw. *Puddle Cruiser* didn't open well—the first fifteen minutes are its weakest. And when audiences are trying to decide if they like your film, starting slow can turn them against you. I saw this phenomenon in person when the one check writer who bothered to come to our Los Angeles distributor screening left at the fifteen-minute mark. Sloss had told the guy that *Puddle Cruiser* was a good, commercial movie, but the guy was bored by the first fifteen, decided he'd been conned, and walked out—right by me.

Conversely, starting a movie well tells the audience that this filmmaker knows what he's doing, so sit back, relax, and enjoy the ride. The best example of this is any James Bond movie.

To counteract our slow start, we decided to perform a live sketch before every screening to warm up the crowd. We figured that if we could get the audience laughing, we'd win them over and be able to move past the *first fifteen*. We tried a few different sketches, but the one we settled on for the biggest stage was called "Billy the Dummy."

Our first screening at the sold-out, six-hundred-seat Park City Library was buzzing off of the word of mouth from the Hamptons. Starting our preshow sketch, Kevin and I walked up to the front of the theater with long faces. I quieted the crowd and told them the bad news.

"Folks, I hate to tell you this, but at the run-through earlier, reel one of the film print"—the first twenty minutes—"got mangled in the projector." The audience groaned. Then I'd say, "Don't worry. Another print landed in Salt Lake twenty minutes ago and is being hand delivered directly to the screening. So we just need to kill a little time." The audience looked at their watches.

Then Kevin would start in. "So, has anyone seen any good movies?" More groaning from the high-powered, overscheduled audience, who were debating whether to get up and bail.

Then our plant in the audience, Paul Soter, would stand up, dead serious, and start heckling us. "Why did you come to Sundance without a backup print? Guys, I'm sorry, but this is really unprofessional!" This would embarrass the audience, who would start to feel bad for us, causing them to shush Paul.

At this point, another audience plant, Steve Lemme, would stand up and shout Paul down for being rude. The audience would usually clap for Steve. Emboldened by the audience support, Steve would then offer to help Kevin and me kill some time.

"You guys are in luck, because I'm a professional ventriloquist and I just happen to have my friend Billy with me." Steve would pull out his dummy (Billy) and start doing a preposterously high-voiced bit, where Billy would insult Kevin and me for being unprofessional because we didn't have a second print. Steve was an intentionally terrible ventriloquist, and the voice he used for Billy was so ridiculous that the audience, sensing a bit, started to laugh. On cue, the back doors to the theater would fly open, and Erik Stolhanske, dressed as a UPS guy, would run in.

"Did someone order a film print?! I've got it right he—" And he would trip, à la Chevy Chase, sending the "film print" flying into the air and unspooling all over the aisle. This always got the biggest laugh, which meant it was time to start the show.

The opening sketch got us through the first fifteen minutes, making the first Library screening a huge hit. After the screening, we did a raucous question-and-answer session—"Who are you guys? Where did you meet? Do you really all write together?" After the Q and A, we threw *Puddle Cruiser* T-shirts into the smiling crowd. We were pulling out all the stops.

After the screening, John told us that many lower-level acquisition executives had been there and were reporting back good things to their check-writing bosses. Screening two was going to be big.

The buzz on *Puddle Cruiser* had made its way around Park City, which made for a packed second Library screening. People wanted to see for themselves what all the excitement was about. The opening bit killed, and the screening was even better. Afterward, I talked to Sloss, who said that decision makers from Trimark and Overseas FilmGroup were there and very interested. Also there were some Miramax execs who were interested and trying to get Harvey Weinstein to come. John told us to keep the excitement going and we'd sell this fucker at the next screening.

The third screening, at the famed Egyptian Theatre, went just like the first two, with big laughs and lots of love. After the screening, John said Trimark and Overseas FilmGroup wanted to partner up, with Trimark taking domestic rights and Overseas taking foreign. They hadn't made an official offer yet, but they were talking about a five-hundred-screen domestic release. *Oh yeah!* Meanwhile, Miramax again expressed interest, and they assured us that Harvey's number two, Meryl Poster, was coming to the fourth screening.

The fourth and final screening was in the lobby of the Yarrow Hotel, where they'd set up seventy folding chairs and projected the film on a fold-up screen. The place was packed, but here's the thing— seventy people, regardless of how much they're laughing, isn't enough to move the excitement needle. Miramax's decision maker was there; she passed. We were frustrated and pissed. If she had come to screenings one, two, or three, we were sure Miramax would have bought the film. *Fuck! Okay, but someone else was going to buy the film, right?* Sort of. We got the five-hundred-screen offer from Trimark and Overseas FilmGroup. Between the two companies, their offer was for zero dollars. *Swingers* had sold to Miramax at a distributor screening for a whopping $5 million advance, and these companies were offering us, in the words of Dean Wormer, "zero point zero." Their pitch was that they would spend the substantial money necessary to get the film in front of audiences and, if it took off, we'd get a share of the profits. We turned both offers down. We just felt in our guts that the big buzz out of Sundance would translate into a better offer later. Maybe we could get some of the decision makers who didn't see it in Park City to come to watch it in LA or New York. *Maybe, maybe, maybe.*

There was some good news out of Sundance. Those raucous screenings had introduced us to young Hollywood, which put Broken Lizard on show business's radar. NBC and ABC execs, who had been at our Park City screenings, were excited to hear our ideas for shows. Broken Lizard on network TV? Because of our R-rated style, it didn't sound like the obvious fit, but maybe we'd adapt and show MTV what they had missed out on.

That February, I went to the Berlin International Film Festival market, where we screened the film for foreign buyers. The mostly German and Dutch crowd appeared confused by our humor. But Berlin was fun. I spent the week with a filmmaker named John O'Hagan, who directed a cool doc about America's first suburb called *Wonderland*. John and I had such a good time that we named our captain in *Super Troopers* after him. We met up with his NYU film school friend, a beautiful, blond, six-foot-tall German girl named Adelheid, who gave us a tour of Berlin. She took us to the stadium where Hitler gave one of those insanely yelly speeches. The same place where he would watch Jesse Owens win four gold medals at the 1936 Berlin Olympics, thus discrediting his theories about Aryan superiority.

That night, Adelheid took us across the Brandenburg Gate into the former East Germany. The billboards on the western side of the gate were bright and colorful, while on the eastern side they were still black-and-white. The cab dropped us off on a desolate street, and we walked down an alley into a courtyard. Adelheid led us down another alley, into another courtyard, and then down another alley to a third courtyard. We were deep inside the bowels now. Finally, she led us up some wooden stairs, where she knocked on a rusty metal door. The door opened a crack, revealing an eyeball and part of some lips. Adelheid whispered a password in German and the door swung open. If this seems familiar, it's because we used this whole gag in *Beerfest*.

We walked up two more flights of stairs to a hoppin' disco, where they were playing American music from the fifties, primarily Buddy Holly. We got hammered on German beer, or as they call it there, beer. Toward the end of the night, Adelheid and I started making out. I could feel the unhappy eyes of East Germany on me. Because of World War II, you might assume Germany is going to be this horrible, racist place, but it's not. At least west Berlin was not. It boomeranged so far the other way that it became inclusive and multiracial and very liberal. The east, though—the east was still a racial work in progress.

When I got home, Kevin, Steve, and I drove down to Austin, Texas, to show the film at the South by Southwest Film Festival. Austin is the gem of Texas. It's groovy, smart, hip, and fantastic, and we were excited to visit the place we had only seen in Richard Linklater's *Slacker.* When we arrived in town, our mind-set was conflicted. We'd won the Hamptons Film Festival, but no sale. We'd kicked serious ass at Sundance and got two offers for zero dollars. Now we needed to come down here and pull off a Texas miracle. We needed to become the first film ever to sell out of South by Southwest. SXSW was beginning to build a name for itself as a hip place to show a film. Tons of filmmakers went, but not as many check writers.

At the opening-night party, we saw Quentin Tarantino talking to Richard Linklater, Mike Judge, and Robert Rodriguez. We sent Lemme over to infiltrate. He stood there for about a minute before bursting out with, "Hi, I'm Steve, and you guys should come see our movie, *Puddle Cruiser!*" It went over like a lead balloon.

The screenings at SXSW were sold out, rowdy, and terrific, thanks to the best film crowds in the country. Austin folk are smart and laid-back, and they get *every single* joke. Sloss brought Richard Linklater to our screening at the legendary Paramount Theatre, which was a big moment for me.

That week, we befriended a filmmaker named Sarah Kelly, who had directed the cool, behind-the-scenes documentary *Full-Tilt Boogie,* which chronicled the making of the Tarantino/Rodriguez film *From Dusk Till Dawn.* We loved the film, and when Sarah saw *Puddle Cruiser,* we formed a mutual admiration society.

Sarah told us that she had been talking up our film to Quentin, who said he was going to come see it. But we had only one screening left. An hour before showtime, Sarah called to say Quentin was coming with ten people and to save them seats. We held eleven seats in the front row, turning away people from the overflowing crowd. Fifteen minutes after the scheduled start, Quentin still wasn't there. We killed some time, doing a really long opening sketch, but still no Quentin. The crowd was restless, and it was time to start, so I signaled to the projectionist to roll the film. On cue, in came Quentin, with Richard Linklater, Mike Judge, and eight others. The screening was great, and the Q and A after was better, with Quentin and Mike Judge asking questions. Afterward, we all went out and got hammered. Amazing, right?

Years later, when we had a deal at Warner Bros., Quentin called me from Berlin, where he was making *Inglourious Basterds,* to ask for a copy of *Beerfest* to show to his cast and crew. I later heard that he put a nod to *Beerfest* into *Inglourious Basterds*—it's the scene where the black-clad Nazi is drinking a beer in the basement bar. He is drinking the beer out of a glass boot.

When we got back to New York, I called John. "Fuck it. Let's take the Trimark/Overseas offer. Let's get the film in theaters." Five hundred screens was a big release for our tiny film. Guess what? Trimark and Overseas were no longer interested. They were offended that we had turned them down and had moved on. *Ouch.*

We moped around New York for a week, back at our jobs and un-sure about what to do next. I was sitting on a lot of debt and had no idea how to move forward. How would we get another film made if we couldn't sell the first one? Then, as if by divine intervention, Sloss called to tell me that Harvey Weinstein had finally watched *Puddle Cruiser,* and he wanted to meet. Was this our last-second miracle in the making?

I met Harvey in his small office at Miramax headquarters in Tribeca. I was dating a Miramax executive at the time, and she deliv-ered me to Harvey's office, mouthing, "Holy shit!" I sat on the couch as Harvey poured on the charm, telling me that his acquisition staff kept hounding him about this movie, so he finally watched *Puddle Cruiser* on a VHS tape in his office and laughed his ass off. He even said the directing was great. I was thinking, *Holy shit! We're about to get a theatrical offer.* Then Harvey shifted gears, telling me that Miramax just signed a deal with ABC Television, and he wanted us to adapt *Puddle Cruiser* to make it one of Miramax's first shows. I should have said yes. I know. Instead, I said, "Harvey, you watched the film alone in your office. This is a huge crowd-pleaser. Yes, let's make the TV show, but buy the film and put it out theatrically first! Let's build the audience!"

He smiled, broadly. "Why don't we test it?" *Holy shit! We were alive. We were finally going to get Harvey in a room with a laughing audience! It was all turning our way!*

Miramax set a date for a recruited test screening and asked us where we wanted to do it, Manhattan or the New Jersey suburbs. We chose Manhattan, figuring that would give us a better chance of getting Harvey there.

The screening was at a theater on Third Avenue and Eleventh Street, just blocks from NYU. Packed with film students, the screening was going great, with steady, big laughs throughout. But Harvey wasn't there. Miramax execs Robert Kessel and Elizabeth Dreyer were there, though, and they were calling Harvey with frequent updates about how wild and raucous the screening was. Harvey told them he was on his way and planned to catch the end of the film.

The movie ended and the credits started rolling—still no Harvey. The moderator stepped in front of the happy audience to solicit verbal opinions. *How did everybody feel about the film?* The reaction was super-positive. Then Harvey walked in, standing in the back, smiling and listening to the positive chat. One of the NYU kids looked back— *Holy shit, that's Harvey Weinstein.* Soon they were all looking back. Guess what happened? One by one, they turned on us. Suddenly, everyone in that room was Pauline Kael, trashing *Puddle Cruiser* for not being part of the French New Wave. If two things had been different, we probably would have sold the film to Miramax. First, we should have tested the film in suburban New Jersey, not the East Village. Never test near a film school. Short of an audience full of film critics, you'll never find a worse audience to rate a comedy. I've tested six films since, and none of them have been within seventy miles of those film school fuckers. Second, had we been able to get Harvey into the room during the screening to hear the laughter, he might have gone with his gut and bought the film. There's just no substitute for having the check writer hear the audience laugh. *Puddle Cruiser* was dead at Miramax, and dead everywhere else.

After the audience filed out, I thanked Harvey for coming and tried to salvage something out of the disaster. "Do you still want to make a TV show?"

Harvey smiled, shrugged, and said, "Bring me your next script and let's start from scratch."

We eventually sold *Puddle Cruiser* to a straight-to-video distributor out of Canada called Oasis. While we were disappointed at not getting a theatrical release, we were able to pay our investors back, plus a tidy profit. Against our wishes, Oasis slapped an unrelated foxy cheerleader's torso on the cover, assuring us that research showed that guys would pick up the DVD if there was a hot girl on the cover. *Ouch.*

But it was time to move on. We needed a new film idea to pitch to Harvey.

CHAPTER 8

—————

Super Troopers:
How It Happened and Almost Didn't

Kevin and I had moved into a house on Twentieth Street between Eighth and Ninth Avenues that Colgate grads had passed down to one another through the years. It was a slightly run-down five-floor brownstone with a backyard and roof and it was called the Flop House. Six guys lived there, and we threw huge parties and smoked a metric ton of grass.

I was a waiter at an uptown restaurant called Busby's along with Erik, Steve, and four other Colgate friends. Waiting tables at Busby's was fun, drunken, hilarious, and sexy, and it formed the basis for our script *The Slammin' Salmon*.

In the summer of 1997, the members of Broken Lizard spent a week at our friend's lake house, which was on the Vermont side of the US-Canadian border. If you paddled a canoe across the lake, halfway there you'd be in Canada. It was a magical week. We played a lot of Ping-Pong, drank and smoked everything in sight, and laughed at what felt like millions of jokes. The soundtrack to the week was the haunting wailing of Neil Young and his album *Harvest Moon*.

At week's end, we headed back to New York City—all of us packed into my car, pitching new ideas for a film for Miramax. When we saw that some college kids had been pulled over by the Vermont highway patrol, we laughed. Gangsta rap was king at the time, with songs like N.W.A's "Fuck tha Police" (1988) crossing into the suburbs and creating a generation of "whiggers." These were preppy white kids, speaking Ebonics and talking tough about cops—at least when there were no cops around. The idea of this power dynamic started a small creative fire, which led to us trading stories about being pulled over by the police. There were some good ones, but Steve Lemme went over the top when he recounted the story that would inspire the opening scene of *Super Troopers*.

A few years after we graduated from college, a friend of ours got engaged and, along with four other guys, rented a van to drive to Montreal, where they planned to throw a bachelor party at the world-famous strip joint Club Super Sexe. Hoping to avoid looking for a weed dealer in Montreal, they hid six joints in cigar tubes to take across the border. They also ate shrooms, timing them to kick in when they arrived at their destination. Included in the group were two brothers. I'll call the older one "Jethro" and the younger "Cornelius," both fake names to protect the guilty. Jethro and the groom were in the same class, while Cornelius was two years younger and tagging along. Cornelius had a secret plan, which he thought would make him a hero to his older brother's friends. He had brought a secret bag of *even more shrooms,* which he planned to break out for a mid–strip club "reload."

Sitting in the long, snaking line of cars at the Canadian border, they could see that the border patrol was pulling a lot of cars over up ahead. They debated. Should they ditch the weed out of the window? Or risk it? They decided to go for it and slid the cigar tubes into the cloth back of the van seat. Meanwhile, Cornelius slid *his* secret baggie of shrooms into another crevice of the rental van. When they got to the booth, the border patrol agent looked at the five twenty-something dudes and selected them to search. The guys got out of the van and watched as a team of agents rifled through their van. Eventually, the head agent emerged, holding six cigar tubes, which he opened, dumping the joints into a little pile.

"Would you mind telling me what these are?"

"Just a couple of joints, sir," said one of the guys, whom I'll call "Smartass."

"Well, whose joints *are* they?" Silence. "Okay. Whose van is it?"

"We rented it," said Smartass.

"You rent a van in the US and it just comes with joints?" asked the agent.

"The good ones do," said Smartass, earning his nickname.

Not laughing, the head agent turned to his underling. "Take these guys to lockup until someone owns up to the marijuana." But then, instead of taking them to lockup, the agent stepped aside for a conference, leaving our heroes to whisper furiously about what to do: *It's just pot. How much trouble can we get into?* Cornelius, though, knew that it was not *just* about pot, so he leaned into the van, snatched his secret bag of mushrooms, and covertly ate them all, licking the bag clean, while the others looked on, dumbfounded.

Then the head agent walked over, making one last attempt. "Tell

me whose marijuana this is or you will *all* suffer the consequences."
Dead silence.

In lockup, the guys debated who should take the rap. Since all had
career plans that they felt couldn't survive a drug charge, no one
budged. The conversation got emotional and weird, as the shrooms
they had timed for liftoff at Club Super Sexe started to buzz in their
ears. Over the next two hours, each of the guys was led into a private
interrogation room, but none of them broke. It had now been three
hours, and while all of them were shrooming, Cornelius was spin-
ning past the twenty-third moon of Saturn. Worse still, Cornelius's
turn at interrogation was coming up, which older brother Jethro knew
would go . . . poorly. So in a gesture of brotherly love, Jethro raised
his hand.

"The joints are mine. All of 'em. Mine." The other four guys
signed a document promising not to return to Canada for a year. To
Jethro, the head agent said, "You, sir, are not welcome in Canada for
seven years!"

As Jethro tells it, he shrugged and said, "So what?"

When Broken Lizard makes a film, the first requirement is that the
story is able to accommodate five male leads. Playing highway patrol-
men fit that bill. It was early in the process but, tonally, we wanted the
cops to feel real, not wacky. Like the hockey players in the great film
Slap Shot, our guys needed to be tough, real, and funny.

We pitched the idea about a Vermont highway patrol unit that was
so bored they made up games to entertain themselves to Miramax
executives Jack Lechner, Robert Kessel, and Michelle Raimo. They

dug it, and Miramax bought the pitch. Kevin Heffernan's mom, Jane, who had recently been pulled over for speeding by the Connecticut highway patrol, gave us the name of the film when she snarked, "Oh, you're making a movie about the *super troopers,* huh?"

We wrote five drafts, incorporating notes from Jack, Robert, and Michelle along the way. Months later, it was time to show Harvey Weinstein. Harvey had been so supportive of *Puddle Cruiser,* and now it was time to take the next step. We'd written a script we were all proud of, so Jack felt confident that Harvey would give us the green light. A week later, Jack called, disappointed. Harvey had read the script and said, "I'm not sure it's funny, but don't feel bad because I don't always know funny when I see it." Miramax was passing. The hint of good news was that Harvey was going to let us have the script back. This was a huge give, because 90 percent of the time a studio will "shelve" a script it's not making, rather than risk letting another studio turn it into a hit. Had Harvey done this, Broken Lizard would have died in the cradle, and we would have broken up having only ever made *Puddle Cruiser.* So, thanks, Harvey.

Now we had to find another studio that would be willing to finance our film. John Sloss sent the script to the two remaining major New York film companies, October Films and Good Machine, but both passed.

Our agents at CAA said it was time to move to LA, where our comedic sensibilities would be more valued. It made sense. We wanted to make studio comedies, like John Landis and Rob Reiner had made, and LA was the center of all that. Erik had already moved out there and seemed to really like it. Kevin and Paul, though, were noncommittal. They weren't going to move to Los Angeles until a job forced them to. Steve and I were on the fence. We understood that Los Angeles was probably a smart move, but we were New York snobs.

New York is a tough, sexy, smart place that calls itself the greatest city in the world. And while I've never admitted that, because obviously Chicago is, I understand why New Yorkers think that way. New York wins at most things—art, media, nightlife, finance, excitement—but it loses to Chicago at niceness, hot dogs, pizza, and sports fandom, and to Los Angeles at show business, and that latter one bothers New York.

So New Yorkers routinely bash LA at every chance they get. *People in LA are superficial. The women are ditzy and have fake tits. It's one big strip mall. Why on earth would you ever want to live there?* Though Steve Lemme and I had bought into this propaganda campaign, we still loaded a U-Haul and made the long drive west. To my view, the bars in LA *did* seem sparsely attended. And how did you get around? Were you supposed to limit yourselves to two drinks? We drank more than that, which worked when you could just hop into a New York City cab. The women in LA *were* hot, but they seemed not to want anything to do with you if you hadn't already made it. And yes, the place did feel like a series of strip malls. To me, New York had it right—Los Angeles was fundamentally flawed.

Before I left New York, I made friends with MTV VJ Karen Duffy (Duff), who told me that if I was moving to LA, I should look up her friend Amy Cohen, who "has LA wrapped around her little finger." Two months later, as Steve and I pulled our U-Haul into Hollywood, I called Amy.

"Hey, it's Jay and Steve. Duff said to call you when we got to town."

Amy jumped right in. "What's your address? I'll be there at seven. We're going to a party."

I hung up and looked at Steve. "I guess we're going to a party."

It was an instant friendship. Amy was hilarious and smart and loved the nightlife. She drove us high into the hills, through winding roads and past groovy houses. This was a part of LA we'd never seen, and, wow, was it beautiful.

We arrived at a party at a fantastic house in the Hollywood Hills. The crowd was eclectic. The guys were comedy writers and the women looked like *Entourage* extras. A famous animation comedy writer walked up holding a salad bowl full of a hundred white pills. (LA was in the early throes of an ecstasy revolution.) We had an amazing time that first night in Hollywood, really loving the shit out of everything.

Several hours later, at another cliffside house party, I walked up to Steve, who was standing alone, staring contemplatively into the distance at the sun rising over Hollywood. As I got closer, I realized he was actually staring at the pool, where two naked models were casually swimming. He smiled and shrugged. "I guess it's not *too* bad out here."

Steve, Erik, Amy, and I became inseparable. An LA native, Amy was totally plugged in. She seemed to know everybody and got invited to everything. We went to the greatest parties, ate at fantastic restaurants, and hung out at bars that would stay open well past closing. I grew to really understand LA. It is a creative person's mecca, filled with lots of really smart people who want to be involved in the storytelling business. Admittedly, before this trip, I had only been to bars on the Sunset Strip, which is kind of like judging New York City after only going to bars in Times Square.

At the time, Amy was George Clooney's assistant, which meant that in addition to running his schedule, she also had to house-sit for him when he was on location. Amy was afraid to stay in the big house alone due to fear of stalkers, so Steve, Erik, and I volunteered to keep her company. We spent weeks sleeping at Clooney's house, feeding his pigs, staying up late, drinking Guinness, swimming, and having a good old time. (Yeah, he knew we were there.)

CAA and John Sloss's strategy was to get *Super Troopers* made at a major studio, so they sent our script to all of the major comedy producers in town, hoping one of them would take a liking to it and set it up. Our first bite came from Bob Simonds, who had produced the Adam Sandler movies *Happy Gilmore* and *The Wedding Singer* at Universal. Bob said Universal dug the script and wanted to make the film for $5.5 million. *That was easy.* We were on cloud nine, until Bob couldn't work his producer deal out. And just like that, Bob and Universal were done.

Next, two of the Farrelly brothers' development guys, Pat Healy and Bradley Thomas, asked for a meeting. Pat and Brad thought the script was great but felt it might work better if it was set in the seventies. Since we wanted to make a film tonally like *Smokey and the Bandit,* we agreed and rewrote *Super Troopers,* setting it in the seventies. Eventually, the Farrelly brothers read it and dug it, so we sat down with them. Peter and Bobby Farrelly cracked us up with their showbiz stories about going to big studio meetings with one testicle out. They tried to get Fox to make the film, but Fox wasn't interested in a film starring total unknowns. None of the studios were biting.

There was one ray of light. Michael Shamberg, from Jersey Films, had read the script and wanted to meet. Jersey was headed by Danny DeVito, Stacey Sher, and Michael. They had produced a lot of smart, great, commercial films including *Pulp Fiction, Get Shorty, Out of Sight,* and *Man on the Moon.* Michael was a big Monty Python fan and understood what Broken Lizard aspired to. He had produced the hilarious film *A Fish Called Wanda,* which starred *Python* members John Cleese and Michael Palin. Though Michael loved our script, he didn't think he could get a studio to put the money up for it. However, he did think it would make a great TV show, so he gave it to John Landgraf, who ran Jersey's TV department (John now runs FX). Landgraf brought us to Fox Television, which paid us to write the TV pilot for *Super Troopers.* In that TV show, we changed the location from Vermont to Reno, Nevada. Yup. Reno. Years later, some guys from the State set their cop show in Reno. It's pretty common for TV shows to try to ride the wave of a successful film, but considering that Broken Lizard and the State were direct rivals, I found it odd that they would do a show that was so similar to our film. Then, they chose uniforms that looked *exactly* like ours. When *Reno 911!* came out, people stopped me on the street to say, "Love your new TV show! Why didn't you name it *Super Troopers?*" And look, we didn't invent funny cops. *Naked Gun* and *Police Academy* certainly came before us. But choosing the *exact same* outfits made it hard for us to make a *Super Troopers* TV show, because both *Reno 911!* and *Super Troopers* are owned by Fox, and they weren't going to do two shows about cops in tan uniforms. To be fair, *Reno 911!* is great and very funny. Every time I've turned it on, I dug it. So, there you have it.

But back in 1998, Fox read our TV script, dug it, but didn't end up making it, which put us at another dead end.

Amy had a ringside seat to our struggles, and as she was also an aspiring producer, she asked if she could help. When we agreed, she immediately brought new life to the film when she gave the script to her boss, George Clooney. When you meet a movie star, and I mean a *real* movie star, what you're struck with is their charisma. As my author friend Michael Craven puts it, "Movie stars have so much charisma, they're paid for it." George Clooney is a charisma machine. We met him at his Warner Bros. bungalow, where he told great stories and did a hilarious imitation of a famous female pop singer ordering chicken Marsala that had us rolling.

Clooney told us he thought our script was great, and he wanted Section Eight, the company he'd formed with *Out of Sight* director Steven Soderbergh, to produce. I had met Soderbergh at Sundance a couple of years earlier, when I'd seen his weirdly hilarious film *Schizopolis*—a film he wrote, directed, and starred in. Soderbergh is a real original. He read the script and had some notes, so I gave him a call. He told me he liked the script but was worried that it needed "something else" to distinguish it from other comedies. *Maybe cops pulling pranks wasn't quite enough.*

He suggested that we should do something like they did in *Point Break,* where the cops wore president of the United States masks. Now, here's the thing about script notes. You have to know which notes to try and which ones don't fit your vision. Soderbergh was doing what producers are supposed to do—he was giving us his honest opinion. But he didn't see the same movie we did. A couple of years later, after he saw the finished film, he put a hand on my shoulder and laughed. "Thank God you didn't listen to me!"

With Section Eight onboard, the plan was to reapproach the studios. When Michael Shamberg heard about Section Eight, he said that since Jersey had developed the TV show, they should be able to produce the film as well. So now our executive producers were George Clooney, Steven Soderbergh, Michael Shamberg, Stacey Sher, and Danny DeVito. But going back to a studio with a script, after they've already passed, only works if you've added a "meaningful new element." Translation: You've hired a movie star to act in the film. When the studios found out that neither Clooney nor DeVito was acting in *Super Troopers*, their response was the same: "We love you, George, Steven, Danny, Michael, and Stacy, but Broken Lizard still isn't famous enough to star in a studio movie." *Okay, this was bullshit. Fuck Hollywood. Fuck this shit. They don't want to make it? Fine, we'll make it indie style, sell it back to them, and shove it up their fucking asses!* (Half of what gets done in showbiz is out of rejection rage.)

I called up Sloss and told him we struck out at the studios and we needed three million bucks to make our film. So he picked up the phone and started shaking the money tree. Being involved with so many indie hits had made John a magnet for film finance. When I was his assistant, Wall Street guys would call, begging for five minutes of his time because they said they had millions of dollars they wanted to invest. We got five meetings. One producer said he'd be willing to finance the film, but only if we shot on video to save money. Since video, at the time, looked like absolute dog shit, we passed. Another guy said he'd finance it if we would put his pal Ben Affleck in the film to play the role of Thorny. I cleared my throat. "Um, I'm playing Thorny."

He smiled. "You play something else. We need Ben." We left.

Then we met Jim, a cool New York producer who was full of energy and loved sports. He said we were going to make *Super Troopers* for $3.5 million. All we had to do was cast a famous actor in the role of Captain O'Hagan—an actor who had "bankable foreign value." A film's foreign value is one of the greatest determiners of whether a film gets financed or not. Okay, you'll need to pay attention for a moment: Foreign value refers to how much money a film is likely to make overseas. Action movies and superhero movies "travel" well;

comedies, less so, because of translation issues and American pop culture references. Films with black actors don't travel well because of foreign racism, which has led to studios green-lighting those films less often, and lightening the skin color of actors on foreign posters when they do. (Yes, I've been made to look almost white.) Actors can bring foreign value to a film if they have starred in films that were financial hits overseas. If you cast a "high-foreign-value" actor in your film, the foreign value of your film goes up, and a producer can go to a bank and borrow money against your film's anticipated foreign box office.

In our case, Producer Jim was looking to cast an actor to play Captain O'Hagan who had enough foreign value that a bank would loan him the money to make *Super Troopers.* Jim made a list of actors who he felt fit the bill. On the list was one of our heroes, John Goodman. John read the script and dug it, and CAA accepted the offer for him to play O'Hagan. And just like that, we were green-lit. *Holy shit! This is really gonna happen!* But then Jim tapped the brakes, saying he "needed to recheck the numbers." After an excruciating week, he came back to us.

"Um, sorry, the bank won't loan me as much money as I thought they would." Jim wanted to go back to CAA to ask John Goodman to reduce his already agreed upon salary. CAA wasn't pleased and the movie fell apart again. CAA was right, by the way. A deal's a deal, and this was embarrassing. With the trust broken, we parted ways with Jim, and we were back in the wind, and out of options. Nobody wanted to make *Super Troopers*—no studios and no independent financiers.

Months passed and we were adrift. We wondered if we should

write a new script, but what would be the point? Financiers telling us that they didn't want us to star in *Super Troopers* wasn't code for *we want you to star in something else.* Some of us were in California and some in New York, so the group's connection was fraying. Steve, Erik, and I wanted Kevin and Paul to move out to LA, but they were reluctant without anything concrete to do. We pondered breaking up and going it alone.

I flew back to New York to re-edit a film by the comedian Mitch Hedberg. Mitch was a hell of a joke writer, and his delivery style included a pace and cadence that were all his own. We were both managed by Dave Miner, who put us together. Mitch's film, *Los Enchiladas!,* was two and a half hours long, and while it was funny and had a lot of great comics in it, including Mitch, Todd Barry, Dave Attell, and Marc Maron, it needed some paring back.

Mitch and I worked in an edit room, looking for ways to make the film funnier and better. Mitch would take fifteen-minute breaks and come back to the edit room wearing yellow sunglasses (the room was dark) and reeking of pot smoke. After a few too many breaks, I said, "You know, if you smoke in here, we'll get more work done."

He laughed. "I didn't want to offend you!" He pulled out a joint and lit it, and our editing sessions got silly. In the end, we trimmed the film down to ninety minutes and it got into Sundance.

A couple of years later, Dave Miner called me with the news that Mitch had died of a heroin overdose in some hotel on the road. So now, that was Farley and Hedberg, and still to come would be the death of the great writer-comic Harris Wittels. Comedy folks, let's be clear: I get it. Heroin is great, but it's the fucking Devil. It's that dipshit Russian game, Russian roulette. Doing it doesn't make you cool. It makes you nerdy. There are plenty of other substances to do that don't kill you and don't deprive us of your comic genius. Don't.

Meanwhile, we had all but given up on *Super Troopers.* I was making the final break with New York by ending our lease on our one-room Broken Lizard office. I was packing up boxes for storage when the phone rang. It was my college friend Cricket Lengyel. Cricket apologized for having to make this call, but her father, Pete, had recently retired from finance and loved movies and had decided to try his hand at script writing. Since I was the only person she knew "kind of working" in show business, she asked if I would consider talking to him. I said, "Sure. Whatever you need."

When Pete Lengyel called, he asked me a lot of questions about the film business and script writing. Pete had written a comedy script and asked if I'd read it, so I said, "Sure. No problem." But then Pete pulled back.

"It occurs to me that I don't really know what *your* qualifications are. Do you have a writing sample I can read?" I was being auditioned to see if I was worthy of reading his script. I didn't love that, but I did love Cricket, so I gritted my teeth and sent over the script to *Super Troopers.* Secretly, I was hoping he wouldn't like it and that I wouldn't have to read his script.

A week later, the phone rang. It was Pete. "So, I read your script. It's funny. I think you're on to something here." I said thanks, thinking, *What could a mid-sixties banker possibly know?* Pete had another question. "What's happening with this movie?"

I paused. I was talking to a (former) investment banker. *Should I tell him the unvarnished truth—that no one in show business thought it was a good bet?* Instead, I told him the other truth. "We're raising money to make it."

And then Pete asked the million-dollar question: "Can you make it for a million dollars?" I closed my eyes. *Was this guy for real?* When you're trying to find money for a film, you meet all sorts of con artists. Many of them *say* they've got the money but then don't come through. I had lunch with a "financier" who supposedly "controlled" a hundred-million-dollar film fund, but not only did I have to pick up the check; I also had to loan him money for the valet. *Red fucking flag!* Why do they go through the charade? Because they want to be near the excitement of Hollywood. They'll tell a filmmaker they have the money to make a film, and after signing a contract, they'll use the filmmaker's name to run around and try to raise the money. When they strike out, and they always strike out, they call you back and say, "Sorry, it just didn't work out."

It happens all the time and it's a huge waste of time. But Pete was different. You could hear it in his no-nonsense banker's voice. I told him I'd talk to my producer and get back to him. I walked the twenty feet over to Rich's office and said, "You think we can make *Super Troopers* for a million bucks?"

Rich said what he always says: "We can do anything for any amount of money; it's just a matter of how much time you're going to have to shoot it and how much money we're all gonna make. With the stunts and fights and actors you want, a million dollars might get the job done, but we'll all get paid scale"—union minimum. Rich asked how real the money was. When I told him that Pete was my friend's dad, he rolled his eyes. But when I told him Pete was a retired investment banker, his mood changed. Rich was a former investment banker, so he knew people who knew people.

"Set up a call and I'll check this guy out. Meanwhile, I'll do a new budget and see if it's even possible."

When we met with Pete, Rich told him that we could make the film for $1.26 million. Pete paused.

"I've got $1.2 million, not a penny more. Take it or leave it." We took it. After a short negotiation, Pete wrote the check and we were in preproduction.

Easy, right?

CHAPTER 9

Casting *Super Troopers*:
How I Almost Played Farva

That we ever got *Puddle Cruiser* made was a minor miracle. And while *Super Troopers* was still a low-budget movie, our budget was going to be seven times that of *Puddle Cruiser*. Plus, it was the first time we were playing characters markedly different from ourselves. *Were we good enough actors to pull that off?* The pressure mounted.

We wrote fifteen drafts of the script before I cast it, to ensure that everyone was writing jokes for every character. When it was time to decide who played whom, the decision came pretty naturally. Since I was the head of Broken Lizard, I ended up playing the head trooper, Thorny. In real life, Kevin tends to be a funny, obstinate naysayer, so we made him the dick, Farva. Steve, in real life, has kind of a macho energy, which he injected into Mac. Paul looked the least like a real cop, so Foster felt right. Erik had a Minnesota gee whiz to him, so we made him the rookie. Truthfully, the only real decision was whether or not I would play Farva and Kevin would play Thorny. That was seriously contemplated.

We hired a casting agent, Jennifer McNamara, who got to work finding the rest of our cast. She landed the great Brian Cox to play Captain O'Hagan, which gave the film a much-needed respect boost. In addition to being hilarious in the great Wes Anderson film *Rushmore* and menacing as the original Hannibal Lecktor in *Manhunter*, Brian also scored as Uncle Argyle in Broken Lizard's favorite film, *Braveheart*. When Brian read our script, he told his agent he wanted in. That's because when Brian was starting out, he always thought he'd be the next Jerry Lewis. Brian saw our film as a way to show the world how funny he is.

The late, great Daniel von Bargen played Chief Grady with just the right amount of sinister exasperation. Daniel and I got off to what I'll call not the best start. On his first day, we shot a scene where O'Hagan comes to the local police station to ask Chief Grady if he knows anything about a cartoon monkey named Johnny Chimpo. Grady mocks O'Hagan, saying they should call in "Bobby the Baboon and Gerry the Giraffe" to see if *they* know anything. On paper, the lines were silly and Daniel played them that way—but that's not how we intended them. We were looking to make a tough, funny film that was more like *Smokey and the Bandit* than like *Police Academy*. After take one, I went to Daniel and said, "Hey, the lines may *seem* silly, but we need Grady to be tough and real. We need him to have gravitas."

He kinda shrugged, and then he did take two. Same result. I went back in with the same note, but I said it a different way. Daniel pushed back. He was worried it wouldn't be funny if he didn't tip the joke. Then he dropped his ace. *You know on* Seinfeld, *we did it this way.*

This is common for first days, where actors and directors feel each other out. The director has a view of how the performance should be, but so does the actor. This early conversation is critical because it sets the tone for the whole performance. Take four was the same. Goofy. At the monitors, Heffernan nudged me.

"I know, dude," I said, heading back in. This time I told Daniel, "Forget the jokes. Just play it tough."

He stared at me, annoyed. "Fine."

And he did. He read it tough, and I loved it. So I went in to tell him.

"That's it. That's the tone." And then I attempted to butter him up. "You're a really good tough guy."

He wasn't falling for it. In his mind, he'd lost this first battle, but he wasn't done swinging. "I've played six generals, four colonels, and three police chiefs. It is what it is." He was basically saying that if I wanted a generic Daniel von Bargen performance, then that's what I was going to get. I left with my tail between my legs.

Later in the day, after finishing another scene, Daniel took me aside. "Tough *and* funny. That's where the joke is. I get this movie now."

Daniel's performance as Chief Grady is my favorite in the film. When he's in the police station basement, asking Farva to spy for him, he's at his best.

"The lice hate the sugar." I fucking love that. Rest in peace, pal.

We wanted a seventies female TV icon to play Governor Jessman, so we were thrilled when Lynda Carter joined the cast. She's hilariously dry in the pre–press conference scene with her aide:

GOVERNOR JESSMAN: "What is this thing, again?"

AIDE: "It's a drug bust."

GOVERNOR JESSMAN: "Cocaine?"

AIDE: "Marijuana."

GOVERNOR JESSMAN: (Sighs) "Then, why are we here?"

I first saw Marisa Coughlan in the Kevin Williamson movie *Teaching Mrs. Tingle*, where she reenacts a possession scene from *The Exorcist*. She is great in that film, and Amy Cohen knew her and convinced her to do our film. Marisa fell in easily with Broken Lizard's rhythm, which made her very popular with us. We named her character Ursula Hanson after our college friend, who was an original member of Charred Goosebeak.

I could talk about a lot of scenes she's great in, but I'll focus on the biker scene. In the script, Foster and Ursula meet in an out-of-town diner to discuss their plan. Worried they'll be recognized, they agree to come in disguise, dressed as "bikers." But the costume director wasn't sure which kind of "bikers" we meant, so she bought both motorcycle leathers *and* bicycle road racer spandex. When we saw the foxy Marisa in her leathers and Paul in his spandex and bike helmet, we came up with the joke that Foster was confused about which kind of biker disguise Ursula meant.

"Oooooh, biker!" This was a low-budget mistake that turned into gold.

Charlie Finn played the Dimpus Burger clerk to perfection. The origin of the character came from Saturday mornings at Colgate, when we'd wake up hungover and drive into town to get large Cokes at Burger King. But the Burger King manager (who had to be Canadian) listed the "large" drink on the menu as "a liter." So when we'd try to order "large Cokes," a voice would come over the drive-through speaker:

"We don't have large colas. We only have liters of cola."

Unwilling to bend to this bastard trying to enforce the metric system in America, we tormented the BK staff, always ordering "large" Cokes, and always being corrected that they only had liters of cola. It was a classic pointless war, which we lost, because they were stubborn and wouldn't give us large drinks unless we called them liters. Score one for Canada.

I actually "discovered" Charlie when we were casting an NBC pilot called *Safety School,* which was based on our first film, *Puddle Cruiser.* I went to the Improv Olympic in LA to look for funny people. Outside, after the show, I saw a tall, lanky dude, with a nasally Chicago voice, smoking a cigarette. He seemed kind of funny, and in the range of what we were looking for, so I approached. "Hey, are you an actor?"

"Sort of," he said, in his trademark voice.

"You want to audition for a TV show?"

"I guess," he said. Charlie later admitted that he'd never been on an audition before. He was also probably wondering if I was a chicken hawk, cruising boys on the boulevard. He got the part in the pilot and, years later, as the Dimpus Burger guy. Charlie is a funny guy and does a great Dennis Miller impersonation.

My high school friend James Grace was hilarious as Officer Rando, the local cop who gets hit in the head with an empty syrup bottle in the diner scene. In college the term "rando" referred to someone we didn't know, as in, *Who's the rando?*

Mike Weaver is the red-haired guy who played Local Officer Smy. Smy tries to dress down Ursula, but she undercuts him by telling him that he has toilet paper on his shoe, which makes Smy apoplectic. Weaver is a hilarious gem of an actor.

Our college friend Dan Fey is the oddball all-star who played Local Officer Burton with spaced-out perfection. Fey also played the part of the hopped-up rugby player in *Puddle Cruiser.*

Jim Gaffigan auditioned to play one of the local cops, but we had already cast our guys, so we cast him as the "meow" driver. Heffernan tried to block him because he and Gaffigan always went out for the same parts, and Gaffigan usually won. We overruled Heffernan, and Gaffigan nailed it in his funny, dry manner. It all ended well, as Heffernan and Gaffigan are now pals. Gaffigan, of course, went on to become one of the biggest stand-ups in the country; so *Hot Pooooooockets to you, Heffernan!*

Philippe Brenninkmeyer's audition for the Porsche-driving German swinger was so good that we cast him before he left the room. Phil always delivers, so we cast him again as the master of ceremonies in *Beerfest.* What an amazing actor. Maria Tornberg played the female German swinger and was hilarious, lovely, and totally game for the sexy silliness the part required.

One of the upsides to taking as long as it did to finance the film was that as we were raising money, and as we were casting, we kept writing—in the end, we shot draft twenty-two of the script. Our low-budget-inspired philosophy was to write the living shit out of our scripts, so that when we arrived on set, we all agreed that what we were shooting was already funny. And if we don't improvise a single line, we'll still be happy. We improvise a lot more nowadays, but *Super Troopers* has only about ten improvised lines.

CHAPTER 10

——————

Making *Super Troopers*:
How We Focused on Jokes We Thought Were Funny

The story took place in a Vermont border town, so we were looking for rolling hills and rural highways. We scouted Big Bear, California, but since all of our crew contacts were in New York, Rich felt that we'd be better able to maximize our budget back east. Eventually, we settled on the small town of Beacon, New York, which is near Poughkeepsie.

Regardless of our confidence in the script, I wasn't feeling confident as a filmmaker. *Puddle Cruiser* had turned out well, but *Super Troopers* was a lot bigger, with fights, car chases, stunts, and real actors. Wouldn't they know that I was a know-nothing fraud? But since nobody wants an insecure quarterback, I faked confidence. The anxiety took a toll on my body. Regardless of eating and drinking everything in Poughkeepsie, stress ate away ten pounds.

THE OPENING

Due to the softness of *Puddle Cruiser*'s opening scene, we invested a great deal of energy in making sure that we didn't repeat the mistake with *Super Troopers*. To that end, we wrote draft after draft after draft of the opening and didn't stop until we finally arrived at a scene that we thought could start the movie right. In a riff on our friends' bachelor party story, our film started with Vermont stoner college kids driving over the border into Canada to get some French fries and gravy (poutine). They are pulled over by the highway patrol, who mess with them before turning to the bigger fish—the speeder in the white Miata.

In an amazing bit of luck for our low-budget indie, we found a six-mile, four-lane highway (two lanes on each side) that, because a bigger one was being built nearby, had mostly fallen out of use. In a funny case of life imitating art, when we needed the on-ramps shut down to traffic, the local cops and the highway patrol got into an argument over who had jurisdiction. The highway patrol said that the ramp was an extension of the highway, so *they* should be the force to shut down traffic, but the local cops said that the highway began at the end of the ramp, so they felt that *they* should be the ones to shut down traffic. In the end, neither force would back down, so the on-ramps ended up being really well shut down.

The stoners drove a sky-blue Impala, which fit the seventies vibe we were going for, but the car broke down after the first pullover. That was a problem since the script called for the stoners to pull back onto the highway after the first pullover. So when Joey Kern (the shotgun stoner) said, "Shit, I was about to pull out my nine and put a cap in that pig's ass," their car was supposed to be moving. With no other choice, we did a quick on-set rewrite and lucked out with two great improvs:

> **ANDRÉ (DRIVER):** "We're already pulled over!"

And

> **JOEY:** "He's already pulled over! He
> can't pull over any farther!"

Those two guys were great, as was Geoff Arend in the backseat, who stole the show when he licked the bulletproof glass. "The snozz-berries taste like snozzberries." (Thank you, Willy Wonka.)

Meanwhile, Erik and I were both doing our best to channel Clint Eastwood. Was that choice going to be funny? We weren't sure, but we liked this couplet:

> **THORNY:** "Do you smell something,
> Rabbit?"
> **RABBIT:** "Fear."

Eventually, Mac, Steve Lemme's character, blows by in a white Miata (we wanted a red Ferrari), and we begin our car chase. Our stunt coordinator, Manny Siverio, really captured the *Smokey and the Bandit* style I was hoping for.

Later, when Mac runs out of the bar and hops into the stoners' car, I get great joy from watching him scream, "You boys like Mexico?!" Steve had come a long way from the day he showed up drunk to our college audition. *Well done, pal.*

THE DINER

After having breakfast at a local diner, the troopers get into a scuffle with the local cops. Kevin thought the scene needed a little Vermont flavor, so he suggested a maple-syrup-chugging contest. The problem with writing a syrup chug into a movie is that you're going to have to do it. Initially, the prop master filled two syrup containers with very thick iced tea, but it wasn't thick enough, so we sent a production assistant to the grocery store to buy the real stuff. Take after take, we drank that sweet, thick syrup down. I drank two full bottles, and Erik drank three. (It's good to be the director.) I'll say this. Over the years, I've put a lot of bad things into my body, but this was by far the worst. When the scene ended, I ran to the bathroom to pull the trigger. Already stepping out was a sweaty-looking Erik, who shook me off. "Don't bother. It won't come up—too thick."

When the crew went to lunch, Erik and I went to my trailer instead, where we shut off the lights, lay down on the ground, and shivered, in the throes of what felt like looming diabetes.

Erik had the afternoon off, while I had to shoot another scene. (It's bad to be the director.)

Afterward I went back to the motel, where I ran into a smiling Erik. "Have you pooped yet?"

"No, I just got back." I grimaced. "But I can feel it coming."

He nodded sagely. "There's a reason maple syrup is part of the Master Cleanse. Hold on tight, matey."

I'll spare you the gory details. Actually, I won't. Things came out of me that I have no memory of ever ingesting. Aside from lots of water and air, I shat what appeared to be a stick with a petrified leaf attached. I shat a fully intact robin fetus.

Today, at restaurants, chefs will often sit down at our table brandishing two bottles of syrup, hoping to re-create the chug. But I just politely tell them to fuck off, as I'll never drink syrup again.

CHOCOLATE SOAP

In the first morning meeting, O'Hagan tells the guys that their ticket numbers are low and that their station is under threat of being shut down. O'Hagan tells Farva, who is under suspension for "the school bus incident," to get coffee for the gang. When Farva pops his head out and asks, "Who wants cream?" we all just stare at him because, though some of us may want cream, no one wants to admit it because of how it might reflect on our manhood. This joke came from my father, who only drinks his coffee black. At the time, I drank my coffee with hazelnut creamer. When I asked my father why he didn't use cream or sugar, he'd just shrug. "It's unnecessary." And while my dad never said a word about my hazelnut creamer, I always felt that he was secretly disappointed that his son didn't drink coffee like a man.

When Farva comes out with the coffees, he has slipped a bar of soap into Rabbit's cup as a "prank." But the bar of soap is so clearly visible that it's a really lousy prank. When Mac sees the soap, he nonsensically suggests to Rabbit that he should bite it to "make Farva look like a dick." Rabbit ignores him, but Mac won't give up trying to get Rabbit to bite the soap. Meanwhile, Captain O'Hagan is trying to tell a story about how much he loves living in Spurbury (the town we named after our Colgate friend Jim Sperber). The script called for O'Hagan to snap on Mac, grab the soap, bite it, chew it, and swallow it. We wanted to show that, though O'Hagan was pissed, he was also enough of a nutjob that he would eat soap to make a point. To make it easy, we made soap bars out of white chocolate, but, on set, Brian told us that he was a diabetic and couldn't eat chocolate. As a fix, Brian bit the "soap," chewed it, and spat it out at Mac.

WHAT'S THAT MEOW?

During the writing process, still a year from the green light, we were in LA meeting on a TV project for NBC and sleeping five to a room in the Travelodge motel in Santa Monica. It was four A.M. and we had been up smoking and joking, getting into some real abdominal-busting laughter. I remember someone saying, "All right now." I have a bad left ear, roughly half of normal hearing, so I asked if he had said "meow." I mishear things a lot, and I get a lot of shit for it. In this case, someone mocked me for my mishear, and then we riffed for half an hour on "meow" replacing "now" in a sentence. We weren't writing at the time, but luckily someone, I think Paul, wrote the riff down on a napkin and brought it back up again at our next meeting. Had Paul not rallied at five A.M. to scribble that down, the meow scene would have been lost forever in the smoke. Take notes in life, folks.

To be clear, *I* didn't invent the meow gag. Not even close. We all did. And this story happened at four A.M., so I'll admit that there could be multiple versions of who said "meow" first. I mention this because Heffernan has a different memory of the night, and you should read his book for that one.

We wrote the scene into the script and rehearsed it, but it wasn't quite as funny as we had imagined. So we tried it in a southern accent. Hearing it that way really unlocked the funny for us. The

Goofing off in the kitchen.

Arsenic and Old Lace.

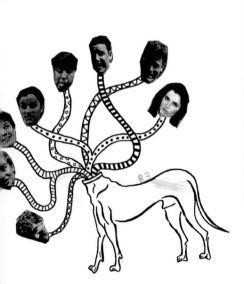

BROKEN LIZARD COMEDY GROUP

Poster for NYC live show. I like weird.

Me in 1991.
I open my mouth a lot in pictures.

Broken Lizard in 1991. The guy in the Yankees hat is Rob Holzer, our piano guy. The woman is Lauren Bright.

Steve and me in Hollywood, 2001. Late night.

The Tinfoil Monkey Agenda.

Groomsmen at Heffernan's wedding, 2001.

"They think I'm Mexican." The diner scene in *Super Troopers*.

I'll never chug syrup again.

"The lice hate the sugar."

Super Troopers premiere, 2001

Lemme, Patrick Swayze, me, and half of Heffernan's forehead
at our *Stuff* magazine party at Sundance, 2001.

Hanging with our British tour manager, Wilko, on the *Super Troopers* tour, 2001.

Steve and me, between shows. Backstage on tour, 2004.

The General Lee. Yeeeehaaaaw!!!

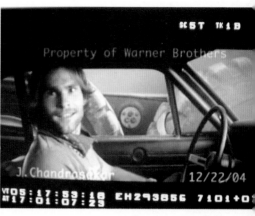

Seann did a lot of his own driving.

Willie and me cracking jokes on his bus,
the Honeysuckle Rose.

The *Beerfest* shoot. Riding this five-man bike was
terrifying because it weighed a ton. I was worried
that it would break all our legs.

She made me wear these.

On the road, playing cards
with Billy the Dummy.

Beerfest poster outside Warner Bros.

Car Ram Rod.

Jon Pack / Fox Searchlight Pictures

Super Troopers 2– with bigger mustaches!

Kevin, Rich Perello, and me on set, in "that most important conversation."

Holy shit. We're in a movie with Rob Lowe.

All photographs on this page are courtesy of Jon Pack/Fox Searchlight Pictures.

problem was that it felt like a bit of a stretch to think that a Vermont cop would speak with a southern accent.

When writing our scripts, we try to achieve balance when it comes to divvying up funny scenes. Since Erik and I had the opening scene, and Paul and Steve had the repeater pullover, and Erik had the German swinger scene, and Steve had the jerking-off-in-the-car scene, it was a toss-up between Paul and me as to who got the lead in the meow scene. Remember, Farva wasn't on the road. Creatively, we could live with a northern cop with a southern accent, but since none of us had ever encountered an Indian with a southern accent, I felt like Paul should probably play the part. And in the end, he really nailed it.

While we were shooting the meow pullover, we were only able to shut down one side of the highway, so the sound of the passing cars was driving our sound guy, David, crazy. Since I was wearing a highway patrol uniform, I walked across the grass median and stepped onto the highway, raising my hand. The traffic stopped dead. "Action!" I yelled, as I watched the feed on a handheld monitor. Was it impersonating an officer? Considering that I was wearing a Vermont highway patrol uniform and I was directing traffic in New York, you bet. Sorry about that, guys.

CHARLIE RICH

Rabbit is washing a patrol car when Farva happens upon him in the garage. In our minds, Farva is a huge country music fan. So Erik called upon a bit of music history that he thought would give the scene some obscure color: In 1975, Charlie Rich, high on painkillers and gin and tonics, took the stage to hand out the award for the Country Music Association Entertainer of the Year, the award that he himself had won the year prior. When Charlie opened the envelope and saw John Denver's name, he pulled out a lighter and lit the card on fire.

In Farva's mind, he is the old-school Charlie Rich, while Rabbit is the new boy, John Denver. Farva goes nose to nose with Rabbit to let him know that he's going down.

This is a good example of how group writing works. Though Erik came up with the idea and wrote the original monologue, he felt that it would be better coming out of Farva's mouth.

GLAMOUR PET

Rabbit and Thorny are called out to a crime scene, but when they arrive, they find that the local cops are already there. Inside an abandoned Winnebago, they find a dead woman—eyes open and facedown in a dog dish. Chloe O'Connor (Rich Perello's assistant) played the dead woman, and she did a nice job not breathing or blinking. While inside the Winnebago, the cops hear a sound and assume it's the killer. It turns out to be a pet pig, which Thorny calls a "glamour pet." We had originally written it as an attack dog, but after our weeks feeding George Clooney's pigs, we decided on this more original idea for a pet.

SHAVING CREAM

After the brawl with the local cops outside the Winnebago, Thorny turns the investigation over to them out of a desire not to deal with the wild hog. This pisses O'Hagan off because he feels like they could have used the murder case to justify the highway patrol's budget and existence. After O'Hagan chews the guys out in the locker room, he leaves, and we reveal that Rabbit has been hiding in a locker full of shaving cream the whole time. The prop master accidentally bought menthol shaving cream, which caused Erik's skin to "really fucking burn!" Since we didn't have time for someone to run to the store and buy regular shaving cream, Erik muscled through and got the scene done.

BOBBY McGEE

Thorny is the coach of his seven-year-old son Arlo's baseball team. We named Arlo after the folk singer Arlo Guthrie. Years later, I would become friends with his daughter, Cathy, who is part of the great and hilarious band Folk Uke. Talking to Thorny at the game is his hippie lover, and Arlo's mother, Bobbi, whom we named after Bobby McGee, from the great Kris Kristofferson song. Bobbi owns a head shop and she and Thorny are swingers, of course.

THE LARGEST COTTON CANDY EVER PUT ON FILM

During college, Kevin and I traveled across Europe together, stopping in London, Venice, Rome, and, eventually, Geneva, Switzerland. While in Geneva we visited a park that boasted the world's longest bench (it's in *The Guinness Book of World Records*). We laughed at how lame the record was and talked about how when we got back to Colgate we would build a bench three feet longer just to fuck Geneva over. We never did, but out of this came the idea for Foster to send Local Officer

Rando a massive cotton candy. And while it may or may not be the biggest cotton candy ever made, we're pretty sure it's the biggest cotton candy that's ever appeared in a movie. So take that, Geneva.

In the same scene, Foster gets up to go to the concession stand and asks the guys if anyone wants anything. Rabbit says, "Hey, see if they've got any chocolate bananas [beat] Foster." Paul loved Bananas Foster, so we honored that love by putting it in the movie.

ENHANCE, ENHANCE, ENHANCE . . .

Distracted by playing the repeater game, Mac and Foster are locked inside the back of a Bunty Soap truck. Back at the station, Thorny is printing an image of the truck driver from the dashboard cam and pretends to "enhance" the photo in an homage to the Harrison Ford film *Blade Runner.*

AFGHANISTANIMATION

In Rabbit's youth, before joining the police academy, he traveled with the Grateful Dead, so he knew his way around a joint. When O'Hagan brings up the marijuana with the cartoon-monkey logo on it, Rabbit offers his (secretly expert) opinion that some drug dealers use cartoon characters to mark their product, like a brand name. When we lived in New York, we had a pot dealer who delineated his different brands with colored stickers. And at a Dead show at Alpine Valley, we bought LSD with Bugs Bunny's picture on it. Though Rabbit is just being helpful, Farva senses a chance to undercut him and says, "Where'd you learn that, Cheech? Drug school?"

We made up the cartoon character Johnny Chimpo to be the pot brand. Paul was into Japanimation, so we started riffing on what country Johnny could be from. After we made suggestions like "Sud-animation," "Chinamation," and "Italimation," someone said "Afghan-istanimation," and we knew we had a winner. Afghanistan was in the news at the time because of the rise of the Taliban. Choosing Afghanistan was also our way to subtly tweak Islam's nose since the religion bans cartoons. We named the monkey Johnny Chimpo because it felt like the kind of generic, Western-sounding name a foreign TV producer would come up with to appeal to Afghani kids.

In the cartoon's fictional backstory, Johnny Chimpo is a monkey who spends his days getting into mischief, while his English butler tries to keep him in line. Johnny Chimpo was a metaphor for Afghanistan, which was generally misbehaving on the world stage at the time, while the butler stood in for the Western powers, who were chastising Afghanistan to behave itself. In the clip of the show, Johnny Chimpo gives the camera a thumbs-up and says the generic English words, "Cool beans!" After 9/11, we seemed prescient for choosing Afghanistan, but it was really just how silly "Afghanistanimation" sounded that drove our decision.

HOW A RANDOM PERSON ALMOST ENDED UP IN A BIG ROLE IN *SUPER TROOPERS*

After Foster and Ursula find the grass in the Winnebago, Foster brings some back to the station, where he and Mac pose for the newspaper cameras. When Mayor Timber arrives, he asks O'Hagan if he can jump in on the photo shoot. Our original plan was to cast ESPN anchor Dan Patrick as Mayor Timber. And when we made the offer to Dan, he immediately said yes, without so much as a meeting or a phone call. That felt strange, but we were thrilled and figured he must just have the acting bug. Then our casting agent called to tell us that she had made a mistake. The Dan Patrick who had accepted the role was an unknown actor from Portland, Oregon—not the ESPN anchor. The mistake had happened because *Portland* Dan Patrick had joined the Screen Actors Guild first and "owned" the name. In the end, we rescinded the offer and got lucky when *Trading Places* alum John Bedford Lloyd agreed to play the part. John was hilarious and perfect and fell in with our tone easily.

For the record, we'd still like to work with the *sportscaster* Dan Patrick.

THE GERMAN SWINGERS

When we shot the German swinger pullover, we didn't budget our time well earlier in the day, so we were left with only two hours to complete the fairly complicated scene before the sun set. I took the approach of shooting only the shots that I thought we needed. When the sun finally dropped, I was worried that we might not have all of the shots necessary to make a good scene. But in the edit room, it cut together really nicely, so crisis averted. Erik is great in the scene, as are the two actors who played the Germans, Philippe Brennink-meyer and Maria Tornberg. This scene has one of my favorite jokes in the film. It's at the end, when we all get back into the car to head to the station. I tell my son, Arlo, to sit on Uncle Rabbit's lap, but Rabbit objects (because of his hard-on): "I don't think that's such a good idea, Thorn."

His delivery always makes me laugh.

FARVA AT THE GAS STATION

During our postcollege cross-country road trip, Heffernan and I saw a sign that advertised a free hot dog with the purchase of a full tank of gas. We thought it was hilarious that there was someone out there who would be enticed to spend $60 to get a 60-cent hot dog. For us, that someone was Rod Farva, who when he came up short on the minimum spend, dumped $3 worth of gas into the garbage to get his dog.

STRANGLEBATION

Mac is parked, radar-gunning cars, when he gets turned on by the image of a woman on a casino billboard. Mac starts to masturbate and then gets into a little autoerotic asphyxiation, or as we nicknamed it, "stranglebation." For the record, I've never done it. Regular, nonlethal masturbation has always been good enough for me. We've riffed a lot over the years about how that had to be the most humiliating way to die—nude, with a belt around your neck, and a hard-on in your hand, with tissues and lotion nearby. *Yech.*

Steve Lemme's girlfriend at the time, Sue Ryan, was the model on the casino billboard. Sue also played Landfill's unlucky wife in *Beerfest*.

A TEN-INCH COCK

My performance in *Super Troopers* is meant to be an amalgamation of the styles of three of my acting idols—Clint Eastwood, Burt Reynolds, and Billy Dee Williams. For the love scene, though, it was Billy Dee all the way. In the (later deleted) scene, my wife, Bobbi, and I make love and then talk about moving when the station shuts down.

The scene had an overly emotional tone, which was meant to lure the audience in before we dropped the big punch line on them. Which was, when Bobbi and I get up to shower, she opens the bathroom door, and the mirror reveals my (Thorny's) ten-inch penis.

We loved the joke, but we were new filmmakers and we were embarrassed, so we didn't even tell the prop master about it. Instead, I called the prop houses myself to ask about making my fake ten-incher, since my own black demon is slightly less. "Yes, hello, I'm making a film and I need a prosthetic penis. Ten inches and brown, though black will do." They hung up on me.

The lady at the second prop house angrily screamed, "We don't do porno!"

At the third prop house, a guy with a big New York accent said, "Take ya black dick and go fuck yahself!"

So we killed the ten-inch cock joke. When we shot the scene, it ended up being just a romantic scene between Thorny and Bobbi. It had no punch line and, frankly, no place in the movie.

After Sundance, the German swingers proved so popular that we brought them back, writing a scene where Thorny and Bobbi swing with the German couple. That was lucky for me because the reshoot allowed me to say five of my favorite words in this order: "Who wants a mustache ride?"

UNDERCOVER

When O'Hagan tells Mac and Foster to investigate the local truck stops to see if they can find anything about the truck driver Galika-nokus, they decide to go undercover. In the original script, they dress as truck drivers, go to a truck stop, and infiltrate a bare-knuckle trucker-fighting ring. To prove that they're not cops, Foster agrees to fight one of the truckers. During the fight, the trucker hits Foster so hard that his fake mustache goes flying. Trying to cover for him, Mac yells, "He punched the mustache clean off of him!" We all thought that was hilarious, though there were internal fights about whether punching the mustache off and getting away with it was too broad for our film's tone. In the end, we didn't have the money to rent a truck stop, so we nixed the bit. Instead, neither Mac nor Foster can drive a truck, so they never make it to the truck stop.

In a bit of good news for lovers of this joke, we found a home for it in *Super Troopers 2*.

IT'S JUST A QUARTER . . .

The idea for this scene came from the McDonald's invention of supersizing. McDonald's workers were instructed to hassle customers into paying twenty-five cents more to get the next size up of a meal. Since I always knew exactly how much food I wanted, I never took the bait on the upsell. Also, to me, the fries in the extra-large always got a little soggy in the end, didn't they? But saying no was never enough, because McDonald's workers would keep pushing. This annoyed the shit out of us, so we wrote the scene where the Dimpus Burger kid, played by Charlie Finn, refuses to give up on upselling Farva.

COUNTER GUY: "Do you want to Dimpa-size your meal for a quarter more?"

FARVA: "Do you want me to punchasize your face for free?"

> COUNTER GUY: "It's just a quarter and look how
> much more you get!"
> FARVA: "I said, 'No!'"
> COUNTER GUY: "It's just twenty-five cents."

I feel Farva's rage.

POWDERED SUGAR

After Farva attacks the burger kid, he's arrested, stripped nude, and hosed down in the basement of the local police station. The local cops also attempt to delouse Farva with powdered sugar, because their chief believes that "the lice hate the sugar." Aside from the sugar, this scene was meant to mirror the one in *First Blood* when the ex–Green Beret John J. Rambo is arrested, stripped nude, and cleaned up with a fire hose. Stallone was nude, so Farva had to be nude.

In our scene, Chief Grady stops the hosing so he can speak with Farva. This would require Kevin to turn toward the camera (and Grady), and he was concerned. "Just don't show my dick, dude."

I smiled. "Don't flatter yourself. No one wants to see that." And then, to reassure him, I told our director of photography / camera operator, Joaquin Baca-Asay, to tilt up when Kevin turned. *Essentially, don't show his dick.*

Joaquin smirked, "Obviously. Who would want to see his dick?"

And so we shot the scene. Kevin was up against the wall, nude, while the local cops hosed him down from behind and scrubbed his body with a long brush. Big puffs of white sugar flew at him as well. When Chief Grady came in, Kevin turned toward the camera, and the cameraman, Joaquin, tilted up to avoid showing his penis.

The story jumps to the edit room, weeks later, where we were watching the raw footage for the first time. In take one, as Kevin turns, Joaquin starts to tilt the camera up—oops, there it was—a second and a half of Kevin's shriveled cock—a cock that seemed to be wider than it was long. A cock that would quickly acquire the nickname "the Tuna Can." Now, to be fair, it wasn't his fault. The water coming out of that hose *was* freezing. At Colgate, I showered with the man a thousand times (in the group shower room), and his cock is bigger than that. So . . . you're welcome, Heffernan.

Seeing his dick on 35 mm film was stunning. Joyous. I looked at him and smiled, but I didn't say anything. He didn't either. To be honest, I don't think either of us was 100 percent sure that we had seen what we thought we had seen.

I rolled take two, and then three and then four, five, and six. There were no cocks in any of those takes.

Then I played the first take again, "the cock take." Bam! I froze the film on his nude dick and pointed! "Ha-ha!"

Heffernan looked at me. "No fuckin' way."

I paused and then parried. "But that's the funniest take, man."

Heffernan shook his head, "We're not showing my dick, dude."

I went for it. "This scene is about Farva's emotional breakdown. He's arrested, covered in powdered sugar, nude, and vulnerable. How much more vulnerable can you be than to show your naked, shriveled cock?" Sorry. I couldn't resist that tiny (shriveled) insult. Then, I went on. "When the audience sees that we're so committed to our sense of humor that we'll do *this,* man, that'll just signal to them that we're willing to go wherever the joke takes us."

He steeled his face. "No."

I tried another tack. "Look, we're liberals. We show naked women, drugs, booze, whatever. If we don't show Farva's dick, we might as well join the fuckin' Republican Party!" His willpower was waning, so I poured it on. "The Farrelly brothers go there. If we're gonna be in the big leagues, *we* have to go there." He scowled, but I was a dog with a bone. "Buddy, you're gonna make film history . . . First dick in an American comedy." (Graham Chapman had shown dick in *Monty Python's Life of Brian*.)

Defeated, Kevin grumbled. "Fine, we'll show my dick." And then, his price: "But next movie, we're showing *your* dick."

I had won. I could afford to be magnanimous. "If the story calls for it, my man. If the story calls for it."

So, in *Club Dread*, he came up with an idea where my character, as a punch line to a scary story, leaps up at a campfire, nude. But the best version of that joke required that I tuck my dick between my legs, thus hiding it from the camera.

In *Beerfest*, Heffernan suggested that my character, Barry Badrinath, would get drunk and then wake up in a field, nude, next to a dead deer, whose throat I'd eaten during the night. It was an homage to *An American Werewolf in London*, so nudity was critical. I did *that* without complaint, but still made sure to keep my dick hidden from the camera.

In *Slammin' Salmon*, a film Kevin directed, my character, Nuts, a waiter, doesn't take his medications and goes crazy in the restaurant. Kevin suggested one way to show that Nuts had lost it was to have him wait tables nude from the waist down. Like any good actor, I dutifully took my pants off. My director commanded it. But I also made sure to keep my dick away from the camera's lens.

Ha! Fuck you, Heffernan! Still no dick!

After we first saw the dick on-screen, I called our director of photography, Joaquin, to ask him what had happened. He told me that when

Kevin turned, he did in fact tilt the camera up, but the image he saw through the lens of Kevin nude, sputtering powdered sugar out of his mouth, was so funny that he thinks he might have laughed—"He-he-he"—which caused the camera perched on his shoulder to briefly dip down, capturing a second and a half of Kevin's historic cock. Awesome.

SHENANIGANS

The troopers have reached a dead end in their investigation and are grasping at straws to save their jobs. Foster and Mac ask Thorny and Rabbit if there were any clues in the Johnny Chimpo cartoon. When the response is that "there was nothing there," Mac suggests taking another look, which leads them to smoke grass and rewatch the Afghani cartoon. When O'Hagan bursts in on the cartoon watching, he snaps, and then vents about Farva's attack on the Dimpus Burger kid. We try to point out that our shenanigans are cheeky and fun, while Farva's shenanigans are cruel and tragic. The word "shenanigans" gets said so much that O'Hagan declares that he will pistol-whip the next guy who says "shenanigans."

The dialogue in this scene is one of my favorite examples of Broken Lizard when we're at our rhythmic best. I can't 100 percent remember where the origin of the scene came from, but I'm 90 percent sure it came from Paul's love of old-time comedy, and I think he wrote the first draft.

I love when Mac asks, "Hey, Farva, what's the name of that restaurant you like with all of the goofy shit on the walls and the mozzarella sticks?"

Farva pops his head out. "You mean Shenanigans? You're talking about Shenanigans, right?"

We're all proud to have been part of that. Since our characters are supposed to be high, two people in the scene (not me) might have taken mushrooms before shooting to achieve the right state of mind.

BULLETPROOF CUP

In the early drafts, this scene was purely informational, focusing on how we (the highway patrol) were going to foil the local cops. But the scene felt too dry, so we made an addition to spice it up.

Under the guise of "testing his equipment," Mac puts on a bulletproof cup and steps out onto the gun range so Thorny can shoot at him. In early drafts, there were blanks in the gun. But we wanted Mac to go flying, so, as filmmakers, we made the buy that Thorny was such a good shot that Mac would trust him not to miss. I was lucky to be a part of this exchange:

> **MAC:** "How're you shootin' today, Thorn?"
>
> **THORNY:** "Dead on, all morning!"

Then Mac sees an errant bullet hole on Thorny's target:

> **MAC:** "What about that little fella?"
>
> **THORNY:** "Oh, that little guy? I wouldn't worry about that little guy!"
>
> **MAC:** "Good enough for me! You're my man now!"

I love that rhythm.

We shot the scene on the gun range of the Green Haven Correc-

tional Facility near Poughkeepsie. There was an outdoor caged hallway in the prison that overlooked the shooting range, where the
prisoners gathered to watch. When Mac (Steve) walked out wearing
only a jockstrap, the prisoners went crazy, hooting and hollering. We
heard sentences like, "I'm gonna rape you!" and "I'm gonna fuck you,
little man!" For Steve, that was disconcerting, but the rest of us
loved it.

GOVERNOR'S PARTY

When Grady and the local cops trick the highway patrol and take
credit for the grass found in the Winnebago, Grady gives a speech
that has one of my favorite jokes in it. In talking about the identity of
the dead female smuggler, he says, "She was a smuggler out of Louisville named Lucy Garfield, or as we like to call her down at the station, the Louisville Smuggler." In the original script, no one laughed
at Grady's joke, so he tried another: "Okay, how about the Kentucky
Doobie?" When no one laughs at that either, Grady moves on. When
we screened the film, the theater audience reacted to Grady's jokes
with silence as well, which caused the energy in the room to nosedive. To combat this, we added the sound of the crowd laughing at
the "Louisville Smuggler" line (essentially, a laugh track), and the scene
played better.

Later in the scene, Farva goes to the bar to order six Schlitzes.
The actor playing the bartender is our producer, Rich Perello. (He's
a bartender in all of our movies.) Later, when Mac punches Farva in
the nuts, a tall white-haired guy walks by. That is our financier, Pete
Lengyel. Without him, there would be no *Super Troopers*.

THE REAL THING

We were always bothered when characters in films used the pea soup trick to simulate vomit. So when our script called for Farva to get hammered at the governor's party, we thought it would be a great opportunity to show people what real vomit looks like.

We saved that scene for last, moving our lights and cameras into the bathroom. When the manager of the party hall heard that we were shooting a throw-up scene, he asked a crew member to stop us. When the crew member told us about the manager's reluctance, we barricaded ourselves inside the bathroom and got to work. Kevin chugged one nonalcoholic beer after another, quickly working his way through five. Then he gobbled a full party-size bag of peanut M&M'S, thinking that the vomit might show up better if it had flecks of color in it. He looked at me and nodded. "I'm ready to roll."

We rolled camera. "Action!" Kevin transformed into Farva, downing one last beer. He looked like he was about to pop, which was what we wanted. So he pulled the trigger and fired off six large-volume pukes in succession. I'm not sure if the M&M'S helped or not, but we all agreed that it was a great success, and we were proud of our artistic authenticity. With the manager pressed up against the door, we cleaned up quickly and hightailed it out of there.

HELL RIDE

After the local cops pull a fast one on the highway patrol at the governor's party, it's clear that our goose is cooked. So we decide to go on one last hell ride, to have a little fun and seek a little vengeance on our enemies. We cuff the traitor, Farva, to the toilet, steal his local police car, and head to Dimpus Burger to torment the kid who may or may not have spit in Farva's burger.

Next, O'Hagan pulls someone over and urinates on the side of their car. While this pullover could be easily classified as mean, we knew that O'Hagan's act was an expression of the highway patrol's anger.

Last, we headed to local police chief Grady's house, where we drove through his mailbox. O'Hagan plans to fight Grady, but since he's not home, he decides to trash his lawn instead.

We "borrowed" the idea of the hell ride from the ending of *Animal House*. In that film, the Deltas get kicked out of school and their house is to be closed. They're angry, so they go on one last hell ride, to exact revenge. At a Directors Guild dinner, I met John Landis and said, "Thanks for the hell-ride idea."

Landis laughed and said, "Oh, I know all about it! Thanks for admitting it." I love John Landis's movies. They've got dead-perfect tone and they're as funny as hell.

ST. ANKY BEER

In the final scene of the film, Thorny and Rabbit are seen delivering a keg of beer to a high school party. We find out soon that they're actually undercover local police who are looking to bust the underage party. The name of the fake beer company they "work" for is "St. Anky Beer." Get rid of the space and it reads: "Stanky Beer."

This was a reshoot. In the Sundance cut, we go undercover as meat inspectors, inspecting a factory. When the factory manager tries to bribe us, we rip off our inspector costumes to reveal our local police uniforms beneath.

The scene was fine, but it didn't get a big enough laugh. So we brought back the stoner boys from the opening, and then the laughs really started rolling in.

After a good opening, the second most important thing a film needs is a good ending.

CHAPTER 11

Selling *Super Troopers*: What It Was Like to Sell a
Movie at Sundance to a Major Hollywood Studio

SUNDANCE—MACH 2

We cut *Super Troopers* in New York, so I couch surfed and sublet places during that time. Four months into the edit, we sent a polished rough cut of the film directly to Geoff Gilmore at Sundance and made sure Sloss told him it was coming. On Thanksgiving night, I was watching the Detroit Lions drub the New England Patriots 34–9 when I got a call from Sloss. We were in. The idea of returning to Sundance brought to the surface a lot of emotion. We had come so close to selling *Puddle Cruiser* but had failed. So, though we were happy to be getting a second chance, we couldn't help but feel like beaten dogs. What if we made *two films* that didn't sell theatrically? We were pretty sure it would mean the end of our careers.

Whether a company buys your film or not is based only on the personal opinions of the acquisition executives and the company's president, who writes the checks. I asked Sloss to set up meetings with the acquisition executives from all of the potential buyers, hoping to make a personal impression. *If a buyer was on the fence about* Super Troopers, *maybe this personal meeting would knock them off of the fence and onto our side.* I met with execs at Miramax, Sony Pictures Classics, and New Line. When I asked Sloss about Fox Searchlight, he said, "Don't worry about them. They're too highbrow. They'll never buy *Super Troopers.*"

THE OPENING SCENE

Jacob Craycroft (our editor), Kevin, and I locked the cut and were feeling optimistic. To my eye, the film felt tough, weird, and maybe even funny—though it was hard to tell, since the biggest crowd who'd seen it was six of our stoned pals in our living room. The scene I was most concerned about was the opening. We had learned the hard way on *Puddle Cruiser* what happens when your film doesn't open well. So, with *Super Troopers,* our highest priority was to write a kick-ass opening that was good enough to dispense with the preshow audience-warm-up sketch. This film needed to stand on its own. But something about the opening was nagging at me. Maybe it was because through three years of development, all of the various producers had given us the same note: *You can't open a movie this way. The audience will be confused because they're going to think that the movie is about the stoners, not the cops.* We stuck to our guns, but now I couldn't help but wonder if the experts had been right. *Was the opening fundamentally flawed?*

On a bitter-cold Thursday in January, we packed our bags for Utah and took a cab up to the DuArt Film lab on West Fifty-Fifth Street to pick up the Sundance print. The story of the indie film movement ran right through DuArt, the lab owned by Irwin Young. Irwin was often a last-second savior to cash-starved filmmakers who ran out of money just before the printmaking process. With Irwin's

credit, broke filmmakers were able to strike prints, take them to fes-
tivals, and sell their films. Irwin had extended us credit on *Puddle
Cruiser* and we paid him back in full. Now he was doing the same with
Super Troopers. After Pete Lengyel, Broken Lizard, Rich Perello, and
John Sloss, Irwin Young was next in line in praying for a Sundance sale.

Kent McGrew (our color timer), Kevin Heffernan, and I settled in
to watch the print that would screen at Sundance in thirty-six hours.
The film started and we watched the troopers pull over the stoned
college kids. We watched Geoff in the backseat eat the pot and
shrooms. We watched Mac blow by in the white Miata. We watched
the car chase with the college kids bouncing around the backseat. We
watched Geoff lick the glass in an homage to Willy Wonka.

"The snozzberries taste like snozzberries."

We watched Mac slam the cop car in reverse. "You boys like Mexico?!"

Finally, we watched the words "*Super Troopers*" come up green in a
cloud of dust. I exhaled loudly.

"We blew it again, dude."

Heffernan turned around. "What're you talking about?" Kent stood
and signaled to the projectionist, who stopped the film and turned on
the light.

"We set out to make a good opening and we fuckin' blew it—
again! This thing fucking sucks." I was pissed.

Heffernan was annoyed. "No, it doesn't!"

I pressed on. "Well, it's not funny. It's *weird*. What the fuck was I
thinking acting that way? We should stop at home before we go to the
airport and get Billy the Dummy, because we're gonna need him."

Kent cleared his throat. "*I* think it's funny."

I shook my head. "It's not, Kent. It's just not. The rest of the film is
fine, but the opening is not."

Though Kevin's confidence was probably shaken, he kept up a strong front. "You'll see. You'll see tomorrow night." The projectionist hit the lights and started the film again, as I sat, sullen, in the dark, feeling doomed.

THURSDAY, 4:30 P.M.

We were in the Midnight screenings series, and we were given a set of times that I thought was perfect: Friday night, Saturday night, and Sunday night, all at the famed Egyptian Theatre on Main Street. When I got to town that Thursday afternoon, I met John Sloss, both for a drink and to take his temperature. He said that acquisition executives from all of the majors would be at the eleven thirty P.M. premiere on Friday night.

"Any check writers?" I asked.

"Let's hope so. How do you think it'll play?"

Not wanting to be the source of my own negative buzz, I said, "Who knows?"

"Are you guys doing an opening sketch? We need to pull out all the stops."

I shook my head. "Heffernan convinced me not to do it."

If you looked at the two of us sitting there, you would have sensed worry. That film had to play well or we were fucked.

FRIDAY, 11 P.M., THIRTY MINUTES BEFORE THE PREMIERE: HARVEY'S SECOND CHANCE

The cast, crew, and I ducked into Cisero's on Main Street for a much-needed pre-screening drink. As we ordered, Erik pointed. There he was, sitting alone at a corner table. Harvey Weinstein himself. *Could we really be this lucky?* Sure, Harvey didn't know if the *script* was funny, but he'd certainly be able to tell by watching the film. We had to get Harvey into the Egyptian.

Marisa had worked for Harvey and his brother, Bob, in the film *Teaching Mrs. Tingle,* so we sent her over to be the tip of the spear. We watched as she charmed him, smiling and laughing. After a beat, she waved me over.

I shook Harvey's hand and dove right in, "Harvey, come see the film you paid to develop. The buzz is good. This is your chance. It'll be a great story." Now, to be honest, there was no buzz, since the only people who'd seen it were the Sundance staff and our living room pals, but everything in show business *is* show business, so . . . Harvey played along, saying he had heard the film turned out well, and he wished he could come but he had a meeting at twelve fifteen A.M. I clamped down. "Come to the first half hour and we'll give you a print to watch the rest tomorrow."

He cocked his head. "Jay, if I come to your screening and walk out, you'll be dead in the water. You won't sell your film."

This was not a time to be meek, so I rolled the dice. "I'll take the risk. We'll save some seats in the back. No one will see you leave."

He smiled. "I'll see if I can work it out." Brush-off? Probably, but short of overpowering him and dragging him to the screening, there wasn't much more to do.

FRIDAY, 11:30 P.M.

The Egyptian Theatre was packed and buzzing with three hundred slightly drunk and/or stoned people. To our eye, the crowd was good and lubed.

Sloss said that execs from all of the majors were there. "Let's hope it's funny," he deadpanned.

"Hey, we just ran into Harvey Weinstein and he said he might come," I said, more hopeful than confident.

John smirked. "Don't hold your breath."

On cue, Harvey walked in and sat down in the roped-off back row. The whole theater turned and the energy in the room went up two notches.

Sundance programmer Trevor Groth gave a great intro, pumping up the film nicely. I gave a small speech and choked up—slightly.

The lights went down.

The guitar score by 38 Special came up, and quickly it became clear that Kevin was right. We didn't need Billy the Dummy. The film was playing and it was playing big. Waves of laughter and surprise rolled through the giddy audience. My favorite moment was when Joey Kern, the kid riding shotgun, says, "Shit, I was about to pull out my nine and put a cap in that pig's ass." As he pretends to shoot . . . *Screeeech!* Through the windshield, you see the police car slam to a stop and kick into reverse, as though the cops could hear every word.

Seven minutes in, the words "*Super Troopers*" came up and the audience roared with applause. My eyes welled up with tears.

Thirty minutes later, I was pacing in the lobby and listening to the crowd when Harvey walked out. He grabbed my arm.

"It's killing! I'm coming back. I'm going to my meeting and coming back!" Off he went into the cold Utah night. The screening continued, getting huge laughs and building momentum. At times, it felt like the crowd was going to rip the seats out. With twenty minutes left in the film, Harvey reentered the lobby.

"I told you I'd come back!" He slid back into his seat, no one the wiser. The credits rolled and the audience cheered, and it was now time for John Sloss to go to work.

When you're trying to sell a movie, what you're looking for after the screening are huddles of acquisition executives in the lobby. Inside these huddles, the executives are polling one another on what they each thought of the film. *Is this something their company should bid on?* As I scanned the lobby, I saw three huddles: one from Fox Searchlight, one from Sony, and one from Miramax, who were joined by Harvey. Harvey motioned me over. He told me we'd made a great film and he wanted the print so he could watch the rest tomorrow. He also wanted to buy us a drink back at Cisero's.

Sloss walked up. "Harvey, you better get it now. I don't know how long it's gonna last."

Harvey smiled and said, "Get me a print."

When the lobby emptied, John said that there were some initial rumblings of interest, but no offers yet. He told us to go to Cisero's and work Harvey over.

I was worried. *Yes, the screening couldn't have gone better, but we'd had great screenings of* Puddle Cruiser *and look where that went. What if it was happening again? What if the crowd response was actually working against us? What if film buyers thought we weren't "indie" enough for their audience?* We were insecure about our place in the independent film landscape. We raised the money ourselves, we wrote it ourselves, we starred in it, and I directed it. We couldn't be more independent. But somehow, maybe the gatekeepers were going to exclude us anyway.

At Cisero's, the cast and I had a couple of cocktails with Harvey and the Miramax staff. It was clear that people were watching. Harvey said he wasn't sure if the film was for Miramax. Maybe it would be a better fit at his brother Bob's company, Dimension. Regardless, Harvey said to check the papers in the morning. He had a feeling that this drink was going to inject some buzz into Park City.

He wasn't kidding. The next day, The *New York Post*'s Page Six ran an item saying that the *Super Troopers* crew was seen cocktailing with Harvey Weinstein late into the night. It was like a buzz bomb went off. Even though Harvey had yet to see the whole film and had as much as told me that he didn't think it was right for Miramax, everyone in town was saying that Miramax was the company to beat. This was chum in the water for Sloss. Instead of his having to call around to the other buyers to gin up interest, they were calling him. *John, don't sell to Miramax. We're interested too. Just hold the film through the next screening. We're bringing our checkbooks.* But don't mistake buzz for check writing—one is fun and the other actually matters.

For filmmakers, Sundance is often a ten-day stress nightmare, where you constantly check your phone, wondering if the mountain reception is fucking you.

In the best-case scenario, a film will sell in a bidding war at the premiere screening. That best case had already blown past us. Not good.

SATURDAY, 11:50 P.M., SCREENING 2: THE EGYPTIAN THEATRE

Because of word of mouth, the second screening at the Egyptian was packed and the crowd was buzzing with anticipation. John said that Fox Searchlight and Film4 were strongly in play.

"What about the print for Harvey?" I asked.

John blanched. "If he wants the film, he'll show up and buy it. If we give him the print and he passes, all of our momentum will disappear.

We're better off with everyone thinking that Harvey is still interested, even if he's probably not. Let's not chase a pass." (Chasing a pass meant forcing Miramax to make what was probably going to be a negative decision.)

The Saturday screening was as good as Friday's. Afterward, I saw more huddles of acquisition executives. A smiling woman walked up, introducing herself as Nancy Utley, head of marketing for Fox Searchlight. She told me they really loved the film. I thought, *Okay, but are you going to buy it?!* When the lobby cleared, I told Sloss I was worried that the air was leaking out of the balloon.

"*I'm* not worried," he said. "Go out and have some fun. We'll sell this thing tomorrow."

So we did. We hit the town . . . hard. It was already two A.M., so we went to an after-party, followed by an after-after-party, and then an after-after-after-party. Finally, at around eleven Sunday morning, Kevin and I wobbled down Main Street, dreaming of our beds. *Mama always said nothing good happens after noon.* Then, my phone rang. It was Sloss.

"Come to my condo. We're closing a deal with Fox Searchlight."

We rerouted to Sloss's condo, exhausted but light on our feet. I was reluctant to tell my old boss that I had been up all night, but he must have sensed it, since he offered us a noon beer. What was one more beer? He told us that Searchlight wanted to buy the film for roughly $3 million. *Three million dollars? We made the movie for $1.26 million. Hot damn!* Then he added that Searchlight was going to pull their offer if we didn't close the deal by ten thirty P.M., the start of tonight's screening. They were worried that Miramax would swoop in and steal it.

We sat for a couple of hours, listening to Sloss negotiate the finer points of the distribution deal with Searchlight's lawyer, Joey DeMarco.

In later years, we'd get to know and love Joey. Once, when we stopped by the office, he went into his wallet and handed each of the Lizards a hundred-dollar bill because he said we'd earned it. Joey died a couple of years later, at age forty-eight, which was a big loss.

I must have looked as tired as I was because John walked over, holding his hand over the phone.

"Get some sleep. You need to be rested for the screening tonight."

We went back to our house, climbed into our beds, and slept the sleep of the dead. My alarm went off at eight P.M., and I immediately listened to my messages—nothing from Sloss. *That can't be good.* I called over and John picked up.

"We closed. You sold your film." I'm not sure I've ever exhaled longer. It was like a massive bong hit of exhaustion and relief. You could hear John smiling through the phone. "Congratulations, man! I'll tell you all about it at the screening."

The Sunday night screening was great but comparatively subdued. Afterward, John introduced me to the excited Searchlight team, including Josh Deighton, Claudia Lewis, Joey DeMarco, Steve Gilula, and of course Nancy Utley. The final advance was $3.25 million, and the film was guaranteed to come out on eighteen hundred screens. Not bad for our little gang from Colgate. Not bad at all. When the execs left, I nudged John.

"Don't bother with Searchlight?"

He shrugged. "Nobody knows anything in show business. Not even me."

Broken Lizard and a big group of pals went back to the house and smoked grass for a couple of hours, wondering, *Did this really just happen?* We awoke to read the front page of *Variety* confirming the details.

The next day was special. It felt like our whole world had flipped right side up. We walked around Park City with those former holes in our chests filled to the brim *with nothing to worry about.*

Stuff magazine threw us a massive party at their five-floor Deer Valley house. One of their execs, whose job it was to make sure Broken Lizard had fun, had his hands full. He is now the star of one of Fox News's most popular shows. All I'll say is that I've seen behind the curtain. Let's leave it at that.

The party was memorable, mostly because Steve, Kevin, and I met one of our heroes. We saw Patrick Swayze standing alone in the kitchen, and we pounced. We talked over one another, gushing about just how much we loved him. He was skeptical. Who could love Patrick Swayze that much? We could! We'd seen *Point Break* and *Road House* twenty to thirty times. We may have gone overboard. Did I mention that ecstasy was big at the time? Swayze's hesitance melted when he squinted at Lemme.

"Wait. You're the guy from that cop movie. That movie rocks!" I looked at Heffernan. *Did that really just happen?*

The rest of Sundance was a dream. We did interviews during the day, and at night we tore it up good. I made late-night friends with the actor Norman Reedus. During a blizzard, we were in Deer Valley and the cabs stopped running, so another friend and I secretly jumped on the back of a snowplow and shivered on the twenty-minute ride back to Park City. I'm still cold. One night, a publicist took me back to her place, stripped down to a leopard-skin G-string, and gave me head on a white fur rug in front of a fireplace. Life was good.

When we got back to LA, we sat down with Searchlight's president, Peter Rice, who asked us, "If you could do anything to the film, what would you do?"

We knew the answer. "We'd cut a few minutes and reshoot the ending. It's just underwhelming."

Peter agreed.

In the Sundance version of the ending, we were undercover local cops who bust a meatpacking factory. It was fine, but it lacked comedy and energy.

We wrote a new ending that brought back the stoners from the opening, and our test scores went up ten points.

Searchlight hired the editor, George Folsey, to help us trim seven minutes. George was the editor/producer of all of the John Landis movies we loved so much, including *Animal House, The Blues Brothers, Trading Places, Coming to America,* and the rest. Folsey is a great guy and had us spellbound with his amazing show business stories, including the time he attended a test screening of *Animal House* in Atlanta mostly comprised of drunk businessmen, who mostly slept. After the screening, John Belushi chewed Folsey out. A week later, they tested the *exact same cut* in Denver for college students, and the place went crazy. Afterward, Belushi hugged Folsey. *Love the new cut, George!*

THE RELEASE

Searchlight loved the movie and they were immensely collaborative on everything from the reshoot to the advertising campaign. Getting the trailers and the imagery right is critical to a film's success, and Nancy Utley and her group just flat-out nailed it. Pulling a page from our *Puddle Cruiser* Winnebago promotional tour, Searchlight put us back on the road, but this time in a rock-and-roll tour bus wrapped with the *Super Troopers* poster. It was a rolling billboard that slept ten and had a kitchen, a master bedroom, and a living room.

We kicked off the tour with a screening at the Mann Village

Theater, near UCLA, and followed that with a party. Around midnight, we loaded onto the bus and drove off into the night, heading for Tucson, Arizona.

Searchlight hired a British tour manager named Derek Wilkenson (Wilkie) to escort us across the country. Wilkie was a rock-and-roll guy who had road managed acts such as the Allman Brothers, the Average White Band, and many others. On the drive, he told us the story of how, at age fifteen, he was hanging out in a roadie bar in England when a guy walked in.

"Who wants to road crew for Led Zeppelin?!" He raised his hand, left the bar, toured around the world, and didn't return until he was seventeen.

Our days went like this: We would wake up in a new town, put on our highway patrol uniforms, and do a round of radio interviews. In the afternoon, we'd hand out free screening tickets to passersby. That evening, we'd introduce the screening and then have dinner. After the screening, we'd do a question-and-answer and then head to a Fox-sponsored party, where we would get bombed with the audience. Wilkie would press condoms into our hands, cackling his rock-and-roll cry: "Come back with these *used* or don't come back at all!"

It was the dead of winter and we did a lot of harrowing night drives. We had bunks, which we nicknamed "coffins" because when you crawled in and pulled the drape shut, it was pitch black. With the road rumbling beneath our backs, we'd awake to a sudden surge of fear brought on by the wheels slightly drifting over a rumble strip. *Had our driver, Dave, fallen asleep? Were we about to fly off the road, or were we just approaching a toll or a rest stop?* Sometimes we'd hear squealing brakes and then feel the awful feeling of the bus sliding on ice. Luckily, Dave was a great driver and always managed to keep us safe.

On Friday, February 15, 2002, *Super Troopers* opened on eighteen hundred screens across the United States. Broken Lizard was in New York City, and we went to Times Square to take pictures under the film's three-story billboard. Our plan was to spend the evening slipping in and out of bars and theaters. Appreciative film festival crowds were one thing. We wanted to know if we could make strangers laugh. At the theater in Times Square, we found out we could. The room was packed and the people were laughing.

At seven P.M., I got a call from Steve Gilula, the head of distribution for Searchlight. He was happy. He said the numbers of the East Coast matinees had been quite good. On Saturday, our numbers went up, which meant word of mouth was good. Peter Rice called and said we could relax. The release was a success. Yeah, they know that quickly.

A couple of weeks after we got back, I was in my Laurel Canyon house, which was in a bamboo forest, on a one-and-a-half-lane mountain road called Gould Avenue. Gould overlooks the Laurel Canyon Country Store and is known for being the street where David Letterman lived during the roaring Comedy Store days. The phone rang and a voice said, "I have Adam Sandler for Jay Chandrasekhar." That's how the powerful do it in Hollywood. An assistant calls on behalf of their boss. Only once it is confirmed that the less powerful person (me) is on the line will the boss get on the line. I didn't buy it. Why would Adam Sandler be calling me? It had to be Lemme pranking me, doing a new Sandler imitation, right? So I said, "Okay." After a few seconds, the real Adam Sandler got on the phone. It was the cool, quiet, subdued Sandler, the one from his movies when he's talking to a kid about something serious. He said he had gone to a crowded theater, ordered a popcorn, and watched *Super Troopers*. He said people were going crazy and that he loved the film. I thanked him, still star-struck.

Then he said, "Don't worry about the reviews. I get shitty reviews all the time, and the people still come. The people are gonna come for this movie." What Sandler was referring to was that *Super Troopers* got a 35 percent Fresh rating on Rotten Tomatoes. (Yes, this is the same movie that *Huffington Post* readers voted the funniest movie of the decade from 2000 to 2010.) My hometown reviewer, Roger Ebert, gave it two stars and said, "I can't quite recommend it—it's too patched together—but I almost can; it's the kind of movie that makes you want to like it." That hurt.

Sandler finished up and said that if we ever needed any help making a movie, we should call him. What he meant was if we had an idea that we wanted him to produce, we should partner up. Wow. Hollywood has the capacity to really blow you away sometimes.

Super Troopers grossed $20 million at the box office, which was good for an indie film without stars, and Searchlight was happy. But it was the massive wave of DVD and VHS that took everybody by surprise. We got lucky. Our film came out at the height of the DVD market, that moment when people actually bought DVDs for their home collections. Millions and millions of copies of *Super Troopers* were sold, which made Fox a profit north of sixty million dollars. Those DVDs were bought by people who smoked grass and watched the movie repeatedly with groups of friends. *Super Troopers* benefited from the old way of watching films, the way we watched at Colgate, when you went to someone's house, looked at their DVD collection, and then just picked one.

CHAPTER 12

9/11: Another Case of Mistaken Identity

On the afternoon of September 11, 2001, I called my mother, worried. Would people think that we were Muslim and attack us? Were we going to have to leave the country? Should I join the CIA? Someone who looked like me would have an easier time infiltrating al-Qaeda than would a Kentucky farm boy. Crazy, I know, but we talked about it. Mom assured me that while 9/11 was insane and traumatic, America had a big heart and would vent for a while, before moving on. "Just be careful," she said. Since the *Super Troopers* release date was still six months away, I selfishly wondered if the country would even go to a film with a brown guy on the poster. It was an insecure time.

On September 12, I put on my most American outfit—a Willie Nelson T-shirt, flip-flops, and some Chicago Blackhawks shorts (not only have I never seen a terrorist in shorts, but I bet there's not a single member of ISIS who digs hockey), and I went to Whole Foods to get a sandwich. As I rolled my cart through the store, I could feel the rage in the angry glares of rich white moms.

On the way back up to my house, I bought one of those American flags for my car. A few days later, in San Francisco, my girlfriend and I went into a tattoo parlor, where I chose an American flag design for my shoulder. And while my girlfriend and I talked about me tattooing Old Glory on my shoulder as an act of patriotism, the unspoken motive in my mind was that it would be *beating repellent*. In the end, I decided against for two reasons. One: I don't like how tattoos look on brown skin. Two: While I feel enormous sympathy for Muslims in America and the awful discrimination they're enduring, *I* shouldn't *have to* brand myself because of a case of fucking mistaken identity.

When I got back to LA, I drove down to Studio City, where I signed up for karate classes, since I was pretty sure my new life would be a series of street fights. Which brings me to our first story . . .

One month after 9/11, I had to take my first flight. The airport was tense, and I was chosen for extra security screening. I get it. I totally get it. But it was embarrassing to be patted down in front of my fellow citizens. I wanted to say, "It wasn't us! We're the Indians! You ever see *Gandhi?* We're the peace guys!" But instead, I just smiled and tried to look nonthreatening.

Later, I was sitting at the gate, reading my *New York Times,* when a guy walked up. Okay, a Muslim guy. He was in his thirties, he had a full-length robe, a full beard, a circular cap, and he was carrying two plastic bags. The man put his two bags down on the open chair next to me. Then he pulled out a prayer rug, unrolled it at my feet, got down on his knees, faced Mecca, and started praying. The whole room turned, staring at him, and then staring at me. You could feel the tension in the room go up a notch. *Are those two Arab men traveling together?*

Now, I'm a liberal guy. I believe that people should have religious freedom, including the freedom to pray after a touchdown, or pray five times a day facing Mecca. That said, the country was a little on edge at the time, and this guy knew that. But he felt strongly enough about his religion that he was going to pray anyway, regardless of how uncomfortable it might make people feel. And that's his right, because this is America. That's freedom. But that doesn't change how the rest of us felt. Personally, I was thinking that if this guy *was* a terrorist about to blow up a plane, wouldn't he pray one last time before he got on? I know, I know. Terrible, but that's what I was thinking, and I'm pretty sure I wasn't the only one. As I watched him pray, I wondered if I should just turn around and go home. Later, I'd be able to tell one of those near-miss stories—*You know, I had a ticket on that flight.*

A very close friend of mine, Ben, has *two* of those near-miss stories. For color, Ben is a six-foot-four, half-Sikh / half-white-American guy I went to Colgate with. In the fall of 1988, Ben spent a semester studying abroad in London. When the semester was coming to a close, Ben bought a ticket home on Pan Am Flight 103, which was to leave London on December 21. When the plane blew up over Lockerbie, Scotland, four Colgate kids were among the dead. Word spread through the grapevine that Ben was one of them. As it turned out, he and some of my other friends had gone out boozing the night before and couldn't pack up their apartment in time to make the flight. So he missed the flight and lived to tell the tale. Score one for hard drinking.

In 2001, Ben was working at an investment bank on, roughly, the eightieth floor of the South Tower of the World Trade Center. After the first plane hit, Ben remembers seeing a printer explode out of a shattered North Tower window and fly by his office. Following his instinct, he grabbed two buddies and jumped into the elevator to get out of there. When he exited on the fiftieth floor to take the next elevator down, a Port Authority cop stopped them. The cop said that they were still figuring out what had happened but that they should all just stay there and await further instruction, because they didn't want a bunch of people running through the plaza with all of that falling debris.

Here's the thing about Ben. Like Burt Reynolds and my mom, Ben has an anti-authority streak a mile wide. He'd been arrested multiple times, once for stealing a cab in Traverse City and joyriding it into Lake Michigan. The other times were for fights and minor drug possession. After the Port Authority cop left, Ben said, "Fuck that! I'm outta here and anyone who stays is a fuckin' sucker!" While I'm certain that *I* would have stayed as the cop had asked, Ben didn't give a shit, and he left. Everyone on the floor followed.

As they headed down the fifty flights of stairs, the second plane hit the South Tower just above the seventy-fifth floor. Ben said it felt like an earthquake, and the temperature in the stairwell went up to what felt like 110 degrees. As smoke filled the stairwell from above, Ben said they all held hands, sang "99 Bottles of Beer on the Wall," and kept pressing down.

Finally, they emerged onto the plaza, where it was pandemonium. In addition to falling, burning plane parts, people from the upper levels of the North Tower were leaping to their deaths to avoid burning alive in their offices.

Because of limited communication, all we knew was that Ben worked on an upper level of the South Tower. Once again, we were all sure that

Ben was dead. On September 14, I was feeling lonely and lost in the world, so I got in my car and drove up to San Francisco to see my girl-friend, Jenny. It was two A.M., and I was speeding up the 5 freeway, lis-tening to NPR's terror analysis, when I heard Ben's voice. He was alive and telling his story to the reporter. Fuck al-Qaeda. Ben has nine lives.

So, there I was, at the gate, watching this guy pray at my feet. Fly-ing, post-9/11, had become annoying for everyone, but more so for Indians (and Arabs). The government told everyone to keep their eyes open. *If you see (a brown person doing) something, say something.* But I'm an American, goddamn it. Okay, Indian American, but I'm no more likely to be a terrorist than some white guy. Probably less so, right, Timothy McVeigh? And as much as I wanted to turn around and go home, I decided, *Fuck you, I'm getting on that plane, because don't let the terrorists win, right?*

Walking down the aisle, I absorbed harsh stares from middle-aged white guys. I smiled a lot, trying to look friendly, and asked the flight attendants useless questions, so that people could hear my American voice. I sat in my aisle seat secretly cursing the prick bin Laden. After a couple of minutes, the Muslim prayer guy walked on, stopping in the seat across the aisle and one row up. He opened the overhead compartment, put his two plastic bags inside, and then sat down. Looking around, I noticed that *all of the white guys in the cabin had taken note of how close the two of us were sitting. Which of these scowling guys was the heat-packing air marshal?* I wondered.

After the plane took off and the seat belt sign went off, Prayer Guy stood up, opened the overhead compartment, and started rustling around in one of his plastic bags. He was digging for what had to be two minutes. Just digging. Everyone in the cabin was watching. Since I was so close, I was staring hard, looking for wires peeking out of the bag. *Was this dude triggering a detonator?* I was staring so hard at the guy, I think he could feel it, because he turned around and started staring at me. Now the two of us were staring at each other, while all of the white guys in the cabin were staring at both of us, thinking that *we had to be in cahoots.*

After 9/11, Mark Wahlberg said that had he been on one of the planes, it would have ended differently. People made fun of him for that, but I understood the sentiment. And if it happened again, there were a lot of people who were ready to stand up and give their lives if necessary to stop it. People were in hero mode. Passengers on my plane were eyeing Prayer Guy and me, and they were at the ready. Meanwhile, *I* was in hero mode too. Because if this guy *was* a terrorist and he made his move, my plan was that *I* was going to tackle him and take him out! I imagined the *New York Post* headline would read: *Indian guy saves the day! We thought they were the same as those other guys, but it turns out they're cool and patriotic!*

Of course, I was worried that if I *did* tackle this guy, the air marshal would be so keyed up by two brown guys rolling around on a plane that he'd just shoot us both. Then it would be like when the white uniformed cop accidentally shoots the black undercover cop, and everyone's sad.

In the end, nothing happened. The guy was not a terrorist; he was just a religiously observant man who wanted to pray. So, I was the racist. I profiled the poor guy for doing nothing more than exercising his America-given freedom. Do I feel bad? Yes, but it felt right at the time, and, man, this shit is complicated.

A year after 9/11, I was walking through Boston in a tuxedo, heading to a benefit for the Boston Public Library. As I turned the corner, I saw up ahead three bald guys leaning against a car. These weren't just any bald guys; they were skinheads—Boston skinheads. Now, skinheads are bad enough, but Boston skinheads are supercharged. Because we all know that Boston is the South of the North. I love Boston, but it has some racial issues.

I always wondered about the origin of skinheads. Was there just this supercool racist who was experiencing male-patterned baldness, so he shaved his head? And then all his follower-racist buddies just copied his style? I feel bad for racists with thick heads of hair, though I guess they can always just join the Republican Party. *Hee hee hee.*

Back in Boston, I was speed-walking past the skinheads when I heard a voice say, "Hey, Muhammad! Islam sucks." Now, let me say this: I get it. People, me included, are furious about terrorism. And before you hop up and down, I know that Islamic terrorists have a beef with America having soldiers over there, but attacking US civilians still feels cowardly.

What I wanted to say to these guys was, "Hey, skinheads, you're pissed at Islam, and I get it, but most Muslims are peaceful. Plus, you're harassing the wrong guy. I'm an Indian. You ever see *Gandhi*? We're the peace guys? So, have a nice day, you bald bigots."

But when you're being racially harassed, lengthy logical statements don't really work, so I just waved and said, "Okaaaaaay!" Unsatisfied with my response, the skinheads chased me. "Hey, dickhead! Fuck your Islam!"

I half-laughed and started half-running. "Okaaaaay!"

But they caught up to me, surrounding me. "Fuck you, Muhammad! You fuckin' suck!"

I thought, *God, I really wished I'd gone to that second karate class.* They started pushing me back and forth. "Thanks fah 9/11, dick!" one yelled in a thick Boston accent. Years later, I'd hear the same exact line, in the same accent, said to an Indian in the movie *Ted*. It would be funnier then.

I contemplated throwing the first punch. Maybe I could knock one out, kick one in the nuts, and elbow the third in the face. It worked for Steven Seagal in *Under Siege*, or at least it did for his stunt double. The skinheads continued to shove me until . . . something happened. The lead skinhead put up his hands, stopping the other two. "Wait a minute? Wait a minute." He cocked his head and looked at me for a beat. Then, in his thick Boston accent, he said, "*Supah Troopahs?*"

I exhaled and smiled. "Yeah!"

The head skinhead smiled big. "Holy shit, dude! Ho-ly shit! That's our favorite movie! We love that movie! All our friends love that movie!" I imagined an outdoor screening of *Super Troopers*, with all the skinheads gathered around a burning cross—where all the guys looked like Farva, with their bald heads and their shitty mustaches.

Then, the leader got shy. "Dude, could we take a pic-cha wit you?"

So, if you see a picture of me in a tuxedo with three Boston skinheads, you've got to understand that I had no choice.

CHAPTER 13

The Macho Contest, aka Wild Times on *Club Dread*

After *Super Troopers,* life in Hollywood changed for us. Instead of being filmmakers who go around begging the studios for money, we were now in the pool of people the studios offered money to. And when Fox Searchlight asked us what we wanted to do next, we told them that we wanted to make a horror-comedy along the lines of *An American Werewolf in London* or *Scream.* We pitched a film where we would play the staff at a snowed-in ski resort. And in the style of an Agatha Christie novel, one by one, we would be brutally murdered. Our Searchlight execs responded as they had to. "Yes, we love it!" It was either that or tell their boss why they'd let the *Super Troopers* guys walk out of their door—and in their competitor's door. Searchlight did make one request, though. Did the film have to be set in winter? Shooting in snow was difficult and costly. Was there a more production-friendly season to shoot the story in? So we compromised: "How about a tropical island?" And *Club Dread* was born.

When people ask me what my favorite Broken Lizard film is, I always say either *Super Troopers* or *Beerfest*. *Beerfest* probably has the best filmmaking. But when they ask which film was the most fun to make, it's not even close. It's *Club Dread* by a mile.

Our initial location scout took place in Australia, in an area called Surfers Paradise. We'd come a long way from scouting Poughkeepsie. While we found some great locations, we got caught up on the issue of extras. The film's story took place in Mexico, and there were no Mexican-looking extras in Australia. We debated flying in a hundred Indians and putting them in sombreros and such but eventually decided that it wasn't worth the cost or the ridiculousness.

So when we got back, Searchlight sent us to the west coast of Mexico, where we found a resort called El Tamarindo. Located two hours south of Puerto Vallarta, El Tamarindo was built by the former Mexican president Vicente Fox for his friends and family to use. It was Mexico's only six-star resort and had thirty-six cabanas, each with its own plunge pool, a couple of private beaches, and a phenomenal oceanfront golf course. For security reasons, it was intentionally hard to get to. It was a thirty-minute drive from the main road, through dense jungle, to the resort.

In addition to Broken Lizard, the cast included the great Bill Paxton, M. C. Gainey, Brittany Daniel, Jordan Ladd, Lindsay Price, Samm Levine, Nat Faxon, Mike Weaver, and Mike Yurchak. Paxton played the rock-star of the resort, Coconut Pete. Coco Pete, a fictional competitor to Jimmy Buffett, had built the resort as an ode to his island lifestyle. Paxton was fantastic. Not only was he enormously prepared and committed, but he was also damned funny. The same can be said of Brittany Daniel, Jordan Ladd, Lindsay Price, and the rest—all great actors who became great friends.

Making a horror movie was fun because it required exercising a different set of mental muscles. Unlike a typical comedy, much of the film took place at night, so we had to work "vampire hours"—shooting all night and sleeping all day.

¿QUIÉN ES MÁS MACHO? MEXICO ES MÁS MACHO.

Some people say that the American male has gone soft, with our Little League participation awards, our desperation for "likes" on Facebook, our hairless bodies, and our male skinny jeans. (Okay, it's me. I said it.) Are we destined to become eighteenth-century France, where men wore white makeup, wigs, and high heels? If we are, the country directly south of us is not. Mexico is wild, relaxed, and un-regulated, as proven by the fact that they still have diving boards at their pools. Mexico feels fearless, macho, dangerous. We frequently quoted Bill Murray from the *SNL* sketch: "¿Quién es más macho? ¿Fernando Lamas o Ricardo Montalbán? ¿Quién es más macho?" In many ways that macho spirit defined our time down there.

On our first weekend off, we rolled into the closest town, Barra de Navidad, which we nicknamed "Christmas Sandbar." We were looking for a dive bar but could find only discos. Finally, we pulled up outside a place called Piper's Lover. It sounded like a strip bar. Not what we were looking for. When I ran in to check, I found a dive bar that opened onto a lagoon. It had a sand floor and a thatch roof, and it was exactly what we were looking for. Then I heard a voice: "Welcome to Mexico! I am Piper." (It's pronounced *Peeper*, so I'm going to spell it that way if you don't mind.)

I looked over to see a smiling, bearded bartender.

"Is this *your* bar?" I asked.

Peeper bowed. "No, this is *your* bar."

We were hooked. We spent a lot of our off time there, includ-ing one night during a massive thunderstorm. Rain was pouring in through the tin and thatch roof, and everyone in the bar was drenched but having a ball. Lightning bolts were slamming into town, causing the lights to flicker and sometimes go out for up to a minute. When I went to the bathroom, I reached for the light switch and saw a blue electrical current running from my hand to the switch. So, I pissed in the dark. There was so much water gushing in through the roof that it didn't matter that I couldn't see the toilet.

Back at the resort, we started having underwater breath-holding contests in the pool. Every day a new record would be set, until Steve Lemme put it out of reach with his three-and-a-half-minute dead float. I almost pulled him up because I thought he might actually be dead. The macho contest had been rekindled, and there would be more to come.

Erik Stolhanske and I rekindled our macho contest at a party, when we reached into a garbage can full of beer and ice. "That's cold," I said.

Erik looked up. "Maybe if you're a wussy from Chicago." *This fuckin' guy.*

I shoved my arm back in up to the biceps and said, "Let's go, Purple Rain."

So Erik did the same. Not wanting to miss out on the fun, our director of photography, Larry Sher, and our cameraman, Rob Barocci, also shoved their arms in. It was brutally, painfully cold. Since Rob and I had done the Polar Bear Club on a twelve-degree New Year's morning in Coney Island, we were talking the most trash. *This was easy compared to swimming in the frigid Atlantic.* Secretly, though, it wasn't. It hurt like hell . . . until it didn't. Soon, the pain was replaced by numbness. *That couldn't be good.* In time, the trash talking switched to who could most afford to live without his arm.

I posited that being a one-armed film director might actually be good for my career. *Did you hear how he lost it? The dude is committed.* Erik countered that he was already living with one leg, so he was more psychologically prepared to lose an arm. Erik and I both mocked the cameramen, asking how they were going to do handheld shots with one arm. I quietly realized that I had made a huge mistake by putting my left arm in because, though I'm righty for everything, I pleasure myself with my feminine hand. *Would I have to retrain myself?*

After ten minutes, real worry started to set in. We'd run out of trash talk, yet it was clear no one was giving up, because now no one was in pain. It was a game where there would be no loser, just four one-armed winners. So when Rob proposed pulling our hands out together, Erik, Larry, and I quickly agreed. Once out, our arms hung dead for a full three minutes. It was scary since we were ten hours from Mexico City, where the best cold-arm specialist must live. When the feeling finally came back, there was much relief all around.

I had a small flirtation going with a Brazilian actress, though it wasn't progressing because she seemed more interested in our stunt coordinator, Fernando. In his sixties, Fernando was a charismatic old-school stuntman and a total badass (think Dos Equis—The Most Interesting Man in the World). When a large poisonous spider was found in our lunch tent, Fernando plucked it from its web and crushed it in his bare hands.

Fernando carried pictures of wild stunts he had done in days past, including a series of photos where a dashing thirty-five-year-old Fernando is seen leaping from one galloping bareback horse to another. In another, Fernando bear-hugs a full-grown leopard, leaps out of a helicopter, and free-falls into a river below. When they hit the water, the enraged leopard swam at him, hell-bent on murder.

Fernando and I were dueling it out for the affection of the actress, and I was losing. And then, suddenly, as it goes with these things, I wasn't. After our final day of shooting, we all went into town to drink one last time at Peeper's. Afterward, at the disco, the actress stuck to me, holding my hand; we even stole a few kisses. At the end of the night, around three A.M., she and I hopped into a cab to head back to the resort. On the way, we stopped in for a late-night snack at a Mexican restaurant or, as they call it down there, "a restaurant."

When we walked in, I saw Erik Stolhanske eating alone at a table. The actress and I got our food and sat down with Erik, who had the Devil in his eyes. Erik got up to pay his bill and returned with a large jar of habanero peppers.

"Pepper-eating contest?"

I eyed the cock-blocking prick, determined not to take the bait. "No, thanks."

"Bok, bok, bok!" Erik clucked.

I held firm. "Nuh-uh."

Erik muttered, "Pollo" (Spanish for "chicken"), and then chewed a pepper down to its stalk, staring at me through quickly watery eyes.

"Not gonna do it," I said, imitating Dana Carvey imitating George Bush Sr.

Then Erik stuck the knife in. "Fernando would eat the peppers."

The actress burst into laughter, agreeing, "Fernando *would* do it!" And then she joined Stolhanske in clucking.

My first pepper was the hottest thing I'd ever eaten, and it caused my lips to burn and my eyes to water.

Erik ate his second. So I did too. We were both sweating, as the actress egged us on. I told him my Indian tongue was far more suited to this than his Swedish tongue, but he just ate a third pepper. So I did too.

We ate our fourth, and then our fifth peppers. We were drenched in sweat, with our mouths on fire. My stomach hurt, and the actress was now trying to get me to stop. *Too late now—I didn't fly down to Mexico* to lose *a pepper-eating contest*. There were only two peppers left. We each ate one, which left us at an unsatisfying draw—a result that Erik found hilarious.

As I paid the bill, Erik reappeared with another pepper jar he'd borrowed from the kitchen.

"Should we continue?"

"Go to hell," I sneered. Erik ate a pepper and then one more to rub it in.

Then he winked. "Hey, can I get a lift back to the hotel?"

Back at the hotel, the actress and I went to my cabana. My stomach was churning and I was sweating, so I threw on my suit and jumped into the plunge pool to try to reset. Trying to get back into the mood, we opened up a couple of beers. Then, Erik showed up, holding a Ping-Pong paddle.

"Care for a little Pong, guy?"

When someone cock blocks you for a little while, it's funny. After college, Steve Lemme and I used to do it to each other so routinely that we'd both always end up alone at the end of the night. Eventually we called a truce. But Erik was not part of that truce, and he was going too far. I stepped out of the plunge pool, grabbed my Ping-Pong paddle, and whipped him like the one-legged bastard he is. As I shook his hand, I whispered, "Now, get the fuck out."

He smiled, but his eyes were focused behind me. I turned to see five more "friends" arriving. They had been up partying when Erik came in and told them that I was having an early morning Ping-Pong party.

I played them all and beat them all, while the actress drank beer and hung around. Finally, at eight A.M., I beat the last cock blocker and sent everyone on their way. And the actress and I finally went to bed. At around two P.M., we awoke and she went back to her room. When she was safely gone, I sprinted for the bathroom, where Satan came screaming out of my anus. As anyone who has been in a pepper-eating contest can tell you, it hurts more leaving than it does coming. Fuckin' Stolhanske.

September 16 is Mexico's Independence Day, and it was a day off for us so we headed into Barra de Navidad. People were eating, drinking, and playing carnival games, including one of genius simplicity. There were two shelves of lined-up empty beer bottles. For 25 pesos, you were given three rocks to throw at the bottles. If you broke a bottle, the man handed you a cold, full bottle of beer. When you finished that beer you handed him the bottle, and he put it on the shelf for you to break again. It was hard to find a reason to stop playing; then Peeper walked up.

"Are you ready for the firecracker bull?"

"What's that?" I asked.

Peeper smiled big. "It's why we're here, bro!"

"Is it like running with the bulls?"

"Yeah, man! But with firecrackers!"

You know, I'd always wanted to run with the bulls in Pamplona. It figures Mexico would up the ante by shooting off firecrackers behind the bulls.

"I'm in," I said.

"Hell yes! I'll get you close!" Peeper pumped his fist.

"Are you going to run too?" I asked.

Peeper shook his head. "Me? No, hell no."

Hmmm. Whatever. This sounded like the beginning of a good story. And what was I going to do? Go back to America with the tale of how I didn't run with the "firecracker bulls"?

As the sun disappeared, hundreds of people started to filter out of the restaurants and into the town square. Noticing the crowd, I asked Peeper where the bulls were going to run.

"It's just one bull," he said. "And right here in the square."

One bull? Hmm, kind of disappointing, but okay.

A Mexican fireworks show started. It felt unsafe, nothing like a show in the United States. Huge rockets exploded really low in the sky, their percussive sound shaking our bodies, and the crowd loved it. *When are they gonna release the bull?* I wondered. *This felt disorganized. Wasn't it dangerous in the dark? Eh, who was I to push our lawyered-up ways on these freedom-loving people?*

Then a huge rocket exploded, low in the air, near some power lines. That planned explosion was followed by a much louder unplanned explosion, which immediately blacked out the entire city. After some investigation, Peeper informed us that a transformer had blown, which meant that the fireworks and cigarette lighters now furnished the only light in town.

I was getting worried. "Peeper, are they going to cancel the bull?"

"Hell no! Nothing cancels the bull!" I told Peeper I wasn't so sure I wanted to run anymore. In the dark, someone could get trampled or gored. But Peeper wouldn't have it. "Gored? What're you talkin' about? Come on, man, I'll show you the bull." He led us through the crowd to an area where a bunch of men were gathered around . . . something. Peeper pointed.

"There she is!"

I looked for a snorting animal with horns, but all I saw was a wire sculpture—of a bull. It was about five feet long, two feet wide, and three feet high and had six wooden handles sticking out of it.

"Oh, I thought it was a real bull," I said.

He looked at me cockeyed. "A real bull in this crowd? What do you think we are, crazy?"

"But what's the firecracker part?" I asked.

Peeper brought me closer. Strung into the frame of the "bull" were literally a thousand bottle rockets, pointing every which way. Peeper explained that when they lit the fuse, six kids would run the bull through town until every rocket had fired.

"Do you want to hold a handle? It's a very auspicious honor."

"Fuck no, Peeper. I don't want to hold the handle!"

Peeper laughed. "Good choice."

Lit only by flashlights, the mayor of the town gave a speech. As it was in Spanish, I have no idea what he said, but the crowd roared loudest when he lit his cigarette.

It was time. Six ten-year-olds ran up, each grabbing a handle of the firecracker bull. The mayor took a big drag off his cigarette, which he then used to light the fuse. Quickly, he scampered off into the dark. And the ten-year-olds started running through the crowd, yelling effectively what sounded like, "Arrriiiiibaaaa!"

Seconds later, bottle rockets started exploding—shooting off in every direction. *Weeeeeeee, kaboom! Weeeeeeee, kaboom!* Twenty to thirty bottle rockets were shooting and exploding every second. We were close, running, hiding behind cars, as rockets slammed into walls and blew up over our heads. Rockets slammed into random crowd members, over and over. One blew up in a woman's face. The kids who were holding the bull got the worst of it. Rockets blew up against their ribs. When a kid would fall away, another would replace him. Happy Independence Day!

Though filming was going great down in Mexico, Searchlight didn't have the same opinion. We were having communication problems. Phone service at the remote resort was so bad that calls would drop, and then the whole system would go down for hours. Getting to the resort required hours of flying and land travel, so no one came down. Searchlight hired two local producers to oversee us—to make sure we were going to bring the film in on time and on budget. But, for whatever reason, the producers were not reporting what we felt was the accurate picture. They told Fox that we were falling way behind and that we were hemorrhaging money. *Maybe they wanted to appear to be saviors to Fox?* I really don't know, because it just wasn't true, as evidenced by the fact that the film came in both on time and *under* budget. Regardless, with four weeks of shooting to go, a narrative was forming and it wasn't good. As my high school headmaster said, "Perception is reality."

Eventually, Searchlight became so concerned that they pressed the nuclear button, sending two people down to rectify the situation. The first was a stunt director named Ernie Orsatti. He was sold to me as someone who would help me shoot the big action finale.

The second was an executive from the bond company. All studio movies are bonded, which means that if a film falls behind and goes over budget, the studio can turn the film over to the bond company, which is really just an insurance company. We weren't behind by more than a day, or over budget at all, but it didn't matter. The bond company was now in control, and their executive was there to make sure that the film was finished on time and within the allotted budget. This executive was there to break a couple of eggs. Which he did, when he immediately fired me. My replacement? Ernie Orsatti, the new director of *Club Dread*.

What the bond guy didn't know was that I was one of the stars of the film. He literally didn't know that. So in firing me, he also lost me as an actor. Then Heffernan quit, as did Lemme, Soter, and Stolhanske, Bill Paxton, Brittany Daniel, Jordan Ladd, M. C. Gainey, and Lindsay Price. The bond company had a new director, but he had no actors left. *Now what?*

After a frenzied negotiation between our new agents at UTA, my producer, Rich Perello, and Searchlight, I was reinstalled as director, the bond guy went home, and the cast came back. We kept Ernie Orsatti, who became our stunt director, shooting a bunch of amazing shots I never could have gotten on my own. In an impossible situation, Ernie busted his ass for us and made the movie vastly better.

When we got back to LA, we dove into the edit, and ten weeks later, we were ready to test a cut. I had my concerns. The opening of the film hadn't turned out as originally imagined. Or maybe it had. In the opening of *Club Dread,* three resort staff members meet in the woods for a sexy threesome. Unbeknownst to them, someone (the killer) is watching. The guy in the trio (played by my good pal Dan Montgomery) is a cocky prick who leads the girls into a Mayan temple for a little privacy. We were looking to mock the terrible decisions horror movie characters make, like when they go in the basement when they really shouldn't.

We were trying to scare the audience, but also make them laugh. We wanted to let them know that we were in on the joke. We wanted the tone of the opening to be different from the rest of the movie—broader and sillier, while the rest of the film would be hip, real, funny, and scary. I told the actors in the opening (three great actors, I might add) to overact. I told them to be dumb people who made bad decisions. Now that the film was done, I was worried that people wouldn't get that we were mocking horror movies. I was afraid they'd experience the overcooked tone and think that we had just whiffed.

When we screened the film, my fears were realized. People were confused by the opening, which then caused them to doubt the rest of the movie. It didn't matter if the rest of the film got laughs, this version of the opening was flawed and now we had a hill to climb. *Someone call Billy the Dummy.*

We went back into the edit, trying out different performances and juggling scenes, hoping to raise our test scores. And though the numbers went up, they didn't go up enough. Each screening said the same thing—the opening needed to be reshot in the same tone as the rest of the movie. There was also a deeper problem. The audience had met Broken Lizard in a pure comedy, and they wanted more of that, not this blood-soaked horror-comedy thing. They wanted another *Super Troopers*. You could feel Searchlight's enthusiasm waning.

In a normal schedule, you edit for three to six months. We were going on a year, which was costing Searchlight money. I suggested reshooting the opening, but the studio had lost confidence and didn't want to spend good money after bad.

Wondering if *we* were the problem, Searchlight went radical. They hired an outside editor. Yup, we were fired again. The new editor came into our room and took over, generating her own eighty-minute cut. But when Searchlight tested her version, the scores went down twelve points. So we were rehired with the direction to wrap it up.

Club Dread opened on February 27, 2004. Though we knew that the film had issues, we still held out hope that *Super Troopers* fans would show up and propel it to a hit. On the Monday before the release, I stopped by the marketing department to take their temperature. "How're we feeling?" I asked.

One of the marketing execs was actually quite optimistic, saying things were looking good because our weekend's competition was weak. I had to agree, though I was concerned about one film, Mel Gibson's *The Passion of the Christ*. We loved *Braveheart* and were worried that this film might be as good. But our executive just laughed. "Don't worry. I think we can beat a self-distributed film about Christ that's in *Aramaic!*" (No studio would finance *The Passion of the Christ*, so Gibson self-funded both the production and the release.) I left feeling confident.

The Passion of the Christ made the odd move of opening two days early, on a Wednesday, and it got off to a brisk start. Who am I kidding? It was breaking records. This film, which was in fucking

Aramaic—a film that no studio thought was a good bet—was selling out theaters across the country. When our film opened on Friday, we stood in the lobby of a Times Square theater, watching as organized church groups handed out free tickets to *The Passion* to anyone who wanted them. Churches had bought out the screenings, hoping to spread the word of God while guaranteeing that Christ's movie was a hit. Meanwhile, *Club Dread*, along with the other movies that opened that weekend, got crucified. Ahem. And while I'm a huge fan of Mel Gibson as a director, to this day, I still haven't seen that movie.

Club Dread was a theatrical bomb, although it would go on to find a big audience on DVD. Today, when fans tell me that *Club Dread* is their favorite Broken Lizard film, my heart warms, because there are a lot of goddamned great jokes in that movie and I truly love it.

In the end, our relationship with Searchlight was a casualty of poor communication and a lack of savvy on my part. It was my first studio film, and I didn't know how to play the game. I should have figured out a way to communicate with Searchlight, so that they could have known and felt confident that their millions of dollars were being minded as well as they actually were. Searchlight didn't want to fire me (twice)—they felt they had to. And in the end, when the film came in on budget, nothing was said on either end, but the facts were clear. Had I communicated better and had we kept the energy positive, Searchlight would have let us reshoot the opening and who knows what might have happened? Regardless, with all of our goodwill from *Super Troopers* gone, our relationship with Fox Searchlight was over, and now Broken Lizard was in the wind.

CHAPTER 14

———

The Dukes of Hazzard: Smoking with Willie, Fighting with Burt, and Other Stories from the Deep South

After *Club Dread* tanked, Broken Lizard was looking for a new studio home, but there were no offers. I was in director jail, which meant I was being blamed for the bomb. We needed help—we needed someone with power to vouch for us again. Thinking about my post–*Super Troopers* call with Adam Sandler, I decided to find out just how big a fan he really was.

When Broken Lizard met with Adam's producer, Jack Giarraputo, he asked us what we wanted to do next. So we pitched him our idea about a five-man beer-drinking team that goes to Oktoberfest to compete in a secret underground beer-games competition. Jack loved it, so he brought us downstairs to pitch Adam Sandler himself. That was surreal. Adam was cool and funny and everything you'd hope for. Adam dug our idea and said that he wanted his company to produce it for us.

We spent the next two weeks pitching *Beerfest* to the studios and eventually sold it to Adam's home studio, Sony. Over the next six months, with notes from Jack and Adam, we wrote roughly ten drafts and then turned it in to our executive at Sony. Walking over to the meeting, Jack was confident that we were going to get a green light. He was used to green lights.

We didn't get the green light. Not even close. Our executive really didn't seem to like the script. After many lukewarm comments, he finally said, "Do these guys really need to drink Budweiser? I mean, wouldn't we root for them more if they drank something imported like Stella Artois?"

Jack stood up and said, "We're going." On the way back to Happy Madison, Jack grumbled. "Fuck them if they don't get it!" Jack called Sony and convinced them to let us make it elsewhere if we could. We couldn't. Everyone passed—Fox, Paramount, New Line, Warner Bros., everyone. And *Beerfest* quietly died (or went into a coma), a casualty of *Club Dread*, no doubt.

Though the phones were quiet for Broken Lizard, my agent *was* getting calls for me to direct other comedies, but nothing really thrilled me. Then, Greg Silverman called. I'd first met Greg when he was an executive at Revolution Studios. He was a big *Super Troopers* fan and was now an executive at Warner Bros. After some small talk, Greg got to the point. "How'd you like to direct *The Dukes of Hazzard*?" I was intrigued. As a kid, I was a huge fan of the show, both for the kick-ass driving stunts and for Daisy Duke's shorts. Plus, outlaw country music had always spoken to me. I loved Willie Nelson, Johnny Cash, Waylon Jennings, Merle Haggard, Hank Williams, Billy Joe Shaver, Leon Russell, Marshall Tucker, Lynyrd Skynyrd, Jerry Reed, Dolly Parton, and June Carter Cash, all of it. Maybe it's because my family originates from the Deep South—Deep South India.

So, I was intrigued. But I also kind of needed it. I had made three movies—*Puddle Cruiser, Super Troopers,* and *Club Dread.* Hollywood loved me for *Super Troopers* because, in addition to it striking a comedy chord with a lot of people, it also made the studio a lot of money. But they hated me for *Club Dread.* Yes, the film had a large group of fans and made the studio money in the long term, but many didn't like it, maybe didn't get it, and felt vindicated when it didn't perform theatrically. I was in director jail, and no one cared about the surprise that was *The Passion of the Christ.* Why a film fails doesn't matter. People just know it failed and they know they don't want to hire the guy who directed the failure.

So I was hopeful when the script for *Dukes* arrived at my Laurel Canyon home. It would be cool, I told myself, to make the General fly again. Sadly, the script wasn't quite up to snuff. It was comedically broader than I thought it should be and the story wasn't all there. So I passed.

Three months later, my agent, Keya, called. "Hey, Warner Bros. has a rewrite on the *Dukes* script. Greg really wants you to do this. This could be big. Will you take another read?"

I read the new draft, really wanting it to be good. It was better, but my earlier notes still applied, so I passed again.

Two months later, the phone rang. It was Keya. "Warner Bros. has *another* draft. Will you take a read?" It's nice to be wanted. And normally I wouldn't read a third draft of anything, but I wasn't doing anything else, so . . . Here's the thing. I didn't hate it. The story finally made sense. The dialogue wasn't there, but there *were* some pretty good scenes. This script had the bones of something I could build on.

A meeting was set at the executive suites of Warner Bros., where *Dukes* producer Bill Gerber and I sat down with Greg Silverman to talk about script and tone. Greg was looking for me to bring some of that *Super Troopers* magic to *Dukes*. I told Greg that his instincts were right, in that *Super Troopers* and *Dukes* were creatively related.

In 1975, Gy Waldron made a small film called *Moonrunners* about southern boys who run moonshine. But it was only after the insane success of *Smokey and the Bandit* that Warner Bros. Television hired Waldron to make a TV show on the same topic. So while *The Dukes of Hazzard* is a TV version of *Moonrunners,* it is also closely related to *Smokey and the Bandit.* Burt Reynolds and Jerry Reed became Bo and Luke Duke. Sally Field in her tiny jean short-shorts became Daisy Duke. Sheriff Buford T. Justice became Boss Hogg. And the bumbling jilted groom became Rosco P. Coltrane. Both *Bandit* and *Dukes* even have hound dogs.

And while I was a big fan of *Dukes, Smokey and the Bandit* was my true love. I loved that film both because of the number of swearwords in it and because of Burt Reynolds's charming anti-authority attitude.

For me, *Super Troopers* was inspired by *Smokey and the Bandit.* I told Greg that I wanted to make a tough, funny *Dukes of Hazzard* with state-of-the-art, ass-kicking stunts. Ten-year-olds need to see that car fly and feel the same sense of awe that we felt back in the eighties. In terms of casting, I said we had to follow *Smokey and the Bandit* by hiring real southerners. *Dukes* had hired northerners to play southerners, which caused it not to age as well. Our film needed an authentically southern cast. We needed two guys to bridge us back to the eighties. Our film needed Burt Reynolds and Willie Nelson.

Greg cocked his head. "To play the Duke boys?"

I laughed. "No, but I'd see that movie!"

A deal was made and we got to work. Warner Bros. is an old-school studio that prides itself on valuing the director's vision, so they were more than amenable to bringing in Broken Lizard to do the rewrite. This was a security blanket for me, because my guys are brilliant writer-comics who understand the importance of tone and structure.

I told the guys that the film should be funny but real. We weren't going to make fun of southerners, and the plot should be as simple as any of the plots that existed in the TV show. We kept two elements of the original script: Boss Hogg would be trying to buy up Hazzard to turn it into a coal mine, and the film would end in a rally race.

Broken Lizard started writing, focusing on the first act, which is roughly the first twenty pages. After six drafts, we turned it in to Warner Bros. so they could see where we were going with it. Meanwhile, Warner Bros. sent Billy, another producer, Dana Goldberg, and me down to Louisiana in a private jet to scout locations. Scouting was hard since the script wasn't close to done, but Warner Bros. wanted us to stay ahead of the process in the event that they decided to go forward. On the flight back from New Orleans, we got a call from Jeff Robinov. He liked the tone and humor of the first twenty pages so much that he had green-lit the movie. Everyone on the plane celebrated. I was concerned. *Shouldn't we wait until we write the rest before we go into production?* But Billy and Dana looked at me like I had two noses. *You don't question a green light, rookie.*

Immediately after the green light, Warner Bros. hired a car broker to secretly start buying 1969 Dodge Chargers. At the beginning of the weekend, you could get a Charger for $2,000. By Sunday, when word spread that the General Lee was going to fly again, the price was $10,000.

Meanwhile, we hired the casting director Mary Vernieu and began the casting process. I told Mary that I wanted the film to be fun and not take itself too seriously. I wanted it to be a classy piece of pop culture. I told her to find great actors who were authentically southern.

We quickly made an offer to Burt Reynolds to play Boss Hogg, and then another to Willie Nelson to play Uncle Jesse. Mary made lists of potential Duke boys and I began a round of meetings. The last major piece was the role of Daisy Duke. This was an important role to me. I went through puberty with a poster of Catherine Bach on my wall. Yes, the other roles were important, but this one was too. When I sat down with Mary to discuss possibilities, I learned from her that larger forces were at play. "Warner Bros. wants to make an offer to Jessica Simpson."

Hmm, Jessica Simpson. Pop phenom Jessica Simpson. Reality TV star Jessica Simpson. The girl who famously wondered if tuna (Chicken of the Sea) was actually chicken. Sure, she was wildly famous, but she wasn't an actor. She was famous for reality TV, the lowest form of entertainment. Snobs would never accept her. I was one of those snobs. I wanted a great southern actress who knew her way around a joke and who could do those shorts proud. Yeah, Jessica was southern, but she was exactly the opposite of what I wanted for Daisy Duke. Compounding the issue was that she was publicly campaigning for the role in the press. The tabloids had picked it up and were constantly referring to her as the next Daisy Duke. She'd even gone so far as to name her new puppy Daisy. *Grrrr.* I told Mary not to worry about Jessica and to first focus on the rest of the cast.

Making two independent films and a low-budget studio film doesn't prepare you for working with Warner Bros., the biggest movie studio in the world. If *Dukes* had been an independent film, I would have talked about my love for Willie Nelson and Burt Reynolds, and then, when their agents ignored our calls due to a lack of money, I would have cast the best "will work for cheap" substitutes. So I was more than a little surprised when Billy Gerber called to tell me that Willie Nelson wanted to meet me.

I froze. "What do you mean by that?"

"He's doing a show in Palm Desert on Sunday. Go offer him the part and get him in our movie."

I drove out to Palm Desert, armed with the phone number of Willie's tour manager, David Anderson. On the way, I gave him a call. A deep Texas voice answered. When I asked him how to meet up, he cut me off. "Just park behind the bus and knock." *Uh, okay.*

I pulled up behind the arena, where I saw Willie's famous bus, the Honeysuckle Rose. I walked up and knocked. The door opened, and standing there was David Anderson, a tall, lean man with an insanely wicked, Texas-style sense of humor. Dave led me past a curtain into the smoke-filled "living room" of Willie's bus. The bus was crowded with pre-concert well-wishers, smoking joints, laughing, and listening to country music. Through the smoke, about twenty feet away, I could see him: the legend himself, Willie Nelson. It was too crowded to move and I didn't know bus etiquette, so I sat down on a couch, wondering, *How exactly does one go about getting country music legend Willie Nelson to sign on to a movie?* I watched Dave whisper into Willie's ear. Willie nodded, looking my way. Then he waved. *Oh shit. Showtime.* I waved back. Then, Willie started over and handed me a smoking joint. "Hey, I'm Willie."

I was starstruck, so I just smiled, grabbed the joint, and puffed and puffed—oops, too much. I burst into an explosion of coughing. Fucking rookie. But here's the thing—I was anything but. I had smoked just about every single day of college and some of the days after. I considered myself a skilled grass smoker. And now, in my big moment, when I was getting to smoke with a man I counted as one of my heroes, I was blowing my lungs out. I struggled to say the words, "I'm . . . Jay," as Willie sat next to me. Then, silence. I was here to *offer* him the role of Uncle Jesse, and Willie was waiting for the offer, but I had somehow lost my voice—I assume from nerves. I couldn't speak, so the two of us sat, quietly, awkwardly passing the joint back and forth. After a long pause, he mercifully broke the ice: "So I hear you're making a movie?"

Still no voice, but I choked out the words, "Yes—you—Uncle Jesse."

Feeling sorry for me, he said, "Do you want some water?" I nodded, and he went and got me a bottle of water. When he came back the conversation went nowhere faster. After more nothing happened, Dave walked back over and told Willie it was time to start the show, so Willie smiled, waved, and started for the exit. And just like that, he was gone.

I spent the show backstage, pissed at myself for blowing the meeting, but loving watching him perform all of his great songs. My high was wearing off and my voice had returned, so I was plotting my postshow conversation with Willie, where I was going to charm the shit out of him to make up for my earlier debacle.

After the show ended, I lurked nearby, watching Willie sign autographs. Eventually, he waved to the crowd and disappeared back onto the bus. I waited a few minutes, since isn't it proper etiquette to wait a few minutes before harassing a country legend after his show? *Who the fuck knows, right?* Eventually, I approached the bus door, but a huge security guy motioned for me to stay where I was. I pointed to my Willie Nelson Family backstage pass, but he just shook his head. And then, the bus started up and drove away. *FUCK!*

The next day, I got a call from Billy Gerber. "Sounds like it went well! Nice job!" I laughed, getting ready for a good mocking, and told him about the Debacle in the Desert. Billy was shocked. "What're you talking about? I just got off the phone with his agent. Willie is in." I laughed.

"I guess he doesn't care who the fuck is directing this movie!"

Everything was going right on this film. Johnny Knoxville signed on to play Luke, which was a big win. Johnny has a wild, real, funny, authentically southern vibe that really helped ground the film.

Then Seann William Scott signed on to play Bo. I loved Seann from *American Pie,* but it was his performance in *Old School* that really put him over the top for me. Sure, he wasn't a southerner, but there were enough southerners in the film that we'd be okay.

Meanwhile, Mary set up several meetings with actresses who wanted to play Daisy. I met a ton of famous actresses in jean shorts. Those were great meetings. When Billy Gerber called, he asked about Jessica. I told him, "No way," but he said I was crazy not to hire her. *She's the most popular girl in the country. We'd be lucky to get her. Plus, she's a real southerner and Warner Bros. loves her. Can you at least meet her?*

I met Jessica Simpson in the garden of the Chateau Marmont Hotel. She came in jean shorts and brought her puppy, Daisy. Truthfully, we got along well. We talked about her dog, her reality TV show, and the fact that she'd never acted before. When the meeting ended, I was unconvinced.

So I kept meeting and auditioning actresses. Meanwhile, the rest of the cast was falling into place. Joe Don Baker signed on to play the governor, Lynda Carter agreed to play Pauline, Kevin Heffernan slotted in as Sheve, and Burt Reynolds agreed to play Boss Hogg. Then Warner Bros. president Jeff Robinov called. "What about Jessica?" When the president of a studio calls, you take it seriously. Appealing to his artistic side, I suggested that we should audition her to see if she could handle the role. Knowing what I knew about nonactors, I knew that there was no way she could succeed.

When Jessica came in to audition, she was a nervous wreck. Her public campaigning had led to this. She had to prove that she could act. She wasn't ready. Her face was buried in the script and you could barely hear her. She was toast—end of story.

When I left the audition, Billy called. "How was she?" I played it cool. "We're sending the tape. Judge for yourself."

When Warner Bros. and Billy saw the tape, they saw what I saw, but they had a different reaction. *You're the director. Can't you teach her how to act?* Warner Bros. was anxious. *It was Jessica's time! The country wanted her to be Daisy Duke. How was this director not seeing what everyone else was seeing?*

Not wanting to stand in the way, I told Billy that maybe I should step off the film so they could hire a director who would agree to hire Jessica. *It's me or her.* Billy wouldn't hear it. Losing the director might pull the movie out of a green light, which could mean that it might never get made. Billy made it clear that I was their guy, period. End of story.

But it wasn't the end of the story. A week later, Billy and Warner Bros. came to me with an idea. They told me to pick my top three Daisy choices for a screen test. The fourth actress would, of course, be . . . Jessica Simpson. At the end, we'd all look at the screen tests and pick the best one.

Here's the thing about Hollywood. It's full of operators and manipulators. I am a manipulator. I do it every day, whether it's sweet-talking an agent or getting actors to say lines they don't want to say. But Billy was the former president of Warner Bros., so he played pro ball. I gamed it out: *My* three choices would be professional, experienced actresses, *who have done screen tests before. They are going to have their lines memorized, and they're going to nail it. Jessica doesn't stand a chance.* So I said, "Sure, let's let the screen test decide." We both left confident that we had outplayed the other guy.

We chose two scenes for the screen test and convened on the Warner Bros. back lot, with a midsize crew and a borrowed General Lee. With a flair for the dramatic, Billy set the audition order, slotting Jessica in last.

As expected, my three top choices came in and nailed it—every line, every joke. They were hot and they were great. I was feeling cocky. Then Jessica stepped out of her trailer.

I didn't envy her. She saw the three famous actresses on the lot wearing their Daisy Dukes. She knew it was me who was standing between her and the role. And she knew that after all of the campaigning she had done, if she didn't get the part, people would make fun of her. She had to be nervous, but she didn't show it. She just smiled and winked and said, "Here we go."

Billy and I watched from the monitors. "Action!" Jessica started in. *Wait. What's this? She'd memorized it. She knows her lines—all of her lines.* Billy and I exchanged a look. *Uh-oh.*

Her first take was good. Her second take was better. In her third take, she improvised a joke. But her fourth take was the best. She'd found an acting coach and she'd worked on the scenes. She had confidence and charisma, and her energy was popping off the screen. The girl seemed to be goddamned glowing. Billy just smiled at me with his Cheshire grin and said, "You're fucked."

I was. When I cut the screen tests together, it was all there. Was she the best actress of the four? No, but she *was* Jessica Simpson, America's sweetheart, and goddamn it, she could act. We had our Daisy Duke.

Two months later I was sitting on a folding chair in the back of a semitruck that was filled, wall to wall, with racks of jean shorts—probably five hundred pair. I was doing rewrites, as Jessica went into a changing room and tried on her top fifty favorites. I'd look up as she'd come out in a new pair, spin around, and say, "What do you think, boss?" I smiled, knowing that the ten-year-old me wouldn't believe it.

Jess and I would go on to become good friends. She's smart and funny and oversees quite a merchandising empire. But one thing bugged me. The girl I knew didn't jibe with the ditzy one from her reality show. When I asked her why, she said that the producers of her show decided to create this ditzy persona. They included her "mistakes"—they used muffed lines or footage that made her look clueless. The ditzier she seemed, the higher the ratings went. And while she never intentionally said anything *stupid,* she did stop filtering herself. She'd just say whatever came to her mind, including her famous "Chicken of the Sea" comment. It's all show business.

Jessica was a great Daisy Duke. It *was* her moment. And when the film opened to $30 million, then the biggest-ever August opening for a comedy, we all knew that a very large portion of the draw was Jess. This became superclear to me when we were on a red carpet in Tennessee with thousands of screaming fans and photographers. I was doing an interview and apparently blocking the view of a paparazzo who was trying to photograph her. Finally, he just exploded, *"Get the fuck out of the way!"*

I slinked away. "Gee, I'm only the director."

A month after the film came out, a package arrived at my office. Mounted in a case was a pair of Jessica's Daisy Dukes. Written on the pocket were the words, "Thanks for giving my ass a chance. Love, Jess."

With the cast in place, I turned my attention to stunts. There was a car chase and a huge jump in *every* episode of *The Dukes of Hazzard* TV show, so the show became a laboratory for innovative stunt-driving technique. But demand for stunt drivers outstripped supply, so the *Dukes* stunt coordinator used to often walk into bars to ask tough-looking blond bartenders a hilarious question: "Hey, you wanna fly the General Lee?" Novice stunt drivers were told, "Keep the wheels straight and hit the ramp at sixty and you'll be fine." Those guys were badasses and they made that show the huge success that it was. Considering how loose the safety restrictions were (and how much coke was being snorted in Hollywood at the time), it's a miracle that there was only one serious injury during the whole six-year run of the show.

When hiring a stunt coordinator for the film, there was only one guy I wanted: Dan Bradley. Dan was the stunt coordinator for the groundbreaking film *The Bourne Supremacy*. When Matt Damon drove his car into the Moscow tunnel in *Bourne,* I knew that car stunts had changed forever. *Was Damon really in that fucking car?* Kids in the eighties were blown away by the stunts in *Dukes,* and modern-day kids needed to have that same feeling. Dan Bradley needed to be the guy to make the General Lee fly.

Dan asked for twenty-five Dodge Chargers, all of which were quickly painted orange. We also bought fifty police cars from *Batman* and repainted those. Down in Baton Rouge, we built a twenty-four-hour garage. Dan would smash the cars during the day and send them to the garage at night for repair. By morning, fixed-up General Lees were sent back out so Dan and his guys could smash them again.

With our cast and crew secured, it was time to move the circus down to Baton Rouge, where I would get another crack at making a good impression with Willie Nelson. The cast was arriving, and Billy and I stopped by Willie's wardrobe fitting to welcome him to town and to invite him to a cast dinner at Sullivan's Steakhouse. Willie said he'd be there. Then Billy's phone rang, so he walked off to answer it. As I turned to leave, Willie winked and said, "Come on over to the bus before dinner and let's get hungry."

I smiled. "You know, Willie, the last time I was on your bus I was a little nervous and, I don't know, I uh ... didn't ..." *I was rambling. Get to the point.* "Well, I just wanna say, I was a pretty big pot smoker in college."

Willie thought there might be more to that sentence, but there wasn't, so he just smiled and said, "Great."

There was an awkward silence, so I added, "I mean, like, I smoked every day."

He raised an eyebrow. "Well, how about that?"

I was the king of the dorks at a festival of dorks. I was dying inside, so I mumbled, "See you later," and walked off.

At around six forty-five P.M., my friend and assistant director Artist Robinson and I knocked on the door of the Honeysuckle Rose for a pre-dinner smoke. For those of you who don't know, the assistant director (or AD) on a film is not the director's assistant. The AD's job is to be the liaison between the director and the crew and to make sure that the director's vision is executed, and executed on an efficient timetable. The AD is like the boss of the crew. Artist is a legendary AD who came up in the go-go eighties and has seen it all. Artist was the first AD on *Breakdown, Face/Off, Jurassic Park III, Men in Black II, Spy,* the new *Ghostbusters,* and many, many more. He's got a deep southern voice, and he was fond of saying, "If you can't drink all night and work all day, you're in the wrong goddamned business!" A Texan and a singer-songwriter himself, Artist was also a huge Willie fan. As we waited at the bus door, Artist turned to me. "Boss, I don't need to tell you how much I appreciate you including me in on this. This is a big moment."

The door opened, and Dave Anderson let us in. We walked back to the kitchen table, where Willie was already sitting with the actor M. C. Gainey, who was playing Rosco P. Coltrane. M.C. is a big, funny, tough-guy actor who played Hank in *Club Dread*. In Broken Lizard we like to cast tough guys who can actually beat you up in real life. M.C. fit that bill nicely.

Artist and M.C. sat on one side of the bench, with Willie across from them. And since I wasn't about to tell Mr. Nelson to move over, I stood. Willie looked up and said, "Shall we?" This was my moment. *Redeem yourself and smoke this joint like the man you are. This is Willie Nelson, motherfucker!* If there were an Olympics for joint rolling, Willie'd take the gold. Actually, he did. He won the *High Times* joint-rolling competition. His opponent rolled and smoked twenty-five joints. Willie did twenty-six. The man is an expert—I'm talking perfectly rolled, lit, and in his mouth in twenty seconds. He passed the joint to me and I took what I felt was a "reasonable starter hit." However, when I exhaled, a massive plume of smoke came out, followed by a series of hearty coughs.

"You gotta cough to get off, partner!" M.C. laughed. But I was fine, and I smiled, coughed some more, and passed the joint to M.C. As I looked to my left, there was Willie, rolling a second joint. I thought, *All right. Two joints, four guys, that's how it goes down on Willie Nelson's bus!* Willie passed me the second joint, and this time, I made sure to take a reasonable hit. I passed joint two to M.C., who then started telling one of his hilarious New Orleans stories.

As I was listening to M.C.'s story, it slowly dawned on me that, regardless of how "reasonable" my last hit was, the damage had been done by my first hit. I had heard that the medical science behind "you have to cough to get off" was that coughing bursts blood vessels in your lungs, which gives the THC a more direct path into your body. That's probably stoner bullshit, but regardless, I was currently higher than a CIA drone. I was dizzy and I had a serious case of dry mouth.

What was in this fucking pot? I needed to quench this thirst, as I didn't want to lose my voice again, so I said, "Hey, Willie, you got a beer? I'm a little parched."

Willie looked up, exhaling a huge plume of smoke. "I don't keep beer on the bus because it leads to darkness."

It's getting pretty dark over here, Willie, I thought, as he started rolling a third joint. M.C. was just getting to his punch line, which caused everyone to burst into laughter. Thinking fast, I fake laughed along but pulled a Clinton and sent the joints by my mouth without inhaling. "Yeah, totally, totally," I said to no one in particular. Since I'm a vaguely talented actor, I got away with it. *I told you this would amount to something, Mom and Dad.*

Artist and Willie were talking about the Austin music scene, while I was so high and dizzy I was wondering if I was going to keel fucking over. And there was Willie rolling a fourth joint. *Dear God. The man's an assassin.* The conversation had kind of hit a lull, and I found myself holding two joints, and Willie was holding the other two, and everyone was looking at me, since I was now the logjam. Since I physically couldn't smoke anymore and I couldn't get away with "my fake-laughing trick," I passed the two joints to M.C. Willie then passed me joints three and four, but I just passed those on as well.

Willie looked up innocently. "What's wrong?"

I waved him off. "I'm good, man. I'm good."

Then he smiled. "Say, 'I submit.'" I looked at him. *Is he serious?* He nodded. "Say it."

And I said it. "I submit, sir."

Willie just laughed. "Big fuckin' smoker!"

While I had sort of redeemed myself with one legend, there was another one down there in Baton Rouge. Maybe I shouldn't tell this story, but I'm going to. See, we have a tradition in Hollywood where movie stars behave however they want to, sometimes poorly, and we on the crew all keep mum. From the studio's perspective, this "gag rule" comes from wanting to keep the star looking good in the public's eye and, by association, the movie looking good. And while I have plenty of stories of stars misbehaving (I worked on *Community*) that I'm not going to tell, this one story is special. And so this one time, I'm going to break tradition.

Burt Reynolds is a fucking legend. His performance in the films *Smokey and the Bandit, The Longest Yard, Deliverance,* and *Boogie Nights* shaped an entire generation of men. Every kid in my neighborhood loved him, and so did the moms, and so did the dads—many of whom grew *Bandit* mustaches. Burt was funny, dramatic, and tough, and he had a twinkle in his eye. And if that wasn't enough, he also did his own stunts. Burt had the quality that all of the great movie stars have: Men wanted to be him, and women wanted to be with him. All of this combined to make Burt the biggest fucking movie star in the world for a good chunk of the seventies.

When we made *Super Troopers,* I told my crew that if we did it right, the film would be tough, real, and funny—it would be a tonal cousin to *Smokey and the Bandit.* My mustache and attitude in *Super Troopers* are all taken from Burt. One hundred percent.

So when I told Warner Bros. that I would make *The Dukes of Hazzard* only if Burt Reynolds played Boss Hogg, I meant it. I put my ass on the line for my hero, and when he agreed to play the role, it was literally a dream come true.

But let me be clear. I'm not naïve. Burt has a reputation for being tough on directors. That anti-authority streak we all love in *The Bandit?* That wasn't acting. That's the real Burt. And on a movie set, the director is the authority. I knew that going in, but when an actor is perfect for a part, I don't care what their offscreen reputation is. As long as they can deliver on-screen, I'm good.

Here's the other thing that complicated our relationship. When Warner Bros. approached him to play Boss Hogg, Burt said, "Sure. Happy to. As long as I can direct the picture." Burt had directed some films in his day, and *I get it—the Bandit, directing* The Dukes of Hazzard? *I'd see that.* But Warner Bros. talked him out of the idea, and Burt signed up anyway.

My experience with Burt on *Dukes* was amazing, hilarious, and, often, chummy. On set, Burt would regale us with a seemingly endless fountain of epic show-business stories. Like the time in the seventies when he was in a New York City nightclub with the offensive line of the New York Jets. In the next booth over, an Italian American guy was sandwiched between the four hottest women in the club. Burt kept looking over, hoping they'd notice him, but the women only had eyes for the Italian. Annoyed, Burt finally walked over and just started hitting on the women, totally ignoring the guy because, as Burt puts it, "The hell with him. I'm Burt fucking Reynolds." After a couple of minutes, the Italian guy had had enough and started talking shit to Burt. Feeling no pain and unwilling to back down in front of the women, Burt challenged the Italian guy to a fight.

Out they spilled onto Forty-Sixth Street on that cold winter night, both drunk and ready to brawl. Burt said they circled awhile, fists up and trading insults. Then, the Italian guy threw a punch. When the punch hit Burt's jaw, he said he had one clear thought: *Uh-oh. This guy is strong.* But, remember, Burt played halfback at Florida State. So he's a tough motherfucker too. The men traded punches for two painful, sweaty, exhausting minutes, and Burt couldn't figure out how the

Italian guy was keeping up—*Who is this fucking guy?* Exhausted, Burt put his hands up. "I'm tired. Can we take a break, pal?"

The Italian guy smiled. "Sure. Why not?"

Feeling like the guy had earned it, Burt extended his hand. "Hey, I'm Burt Reynolds."

The Italian extended his hand. "I'm Mario Andretti. Nice to meet you." That was the beginning of Burt's friendship with one of the greatest race-car drivers in the world.

As good as Burt's stories are, it's his style of storytelling that demands your undivided attention. Burt starts a story with his normal speaking voice but then gets progressively quieter as the story continues, so that at the climax of the story, he's actually whispering, which forces you to lean in so close that your ear is almost touching his lips. It's an incredibly effective way to get people's attention—especially when executed by the master.

There's a special place in America's heart for actors who do their own stunts. Whether it's Steve McQueen, Jackie Chan, or the great Burt Reynolds, doing his or her own stunts lends an actor a dose of *real* toughness. Times have changed, though, because in today's Hollywood, unless you're part of the *Jackass* crew, you're usually not allowed to do your own stunts. One reason is that visual effects have become so sophisticated that it has kind of become unnecessary. And the other is that studios don't want to risk a production shutdown from an unnecessary actor injury. But in the seventies, Burt became famous for doing his own driving and fighting in *Smokey and the Bandit,* for really playing football in *The Longest Yard,* and for doing his own stunts in the movie *about* stuntmen called *Hooper.* Of course, there was a price to pay: physical pain, specifically back injury. Put simply, the man's back hurt, which I knew before he arrived in Louisiana.

We had been shooting for a few weeks when Burt arrived in Baton Rouge. In *his* first scene, Boss Hogg pays a visit to the Duke boys, who are locked up in an Atlanta jail. The scene was five pages long and Burt had huge chunks of dialogue. After I ran a rehearsal, it became clear that Burt didn't have the best grasp of his lines yet. Maybe he thought he could do what he did on *Smokey and the Bandit* and improvise. Burt told me that the *Smokey and the Bandit* script was only sixty pages long (a typical script is 120 pages), and he, Jackie Gleason, Sally Field, and Jerry Reed improvised the rest to brilliant results. But that wasn't possible in this scene, as Boss Hogg's lines advanced the story in relevant ways and also set up some decent jokes. I needed Burt to at least get close to his scripted lines.

One of the main jobs of a film director is to make the actors look good. We set camera angles that are the most flattering, we choose clothes that make them look their best, and we give them advice on how to maximize their performance. And when an actor shows up not quite knowing their lines, there are ways to make sure that their performance doesn't suffer. The best trick is just repetition—if actors do enough takes, eventually they'll perform their lines well. Then it's just a matter of spending the time in the edit room and cutting together the best reads of each line. Yes, it can be a lot of cutting, but the actor will look good and the audience will feel that the actor they love is amazing in the movie. And that's the whole point—directors are there to make the actors look good.

That day, I decided repetition was the solution. So we were doing a lot of takes, but still not making much progress, and Burt was getting annoyed. So I reached into my bag of tricks and asked Kevin, our second assistant director, to make cue cards with Burt's lines written on them. This would shorten things for sure. But Burt didn't love having cue cards on his first day, and he let me know it. Talk about a lousy start to our relationship. We didn't "fight" that day, but there was tension in the air, which was a bummer because, in case it's unclear, Burt Reynolds is one of my heroes. Eventually, something clicked and he figured out the words and started drilling it. And in the final film, Burt's performance in the scene is both great and hilarious.

And best of all, the next day, Burt showed up knowing every line. He was the great Burt Reynolds I had grown up with—smart, funny, and sly. I couldn't have been happier.

But the day after that, he didn't know his lines again. So we had to shoot a lot of takes. Shooting a lot of takes was fine for me, but it was annoying the shit out of Burt, whose back was hurting.

It went like this the whole shoot, alternating between Burt knowing his lines and drilling his performance, and not, and then having to shoot a lot of takes to make it great. I even offered to run lines with him after work, but he said it wasn't necessary.

Compounding the problem was Burt's back pain, which was why he wanted to shoot fewer takes. So, *my* choice was to either shoot a performance that wouldn't deliver the Burt Reynolds America loved, or shoot more takes, knowing my hero's back was hurting. I chose the latter. We'd go back and forth, with Burt yelling at me for shooting too many takes, and me countering with, "Just trying to make it good, sir!"

He would then fire back with, "Goddamn it! Roll film!" And we'd shoot another take.

There's a scene in *Dukes* where Uncle Jesse argues with Boss Hogg in his office and then punches him, sending Hogg flying over a desk. Here was my choice: Either hire a stuntman to double Burt and do the backward flip over the desk, or let Burt do the flip himself. Since

Burt was nearly seventy and had an injured back, I made the decision to hire the stuntman. For a million reasons, it felt like the right thing to do. I knew Burt might be annoyed, but I did it anyway because I was trying to protect him. And, no, I didn't tell him. Because I knew he would say that he wanted to do the stunt, even though it was unnecessary. Honestly, I didn't want to put him on the spot.

I decided to shoot the stunt first to get it out of the way. When we were done, I would bring Burt in to shoot the dialogue. I positioned the camera behind the desk and told Willie to say his final line and then throw a stage punch at the stuntman, who would then throw himself backward over the desk. This was a big moment for the stuntman, because all stuntmen revere Burt. They feel like he's one of them. And now this guy was getting a chance to do something that almost no one else has ever done. He was going to *double* the great Burt Reynolds.

The stuntman, who was dressed in Boss Hogg's white suit and wig, did the stunt four times, and the result was brutal, chaotic, and fantastic. This dude flat-out nailed it. Now it was time to call Burt to set so we could shoot the dialogue. I flipped the camera around so it was now facing Burt. And when he arrived, I told him what I needed: Willie was going to throw his fake punch, and then all Burt had to do was jerk his head. In the edit, once Burt jerked his head, I'd cut behind him to the stuntman flipping over the desk.

Burt cocked his head. "Stuntman?"

"Yeah," I said. "It's a pretty gnarly stunt and I didn't want to risk you hurting your back anymore, so . . ." Burt just stared at me. Trying to fill in the awkward silence, I said, "Burt, the flip went great. The stuntman really nailed it." I pointed to the stuntman, who waved.

Burt didn't even look at the guy. He just whispered, "But I'm Burt Reynolds."

"Burt, *I* made the decision because of your back."

He exhaled. "Let me see the stunt."

I said, "Yeah, okay. Roll playback on the stunt, guys." Burt made his way to a monitor and sat down on an apple box, his face inches from the screen. Willie and I, along with the stuntman, folded in behind Burt to watch the stunt as well. I eyed the stuntman, who was smiling. I knew he really wanted to impress Burt.

We rolled take one, where the stuntman flipped backward over the desk. It was a good take, but Burt just sighed. "Take two!" This one was better, even more violent. Burt shook his head. "Three!" We rolled take three, which was even better than the last, but Burt just covered his eyes, exhaled, and whispered, "Four." I looked at the stuntman, trying to reassure him, but he looked shell-shocked, in his white suit and white Boss Hogg wig. Take four was big, with the stuntman going over the desk and taking everything with him (the lamp, phone, everything). *You can't do it better than that.* But it didn't matter. Burt stood up and screamed, *"Roll camera!"* even though actors don't have the authority to do that. As Burt strode off, I looked at Willie, who smiled and winked.

With the camera facing Burt, Willie said his line and threw his stage punch. Then Burt threw his almost-seventy-year-old body over the desk, taking everything with him. I winced. *That looked great, but it had to be painful.* Burt stood up, looking at me. "Any notes, Orson?" He'd taken to calling me "Orson" after, of course, Mr. Welles. I said, "Burt, that was great. I think we've got it—"

He cut me off, "I need another one." Take two was fantastic and brutal—frankly perfect. And I told him so, but he shook me off. "I can do better." I looked at Willie, who winced.

Take three was even better than two—nasty. When Burt looked

over, I tried a different strategy. "What do you think, Burt? Do you think we've got it?" But he just scowled.

"I'm not feeling it yet." He was right. Take four of this legend flipping backward over the desk *was* his best take. This time, he stood up, punched the air, and yelled, "Now, *that's* how you get punched over a desk!"

And then this happened . . .

A few weeks later, we were shooting the climactic rally race in which Bo Duke races in the General Lee. We needed to shoot aerial shots of the cars crossing the finish line, so we hired a camera helicopter for the day. At the finish line, on the dais, were local dignitaries including Boss Hogg and the governor, played by the great Joe Don Baker. As I was climbing into the helicopter, my AD Artist Robinson's deep southern drawl came over the walkie. "Boss, Burt's back is hurting. Can he go home?"

I answered quickly. "Of course. Put the stand-in in Hogg's white suit and tell Burt to have a great afternoon." Then I jumped into the helicopter and we flew around for three hours, shooting wide shots of cars racing and crowds cheering. From the helicopter, I could see the stand-in, in Boss Hogg's white suit, waving. All was good.

But here's what happened on the ground: Artist approached Burt and said, "Burt, we're good. You can take the rest of the day off." Apparently, Burt smiled and started walking off the dais. Next, Artist approached Joe Don Baker. "Joe Don, you can go. Have a nice day."

But Joe Don just shrugged. "Ah, what the hell? I'll stay."

When Burt heard that, he stopped and said, "I'll stay too." Now, to be clear, there was zero need for either of them to be there that day. There were thousands of extras on the ground, and you can't recognize faces from the height we were flying. My hunch is that Burt respected

Joe Don and decided that he wanted to do the right thing and be there for his fellow actor. So that stand-in in the white suit wasn't a stand-in at all. It was the too-small-to-be-recognizable-from-a-helicopter Burt Reynolds, waving at cars whizzing by for three hours.

The next morning, we were getting ready to shoot a scene with Burt and Jessica. Jess was on set, but Burt was a no-show. "Where's Burt?" I asked.

Artist radioed to his second AD, "Kevin, where's Burt?" About fifty yards away, I saw Kevin, the second AD, speak into his walkie. After about a minute, a production assistant, or PA, whispered something to Kevin. Then I watched a worried-looking Kevin make a beeline for Artist, whispering in *his* ear.

Finally, Artist walked over to me and Billy Gerber. "Boss, Burt won't come out of his trailer. Says he wants to see you, Billy, me, and Kevin in his trailer now."

"Why?" I asked.

Artist shrugged. "Probably has something to do with you flying around for three hours while he stood around onstage yesterday."

"But I said he could go . . ."

Artist put his hands up. "Oh, I know. I told him." Then, smiling: "But he stayed."

The PA who delivered the Burt news led the four of us on the half-mile walk across the fairgrounds to Burt's trailer, where he knocked. "Mr. Reynolds?" he said meekly. Silence. We looked at one another, not sure what to do. So the kid knocked again.

Wham! The door flew open. And there was Burt, wearing his white Boss Hogg pants, white shoes, and a white tank top. Apparently, he'd only gone through partial hair and makeup, since the sides of his hair were white but the middle was black. "*Get the fuck in here!*" he roared.

So we filed in: me, Billy, Artist, Kevin, and the confused PA, who frankly just got caught up in the shuffle.

Burt sat down and we formed a standing semicircle around him. To say he was pissed is a preposterous understatement. He was frothing mad, spitting mad . . . at me. "You know, I've directed a couple of pictures in my day, and one thing I learned is that there's not a lens on the planet that can see my face from a fucking helicopter!"

Trying to calm him, I said, "I know, but Burt, I said you could lea—"

Stabbing a finger at me, he shouted, "Shut the fuck up! Learn when to shut up! You know I've done a lot of stunts in my life! In my life, before *you* showed up in Hollywood, Orson! And you know what? My back hurts! And for you to think it's okay to fly around in a fucking helicopter while I stand around for three fucking hours is *bullshit!*"

Artist piped up. "No offense, Burt, but I *did* say you could go."

Burt ignored that and moved on. "What is this fucking movie anyway? I mean, *how many fucking takes do we have to do?!*"

I exhaled. "I'm shooting the minimum number of takes we need—"

"I learned how to act from a man named Jimmy Stewart!" Burt growled. "Is that good enough for you?! *Is it?!*" I wasn't sure how to respond. Then there was a knock on the door. "*COME IN!*" Burt bellowed. The door opened and we all turned to see a nurse meekly enter, and she was carrying a little black bag. She stood there for a moment, feeling the tension. Burt motioned her over. "Let's do it!" The nurse tiptoed over to Burt and pulled out a syringe, which she started filling with liquid. Simultaneously, Burt stood, turned away from us, pulled down his white pants and underwear, and bent over. The nurse injected Burt, and he pulled his pants back up and shouted, "*Now, get out!*" The nurse exited and Burt sat back down, but he now seemed to have lost his train of thought. "Painkillers." Grumble.

"Mmmph. They say Demerol is as good as Percocet. *It isn't!"* Then, quietly: "It isn't. Now, I like Percodan. But it's harder to get . . ." Long silence. I swear to God, the next sixty seconds was a monologue on the efficacies of various painkillers. The pain shot was really taking effect, and Burt was mostly mumbling. Me, Billy, Artist, Kevin, and the PA were now all looking at one another like, *Now what?* Personally, I was on the edge of nervous laughter, because having one of my childhood heroes ream me out, while on painkillers, ranks as one of the highlights of my life. Soon the haze started to lift and Burt's intensity returned. "I should have directed this fuckin' picture! I could've made a *good* movie!"

Then he started going around the room pointing. First at Billy Gerber—"I like you, Billy." Next was Artist: "I like you too." Next Burt stabbed a finger at second AD Kevin: "I don't like you!" (Kevin's job was to tell him what time to come in every day.) When Burt swept his finger right, he looked momentarily confused as he eyed the random PA. "I don't *know* . . . you?" But then he moved quickly to me: "But I don't like you! I saw your movie—Super Dooper Pooper Scooper! You want to see a real movie? Watch this!" Burt grabbed a DVD case off the table and Frisbee'd it at me, hitting me in the chest. I caught it and looked down at the label quickly before Burt stood up screaming, *"Now, get the fuck out!"*

As we filed out, I tried to salvage things: "Burt, I'm sorry that—"

He stepped toward me, grunting low, *"I said get out!"* So I left.

As we were walking away from Burt's trailer, Artist said, "Boss, I would never let another man talk to me like that."

I shrugged. "Artist, we have a week left. I need him in the rest of the movie. What was I supposed to do? Fight him? The dude's almost seventy and a tough seventy at that."

Artist nodded. "Well, what do you want to do now?" I didn't have an answer for that.

Then Billy asked, "What movie did he give you?"

I held up the DVD. Printed on the cover was the title: *Burt Reynolds— Why My Back Hurts*. I swear this is true. The five of us went to my trailer and popped in the DVD. And let me say this. It was amazing. It was five minutes of footage of every stunt Burt Reynolds has ever done ... set to classical music. There were shots of Burt, as the Bandit, speeding in his black Trans Am and crashing. There were shots of him running with the football and being brutally tackled in *The Longest Yard*. There was a shot of Burt leaping off a second-story building and grabbing on to a tree branch, only to have the branch snap and send him crashing to the ground. There were bar fights, kicked-in doors, being thrown over tables, Burt and a guy fighting, rolling ass over teakettle down a huge hill. When it ended, I looked around at everyone, and do you know what they were doing? Smiling. And so was I. And the only thought running through my head was, *Man, if Burt Reynolds isn't the coolest motherfucker on the planet, I don't know who is.*

When we came out of the trailer, we heard over the walkie that Burt was walking to set. Back on set, Burt was all smiles, and he absolutely nailed the scene. He knew every line, was charming and funny and cool.

And this awesome version of Burt continued through the whole last week of the shoot. Meanwhile, nobody said anything about what had happened in the trailer. Burt and I just pretended it had never happened.

There was one small blip. On the last day, Burt was having trouble remembering a line. After a couple of tries, he snapped, "Goddamned stupid Indian!" (Pause.) "Not you! Me! You're an Indian, but I'm the other kind of Indian!" I learned in that moment that Burt is part Native American.

On the last day, we shot a big scene in the Dukes' barn. Everyone was there—Burt, Willie, Johnny Knoxville, Seann William Scott, and Jessica Simpson. When the scene ended, the movie was over and we started hugging, saying our good-byes.

When Burt saw me, he put his arms out and pulled me in for the tightest hug ever. Burt put his lips right next to my ear and whispered fiercely, "Will you ever forgive me? Will you *ever* forgive me?" It was cool, amazing, emotional, and hilarious. I felt like I was in the movie *Deliverance.*

And that's why I love Burt Reynolds. He's a passionate, hilarious, crazy badass who I fucking admire. And maybe sometimes artists have to be a little crazy to channel whatever it is that makes them great. I went into the film loving the legend. And I still love him and love his performance as Boss Hogg. He's brooding, evil, funny, and charming. It's everything I had hoped for. And as far as this story goes, I hope to God he's not mad at me for telling it. *Will you ever forgive me, Burt? Will you ever forgive me?*

The Dukes of Hazzard had a huge opening weekend. It grossed more than $30 million, making it the number one movie at the box office. The film would go on to make Warner Bros. close to $200 million worldwide. And while that was great, it did take some critical lumps. Why? It's a good film, and I tried as hard on it as I did on my other films. But the press was ready to pounce. Whether it was the Confederate flag, or Jessica, or the fact that the studios had developed a bad habit of making every seventies and eighties TV show into a movie, the press was drooling for a failure that didn't come. Don't get me wrong. I understand the sentiment. There *are* too many TV show–inspired films and too many superhero movies and too many remakes.

When the dust settled, I sat down with studio head Jeff Robinov, who offered me a production deal. He said Warner Bros. wanted to be in the Jay Chandrasekhar business. I told him that it was really Broken Lizard's jokes that fueled *The Dukes of Hazzard* and that the deal should be with all of us. He agreed and, just like that, Broken Lizard had offices on the Warner Bros. lot.

CHAPTER 15

Jackass Number Two: The Story Behind the High-Wire Act That Was My Collaboration with Johnny Knoxville and the *Jackass* Crew

I was in my Laurel Canyon house one morning when the phone rang. It was my friend Johnny Knoxville, and he had a question: *Would I consider being in the sequel to* Jackass? My danger-warning alarm started ringing. During the making of *The Dukes of Hazzard,* Johnny and I had become good pals, but I didn't trust him. Well, I trusted him, but a friendship with Johnny required being on guard at all times because of a game he played with his *Jackass* pals that included sudden, unexpected punches to the balls. (Apparently, the game originated when Spike Jonze and he used to surprise-break dinner plates over each other's heads in restaurants.)

After Johnny drilled my nuts a couple of times, and I returned the favor a few more, we both moved to phase two of the game, which was to cover one's nuts (*out of respect*) when in the presence of the other.

Look at any photograph from *Dukes* and you'll see both of us with our hands in this "defensive position."

When Seann William Scott made the mistake of going into a porta potty on the *Dukes* set, Johnny sprinted up and mercilessly rocked it back and forth, almost tipping it. Seann came out laughing, but rattled. After that, everyone just pissed *next to* the porta potties. The lesson with Knoxville was clear: Watch your back.

But I'd be lying if I said I wasn't intrigued, because I was a massive *Jackass* fan. I remember watching the first film at the Beverly Center. Holy shit. I was blown away, screaming with laughter. I went again two days later and loved it just as much. Afterward, I went into a creative funk, telling Heffernan that it didn't matter what we did. Nothing prewritten would ever be as purely funny as *Jackass*.

So on the phone that morning, I asked Johnny what he had in mind. The "stunts" in *Jackass* required being willing to risk bodily injury. I was probably willing to do that, though I was aware of how beat-up the *Jackass* guys were from their years of comedic violence.

Johnny, who had never ridden a motorcycle before, once attempted to pull a backflip on a motocross bike. This required hitting the ramp at forty miles per hour. On the way up, Johnny was supposed to pull back on the handlebars, which would induce a backflip. He was unsuccessful on his first five attempts. On take six, he pulled back on the handlebars, but the bike didn't flip. Instead, Johnny separated from the bike at its peak and fell, landing hard on his back. Then the bike landed on him, with the handlebars slamming brutally into his crotch. When I saw him a few weeks later, he jokingly told me that he "broke his dick," which was half true. Yes, he did have to piss through a catheter for the next two and a half years, but he was still able to have sex and father two more children.

Johnny told me to come over to his house, where he would explain what he had in mind for the sequel. I drove east on Mulholland Drive to his Beachwood Canyon home, where he was waiting with film-maker and *Jackass* collaborator Spike Jonze. Spike is one of my favorite filmmakers, a real innovator. Though I love all of his films, my favorite is *Being John Malkovich*. It's a stunningly original film that would never get made in today's retread-obsessed Hollywood.

Knoxville handed me a coffee as he recounted a story from the night before when he had urinated into a beer can, chilled it, and then used his ten-year-old daughter to deliver the "beer" to his friend. When the friend took a sip of cold urine, Johnny and his daughter cracked up, big-time. *Beware the spawn of Jackass.* I eyed my coffee as Johnny started in. "Do you know who Ehren McGhehey is?"

"I do," I said. "Danger Ehren." Ehren was in the *Jackass* crew and was famous for attempting some of their more dangerous feats, which had caused him to lose a couple of teeth in the process.

The "stunt" they wanted to talk about was called "Terror Taxi," and Ehren was going to be the star of it. In the bit, Ehren would dress in a Middle Eastern robe and checked headdress while sporting a glued-on human-hair beard. Next, he would strap on a fake dynamite vest and call a cab to take him to the Burbank Airport, where hidden cameras would capture him *dicking around* with passengers, flashing his dynamite vest, and making jokes about blowing up airplanes.

If you are shocked, you know how I felt. As it was 2005, anyone dressed like Yasir Arafat who showed up at the airport with a dyna-mite vest was going to be shot on sight. When Ehren raised this concern, Spike, Johnny, and *Jackass* director Jeff Tremaine assured him that the FBI was aware of the gag and would make sure that no harm came to him. Ehren agreed, but since the first part of the gag required him to make plane-bombing jokes with the cabdriver, Ehren had another concern. *What if the cabdriver has a gun?* But he was told that the cab company was also in on the gag. While the cabdriver would be totally oblivious, the cab company had promised that the driver they sent would *under no circumstances* be carrying a gun. Satisfied, Ehren consented, and the wheels were set in motion.

What Ehren *did not* know was that he would never make it to the Burbank Airport. Instead, he was the mark in an elaborate con. The *Jackass* crew was double-crossing him by making the cabdriver a plant whose job it would be to flip the script on the unwittingly clueless Danger Ehren.

Knoxville smiled. "We want *you* to be the cabdriver." They described how they hoped the con would go: Once in the cab, Ehren would start harassing the cabdriver (me) by making sexual jokes about my wife. This was supposed to make me angry. Then he would move on to jokes about hating America and blowing up planes, which would make me even angrier. When he finally flashed his dynamite vest, I was supposed to screech the cab down a preorganized alley before coming to a stop in a walled-in courtyard. Then I was told to turn around and punch him square in the mouth, with the goal being to stun him. Next, I would pull a fake gun, and drag the stunned Ehren out of the cab and onto the ground. Finally, in order to establish animal dominance over him, I was supposed to hard-stomp him several times before shoving the gun in his face and forcing him into the trunk.

Johnny smiled. "Easy, right?"

I shifted in my seat. As a brown guy, I had made it a policy not to mess around with jokes related to terrorism. I'd heard enough stories about Indians getting beaten when they were mistaken for Middle Easterners. In fact, it had once almost happened to me in Boston. But in this bit, I was kind of the terrorist-thwarting hero, so maybe? Plus, I was sitting across from two guys I admired the fuck out of—two guys whose artistic/comic taste I trusted—because while Knoxville may seem crazy, the man is a true artist.

Jeff Tremaine, *Jackass*'s director, recounted a story about the opening scene of *Jackass Number Two*. Their goal was to re-create the conditions of a firing squad, so Johnny would be blindfolded and smoking a cigarette while wearing a red shirt and standing in a bullring. When a furious, full-grown bull was let loose, the hope was that it would lower its horns and run over Knoxville. And in take one, that's what it did. The bull hit Johnny in the legs, flipping him ass over teakettle. It was perfect. Afterward, the elated *Jackass* crew ran in to congratulate their fearless leader. But when Johnny stood up, he noticed that the end of his cigarette was wet. It had been drizzling that morning, and Johnny was worried that the rain had snuffed out his cigarette *before* the bull had hit him. Jeff said he thought that the cigarette was still smoking and, regardless, *the take was fucking perfect, so all good.* When Johnny watched the playback, he was right—the cigarette was snuffed out by a raindrop seconds before the bull made contact. To Knoxville, the snuffed-out cigarette meant that the firing squad vibe had *not* been achieved. So he said, "We have to do it again." So they reblindfolded him, lit a new cigarette, and loosed the bull a second time. The fourteen-hundred-pound bull hit Johnny's legs, flipping him into the air like a rag doll—*again*. That's the take that's in the movie.

Still, I was worried. *What if this whole thing was an elaborate triple cross of me? What if I was the lamb, and Knoxville, Spike, and Ehren were setting me up for the slaughter?* I brought this up to Knoxville, who said that he understood why I was worried, but he promised that he was being straight up with me. *Of course he would say that.* Knowing I was never going to be totally assured, I said, "I don't believe you, but fuck it. I'm in."

On the day of the shoot, I arrived at Knoxville's house early for wardrobe. On the rack were two choices: a billowy authentic Indian outfit and an American one. Knoxville and Spike chose the American one because they felt it would draw less attention to me. I wondered aloud, *Ehren was roughly thirty. Wasn't there a decent chance he had seen one of my movies? Maybe I should do an Indian accent to throw him off the trail.* But Knoxville said that he wanted Ehren to be the only one doing a fake accent. He wanted contrast. Plus, he said, "Don't worry about Ehren recognizing you. He is so wrapped up in trying to do a Middle Eastern accent that he won't even notice you. And try not to laugh, because his accent is fucking terrible!"

Next, I got in the cab and drove the prearranged route five times to make sure I didn't fuck up. There would be a follow van, which the *Jackass* guys would ride in, that was outfitted with monitors so they could watch the feed from the hidden cameras. Finally, *Jackass* director of photography Dimitry Elyashkevich, who would also be in "Arab garb," would accompany Ehren and would also be holding a camera.

Before I left, Jeff Tremaine took me aside and told me that the FBI would be following the prank at a distance. If the cab went within a mile of the Burbank Airport, the FBI would force the car to the side and end the gag. "So, whatever you do, stay the fuck away from the airport." *The FBI didn't trust Knoxville either.*

At the last minute, Knoxville decided that it would be funnier if I bitch-slapped Ehren instead of punching him. I was relieved, because punching felt too violent. Spike said slapping was fine, but I needed to slap him hard. *Ehren needs to feel dominated. He needs to be the beta dog ced-ing control to the alpha.*

Lurking nearby was a hairdresser who was holding an electric ra-zor and a ziplock bag. I waved her off. "I'm wearing a hat, so I don't need my hair done."

"No, Johnny asked me to get your pubic hair," she said.

Across the room, Knoxville perked up. "Oh yeah, Ehren's beard is going to be made out of our pubic hair. Any chance we can get some of yours? And can we film it?" *This fuckin' guy.*

The cameraman recorded me shaving my pubic hair in the bath-room, and now it was time . . .

I picked up Ehren and Dimitry in the cab, and off we went. Ehren started in with his horrible "Middle Eastern" accent, making fun of my wife's boobs, while I pretended to get mad at him. Then Ehren started talking shit about America and making cracks about blowing up planes. So I got angrier. Though he hadn't shown me his dynamite vest yet, I figured it was time to pull into the alley anyway. But in all of the excitement, I had gotten lost and made a wrong turn. Worse still, I was now driving right by the Burbank Airport. *Oh fuck!*

Ehren noticed and yelled, "Hey, there's the airport!" But I just floored it, hoping to outrun any FBI cars that might be about to take us out. Finally, I found the alley. Ehren was freaking out that I was clearly not going to the airport. When I pulled into the walled-in courtyard, he really started losing it. On the roofs of the buildings were police snipers, who were there in the event that Johnny Knox-ville was pulling a fast one. I screeched to a stop, turned around, and—*Whap! Whap! Whap! Whap! Whap!* I slapped him in the face eight or ten times, hard.

Panicked, he threw money at me, trying to buy his way out. But I kept hitting him, so he showed his dynamite vest and threatened to "blow us up right now!"

I grabbed my fake gun, jumped out of the car, yanked open the back door, dragged him onto the ground, and kicked him a couple of times, hard. He had dropped his accent altogether and was now saying, "I've got a bomb, dude!" He got up, so I slapped him again, using the gun to force him to the ground. He was panicking, totally breaking character and screaming at the *Jackass* guys, who were now out of the follow van, "This guy's got a fucking gun, dumb shits!"

I popped the trunk, shoved the gun in his face, and, channeling every cop show I had ever seen, screamed, *"Get in the fucking trunk!"* He didn't want to, but Dimitry, who was there to help me, said, "Ehren, do what he says, he's got a fucking gun." So he did. Ehren got into the trunk. *Wham!* I slammed it shut. *Holy shit! This thing had worked!*

Then came the offscreen theater, as Dimitry and two other *Jackass* crew members, Brandon "Bam" Margera and Preston Lacy, ran in to *try to talk me out of my gun, explaining that they were just filming a movie.* Someone ran in with two wooden blocks, slamming them together, making the exact sound of gunshots. Then Bam screamed that he was shot! *See, these guys are artists.*

Then I got back in the car and drove a bunch of doughnuts, as the still-mic'd Ehren panicked: "Get me outta here! Oh shit! I'm gonna fucking die! Why did I agree to do this? It wasn't even my fucking idea!"

When I stopped the car and popped the trunk, a confused Ehren crawled out. Then came the sound of his friends laughing. Ehren's reaction was rage coupled with relief. Seeing me standing there, laughing, he was confused. "Are you some kind of fucking actor or something?"

Offended that he didn't recognize me, I said, "Come on!" He hugged me in relief.

Finally, Knoxville came in with the final insult, informing Ehren that his beard was made out of our pubic hair. When Ehren found that out, he puked, finishing the prank off in poetic fashion. Good fun.

CHAPTER 16

Beerfest: Origin Story

We're going to go back in time now, back to the movie that we couldn't get made after *Club Dread,* but now possibly could. I'm talking about *Beerfest.* But first, here is its origin story.

After the successful US release of *Super Troopers,* Fox Searchlight decided to send us to Australia to promote the film there. Mildly concerned by the reports of our fun-filled drinking on our US tour, Searchlight's then president Peter Rice made a surprise visit to the airport to see us off. He smilingly asked us not to drink *all* of the booze in Australia and told us our nickname at Fox was "Drunken Lizard." We laughed and assured him that we'd represent Fox well, and off we went.

We loved Australia. Not only is the country beautiful and hip, but the people in Australia are rebellious, funny, and less concerned about social strata than Americans are. In Sydney, the president of Fox Australia was giving Heffernan and me a tour. We were riding in an elevator when a twenty-year-old dude got on. Now, in America, if a twenty-year-old saw the president of the studio on an elevator, he'd wait for the next one. Not this kid. He got on. Then, after we ascended for a bit, the kid looked the president up and down and said, "Oy, my sister has that same shirt."

Without missing a beat, the president said, "Yeah, she left it at my apartment last night. Nice girl." They both laughed as the doors opened, and we all got off.

Baffled, I asked the president who that was. He shrugged. "I think he's an intern." That's Australia.

We were there for the two-week lead-up to the release of *Super Troopers*. Promoting in Sydney, Brisbane, and Surfers Paradise, we were paired with two Australian publicists named Leslie and Leonie.

We were struck by how much Australians loved to drink. We left a bar at two A.M. and saw a drunken guy run facefirst into a tree. Down he went. Laughing, he propped himself on his elbow and used his legs to propel himself around and around in the dirt patch like a cartoon character.

While our promotional screenings in Australia were going great, the fact that we were total unknowns there made it hard to get the media's attention. To juice things up, Fox asked us to wear our trooper uniforms for all of our appearances. We groused a little, joking that looking like cops wouldn't make us very popular in this former British penal colony. We took a grassroots/volume approach to promotions, showing up literally anywhere that would have us.

Dressed as cops, we went to a mall and stood on a six-inch stage in the food court, while a guy who was inexplicably wearing a tuxedo introduced us to moms and their children. "Ladies and gentlemen, say hello to the Super Troopers from America!" A smattering of applause.

"You should go and see their movie!" The moms looked confused. *Wait, the cops are in the movie?*

They took us to a tire-store opening where we ate meat pies and cut a "Grand Opening" ribbon, while confused families looked on. Everyone just thought we were real cops.

Sensing the awkwardness, Leslie pivoted. "There's a beer garden nearby. Let's pop in. Your people are bound to be *there*, right?"

"You mean because they're drunks?" I asked.

"Yes."

We filed into the packed beer garden, found a table, and started drinking. After a few pints, Leslie talked the manager into letting us go onstage to tell the crowd about the film. We were hesitant. The manager grabbed the microphone, calming the rowdy four-hundred-person crowd. "Ladies and gentlemen, I want you to give a warm welcome to the Super Troopers from America!" The crowd slowly stopped talking to study us. As we five cops walked onstage, one chippy Aussie yelled, "Fuck you, coppers!" The whole place burst into laughter. Hoping to turn around a looming disaster, I grabbed the mic and started vamping, telling the crowd that we weren't real cops but that we were in a movie about cops who like to play pranks. No one was listening. They were all talking again.

Trying to regain their attention, Steve grabbed the mic and yelled something I thought he shouldn't have: "Russell—Crowe—sucks—kangaroo—dick!"

Look, we're all big Russell Crowe fans, but we needed a spark, and we got one. The crowd exploded with amused rage. People jumped to their feet, shouting at us. Heffernan jumped in: "We want to challenge any five guys to a boat race!" And then the place really went off! Hands shot up. Huge guys pushed toward the stage, desperate for a chance to defend mother Australia against these random, insulting, fake cops from America.

Five large Aussie blokes took the stage to compete against us in a boat race. There were two five-man teams lined up against each other. The first guys on each team start the race by chugging their pints. Then you go down the line, with guys two, three, and four. The fifth guy on each team (the anchorman) drinks two pints, and then the race goes back up the line, ending with the first guys again.

We came out of the gate hot. I beat my guy, Erik beat his guy, and Steve beat his guy. We had a full-beer lead and the crowd was shocked. Then Paul started slowly gulping. I'll spare you the details, but the Aussies regained the lead. But it wasn't over, because we had Kevin Heffernan, who is the fastest chugger in Broken Lizard. Kevin and I have chugged roughly a thousand times, and I'm 0 and 1,000 against him. Kevin slammed his first and then his second pint, regaining the lead for Team USA! But now it was Paul's turn again—gulp, gulp. In the end, the Aussies won by half a beer. After the win, all four hundred Aussies stood and screamed all matter of outback insult at us.

So we had arm-wrestling contests with the same five guys and, much to their surprise, we won those. The energy was peaking as people were pounding their fists and their pints. Leslie reminded us that we were there to promote *Super Troopers*. So Lemme grabbed the mic. He put his hands up, calming the crowd. "People, if I can have your attention! I just wanna say something!" he yelled. The crowd quieted, eyeing the drunken little cop. "We had a lot of fun today, but I want you all to remember that . . . *Crocodile Dundee fucks koala bears!*"

Arghhhhaahahhah!! The place blew up. People started throwing food and half beers at us. Did they care about Crocodile Dundee more than they did about Russell Crowe? I doubt it, but it sure seemed like it. Regardless, it was clear that it was time to go. So Leslie and Leonie shoved us out the back exit and into the waiting van. *Screech!* We disappeared in a cloud of dust, loving life. Then Heffernan leaned in: "Hey. That could make a good movie." And the idea for *Beerfest* was born.

Years later, after the success of *Dukes* . . .

Studio president Jeff Robinov had given Broken Lizard a suite of offices in the Motel Building on the Warner Bros. lot. Soon after we moved in, I met Jeff in his office, where he asked me what I wanted to do next. When I told him we wanted to make a film about an international beer-drinking team that competes against other countries' teams in beer games, he cocked his head. "You're serious, right?"

"We have a great script."

"If you think it's great, I'm sure it is. Can you make it for $13 million?" he asked. "That's the lowest number we can make a movie for here. I don't have to ask permission for that."

I said, "Sounds like a good number, but Sony owns it."

He said Sony owed him a favor, and within weeks, Warner Bros. had bought the rights to *Beerfest* and Jeff had green-lit the movie. It was that easy. After years of running around raising money and/or navigating the roadblocks put up by the various low-level development executives, this was different. This was rarified air. We were talking to the boss. And the boss didn't want to talk about script notes. Thanks to the success of *Dukes,* Warner Bros. trusted us, and proved it with a quick green light.

As much as we wanted to shoot in Germany, economics dictated that we shoot closer to home. Since Warner Bros. had a new production relationship with New Mexico, we were asked to see if we could figure it out there. This would require doubling Albuquerque for

Munich, so we adjusted the script so that the arena and, frankly, most of the Germany scenes would take place inside. And yes, the rumor is true. The *Beerfest* arena was inspired by the Jean-Claude Van Damme film *Bloodsport*.

We wrote twenty drafts of the script before I cast it—again, to ensure that everyone was writing jokes for every character. We needed brothers and felt that Erik and Paul were the most visually similar, so they got the parts of Todd and Jan Wolfhouse, respectively. To round out the rest of the drinking team, we decided to create drinking specialists. We wrote a part for a scientist who would use science to devise faster ways to drink. We wrote a part for a gluttonous volume drinker who would be our anchorman in chugging contests. And we wrote a part for a beer-games specialist, a ringer who knew his way around a quarter.

Steve Lemme had a high school friend named Finkelstein who was a genetic scientist. The real-life Finkelstein told Steve that part of his job was to masturbate frogs to collect their sperm. We didn't need to add any comedy there. Lemme modeled Finkelstein's hairstyle after Sean Penn's in *Carlito's Way*, which meant he had to shave three inches of male-pattern baldness into the front of his scalp, daily. On the weekends, Lemme would let his hair grow back, but it created an ugly stubble effect that looked even worse. Lemme actually endured a few anti-Semitic encounters in Albuquerque, where guys called him "Jewboy." For a non-Jewish, half-Spanish, half-Argentinian kid, that was surreal.

One of our *bigger* friends at Colgate was nicknamed "Landfill." Heffernan, who is our biggest guy and who also happens to be our fastest beer chugger, snagged that part.

That left me to play the beer-games specialist. We named the character Barry Badrinath, after one of my childhood friends. And we wrote a scene where the Wolfhouse brothers go looking for and find Barry working at a circus, as a weathered circus roadie. Something about that felt too cute, so we switched it, last minute, making Barry Badrinath a male prostitute who peddles his wares near an overpass. When they find him and ask him to join the team, Barry tries to show them how good he still is at beer games, but he can't land a single quarter in the cup. The brothers leave, dejected, and head back to their bar. Then Barry bursts in, drunk, and drills one quarter after another, finishing with the oft-heard quarters line, "I'm better when I'm drunk."

In addition to Broken Lizard, the cast included Donald Sutherland, Jürgen Prochnow, Mo'Nique, Cloris Leachman, *Dukes* and *Club Dread* alum M.C. Gainey, and *Super Troopers* alum Philippe Brenninkmeyer.

We approached Donald Sutherland because, once upon a time, he had played a professor in one of our favorite films of all time, *Animal House*. Sutherland was cool, and his being in the opening scene lent our film an air of much-needed gravitas.

Cloris Leachman played Great Gam Gam, the boys' kindly grandmother, and was fully willing to go wherever the joke took her. I love Cloris, and I think the feeling was mutual because she would not allow us to shoot an inch of film until she and I kissed (in front of the crew) for thirty seconds . . . every morning. I'm an actor's director.

Jürgen Prochnow was dark and hilarious as Baron Wolfgang von Wolfhausen, the elder statesman of the Germans. The highlight for me was the scene where he is piloting the German team in a cramped submarine. He flips out on his guys for grab assing, before apologizing, "Sorry, I had a bad experience on a U-boat once." This, of course, was a call back to his legendary performance in the German submarine film *Das Boot*. It was cool that he was willing to do that.

Mo'Nique was terrific both as the villain and as Barry Badrinath's lover. While we had written some good lines for her, it was her improv that stole the show and ended up in the movie.

We have a theory about bad guys. Kevin Heffernan and I lived in New York City for ten years, and we saw a lot of movies. Afterward, we'd often argue about whether the bad guy was tough enough. If we thought we could beat up the actor playing the bad guy, he wasn't tough enough. It was the same with James Bond. Bond had to be tougher than us or he was no good. (There has been only one Bond whose ass I thought I could kick, and he didn't last long.) The villains in *Beerfest* are five brothers, who are cousins to our heroes, and make up the German drinking team. We wanted a mix of actors, some who would be scary and some, funny.

Nat Faxon, who played a small part in *Club Dread*, played the German brother Rolf. Nat's Rolf is menacing and fucking hilarious. My favorite is when he imitates Schwarzenegger, "Do it! Do it! Kill me now!" Years later, Nat would go on to win a writing Oscar with Jim Rash for their adaptation of the book *The Descendants*.

We targeted Will Forte to play brother Otto. Will was in his fourth year of *SNL*, and in New York, so I was unable to audition him. I loved him on the show, and Nat Faxon had performed with him in the Groundlings and said he was top-notch. After I gave him the part of Otto, we spoke on the phone. I asked him how his German accent was, and he broke into a few words of something that sounded distinctly Chinese. Then he laughed, nervously, and said he would work on it. When Will arrived in Albuquerque, his German accent was flawless. Will was also an impressive chugger. During the shoot, we did a scene where the Germans had to show their drinking prowess. Will volunteered and pounded a pint of beer in about three seconds. We were blown away. That night, we all challenged him to chug-offs, and he beat every one of us.

Eric Christian Olsen played brother Gunter with bizarre hilarity. I had worked with Eric a couple of years earlier when I directed him on the show *The Loop*. The dude had charisma and great timing. Eric is now one of the stars of the long-running show *NCIS: Los Angeles*.

There was a point when Jimmy Fallon was going to play one of the German brothers. I sat with him for two hours at the Chateau Marmont while he rolled through his massive repertoire of impersonations. (My favorite was probably Woody Allen.) Jimmy was cool and a *Super Troopers* fan, and he agreed to be in the film. But in the end, he got cold feet and dropped out.

With our funnymen in place, we needed some danger. Our casting directors, Mary Vernieu and Venus Kanani, whom I'd worked with on *The Dukes of Hazzard*, found us a giant of a man in Ralf Moeller to play the role of the eldest brother, Hammacher. A real German, Ralf was six-ten, had a deep voice, was a former Mr. Universe, and was friends with Arnold Schwarzenegger. Ralf was exactly what *Beerfest* needed.

The final brother role of Schlemmer went to acting novice Gunter Schlierkamp. At six-one, 275 pounds, Gunter was a veritable brick shithouse of a man. He was a former competitor in the Mr. Universe competition, and had a sweet high voice that reminded me of Chicago Bears great Walter Payton. Payton's voice was deceiving, because that man could run you over like a speed train. Gunter possessed that same energy. He did an imitation of a sex-crazed ape that climaxed with a ferocious chest beating that was both terrifying and hilarious.

Neither Ralf nor Gunter had ever heard of the mall store Hammacher

Schlemmer, which we named them after. Regardless, Heffernan and I felt confident that we couldn't beat up *these* bad guys.

At Colgate, we used to do a thing called a "half-hour party." We'd go into a cement room in our basement with kegs of beer, bottles of whiskey, and joints and bongs. We'd start a timer and then we would just try to smoke and drink as much as possible before the buzzer went off thirty minutes later. I partook in only one half-hour party because I got unnecessarily fucked-up—not a pleasant end to the night. Regardless, to up the ante in these parties, we invented something called . . . "the Strikeout." In a Strikeout, you inhale a bong-load of smoke, then chug a beer and do a shot of whiskey before exhaling the smoke. Again, I don't recommend it. It gets you wasted in a way that's really unnecessary. *Take your time. No need to rush. Seriously.* In the film, the American team goes to a college house party to test their mettle against some "college drinking professionals." At the party, Finkelstein, played by Steve Lemme, is challenged to a Strikeout. Like Daniel Day-Lewis, Steve is a method actor who likes to be referred to by his character's name. On the day before we were to shoot the Strikeout, Finkelstein approached. "Jay, everything's gotta be real tomorrow. Real whiskey, real beer, real pot!" Fink, as he was nicknamed in the movie, was worried that people would see the scene and grouse that we used fake stuff. So we got him the real stuff.

In take one, Fink inhaled the bong, chugged the beer, downed the shot, and exhaled a beautiful plume of smoke. He nailed it. It was a beautifully perfect Strikeout. There was nothing to improve on, so I told him that the lighting wasn't great and we needed to do another take. After our ace director of photography, Frankie DeMarco, pretended to change the lighting, Fink did take two. He nailed that one too, but I made up a reason why we needed another. After six takes, poor Fink was finished—TKO. Funny guy.

After shooting, Heffernan and I held nightly parties at our house. The weekday parties were just games of beer pong and hanging out. The weekend parties went late. During one Friday night fete, the doorbell rang. It was the cops, there on a noise complaint. Walking to the door, I whispered to people to hide the smoking bongs.

At the door, Officer One was gruff. "Do you live here?!"

I kicked into charm mode. "I do, Officer. Sorry, are we being too loud?"

The cop didn't answer. He just cocked his head and then mumbled, "Uh, never mind." His partner looked at him like he was crazy, but Cop One just dragged his partner off and mumbled, "Just have fun. Have a good night." I closed the door, unsure of what exactly had just happened. *Maybe they had bigger fish to fry?* After all, Albuquerque was the per capita murder capital of the country. Fifteen minutes later, the doorbell rang again. Standing there were eight Albuquerque policemen. *Oh shit. They'd called for backup.* Cop One smiled. "*Super Troopers,* right?"

I said, "Yeah," sheepishly.

All of the cops shifted on their spots, happily. "Can we come in and party? We're huge fans," Cop One asked through grinning teeth.

I swung open the door and in they filed. People in the party who had just seconds ago been smoking joints were shocked. But the cops adopted nonthreatening poses and made everyone feel fine. After about an hour of partying, the cops had to go and asked us for a group picture. Yes, some of my more adventurous college friends were holding bongs in the back row. The cops asked us not to share *those* pictures, and we didn't. That was the moment when we came to realize how big an impact *Super Troopers* had had in the law enforcement community.

Doing boat races in real life was fun, but we wanted to give it a visual twist in the movie. We were inspired by the time when, back in New York, Erik, Steve, and I were waiters together. After our shift one night, we, along with Chef Dave, went to a bar called Richter's. Chef Dave was a little man, but he talked a big game about his beer-chugging prowess. Richter's had two glass beer boots, so the challenge was set. It was Chef Dave versus Erik in a boot chug.

Erik, Lemme, and I laid down our night's wages on the bar, some $360 in all. Then, Chef Dave, in what felt like a pointless display of machismo, said that you were disqualified if you spilled a drop. To which we said, "Obviously." But Chef Dave had an ace up his sleeve. The chug began. Chef Dave was fast, but Erik was faster. *No shit. Colgate, right?* As they got to the ankle of the boot, Erik kept guzzling, but an air bubble formed, which caused the remaining beer to explode all over his face. Meanwhile, Chef Dave casually turned his boot sideways, which dissipated the bubble and allowed him to finish his chug without spilling a drop. Chef Dave knew the secret of the boot and collected our money as he laughed in our faces. Though poorer, we were impressed. More importantly, we had a memory that would come in handy later when we invented "Das Boot!"

I first met Lee Haxall when she was my editor on *Arrested Development* (more on that show later in the book). Lee had an innate understanding of *Arrested*'s rhythm, and since Broken Lizard's rhythm was similar, I hired her to cut *Dukes,* and then *Beerfest.* Heffernan and I sat with Lee for a few months and got a two-hour cut that we liked. When we showed it to fifty of our friends, we knew we were on to something. We trimmed ten minutes from the film and then set a date to test it. One day before the test, we screened the film for Warner

Bros. president Jeff Robinov. Jeff typed into his BlackBerry during the whole screening, which made me sad. *Did the movie really mean that little to him?* After the screening, Jeff said, "I think this is really funny. It is funny, right?" he asked, since he did watch it alone in a room. Having seen the response of our fifty friends, I told him that I was confident that it was. Then he said, "Here are my notes." An assistant walked up with his typed-up notes, fresh off the printer. *Jeff hadn't been texting; he'd been writing notes the whole time.* Big relief.

The next day we tested the film, and the scores were great— better than *The Dukes of Hazzard*, which were the highest scores we'd had to date. Enthusiasm at the studio was high.

For the promotional tour, Warner Bros. arranged screenings and keg parties in all of the major cities across America. Before we arrived, beer pong tournaments were held, with the winners earning a chance to play Broken Lizard when we came to town. We played every night for six weeks, and we became great—pro ball. Of the hundreds of games we played, we lost fewer than twelve. It was glorious to listen to cocky college kids talk trash before we smoked them. We had swagger and very few stood a chance.

The campaign for *Beerfest* made me nervous. I realize that the film had the word "beer" in the title, but we had endeavored to make the smartest, funniest drinking movie ever. Yet, reminiscent of *Puddle Cruiser*, our *Beerfest* poster had two hot blondes on it who were not in the movie. Further, the TV ads seemed to emphasize the noise and the action, not the intelligence and the wit. We expressed our concern, but our marketing executives were the same exact ones who had absolutely drilled the *Dukes* campaign, so maybe they knew better? And to be clear, this is not science. There is no right answer. We all looked at the materials and we made decisions together. And the marketing team chose the campaign they believed would reach the widest audience and make the most money.

Then, when a release date opened up that was a mere three months away, Warner Bros. gave us a choice: Either take this early date or wait nine months for the next opening. They promised to spend a lot of money on the campaign to make up for the short window. It didn't quite work. In the end, *Beerfest* made a ton of money on home video and pay-per-view, but the theatrical results, especially considering the high scores, were disappointing. As successful as *Super Troopers* was, we weren't exactly movie stars yet, so the noisy campaign plus the short exposure period didn't bring our fans to the theater. This is only my opinion, but had Broken Lizard been less impatient and taken the later date, and had we had a more sophisticated campaign, I think our theatrical results could have been big. A few years later, we saw the campaign I wish we had had when Warner Bros. promoted the film *The Hangover. That's* how you sell a party movie without stars.

A few weeks before *Beerfest* opened in Germany, my old pal Kevin Cooper sent me an article from a Munich newspaper that detailed a movement to ban the film there. Though the writer of the article had yet to see it, he was certain that our film would make German culture look bad. To which we said, "It was probably the Holocaust that did most of the damage." In the end, the film did not get banned, and Germany would go on to become one of our biggest markets. In fact, last year, we held a Beerfest tournament in Chicago and two guys flew in from Berlin. What a joy it was to listen to them gush over *Bierfest* in their real German accents.

Beerfest initially had a different type of fan than *Super Troopers*. We were suddenly being approached by clean-cut Republican-looking types who felt we had made a movie for them. One young Republican said, "I heard you made another movie, too, though it's supposed to be some kind of a stoner movie, right?"

"*Super Troopers?*" I asked.

He pointed. "Yeah, that's it."

To which I said, "I guess I can see why you think *Super Troopers* is a stoner movie, but, truthfully, they're probably both stoner movies, since grass played an integral part in the creation of both."

Beerfest, at its core, is an ode to binge drinking. And I'm fine with that. It's easy to look back on your high school, college, and postcollege years and judge them harshly for the amount you drank or drugged. I'm not willing to do that. Those years were fun and I loved them. I'm lucky—frankly, all of us in Broken Lizard are lucky that we don't have the alcoholic gene. Were we drunks? Yeah, and for decades, but it was never a problem. And I wouldn't change anything, because it was fun and bonding and partly responsible for the beginnings of a whole lot of lovely marriages. Yes, some people can't handle booze because they can't stop drinking it. Yes, some people drive drunk, and some beat their lovers, wives, and children. But most don't. Most people drink a little bit on most nights, and more on the weekends—sometimes to get drunk, have fun, and then get up on Monday and go to work. I don't drink like I used to because I have a wife and kids and a job. But when I didn't have all that, and I could drink as much as I wanted, I still never beat my girlfriend. So it all depends on who you are. Is beer responsible for fights at football games? Sure, but it's also responsible for an intensity of friendship that can only be forged late at night in a rush of alcohol, grass, and whatever. If you read the newspaper, most of the stories about alcohol are about the evils of binge drinking. What about some stories about the joys of drunkenness? In TV and movies, we spend a lot of time focusing on addicts because their plight makes for good drama. But they're in the vast minority, and maybe less time should be spent on them. And to be clear, I'm sympathetic. I have a good number of friends who quit drinking because they had trouble with it. And that's good. Don't drink if you can't, but the media shouldn't make the rest of us feel bad about it when we don't have the same issues.

The big question surrounding films like *Beerfest* is, does the film *reflect* culture or *affect* culture? *Animal House* came out in 1978 and dramatically affected the next twenty-five years of fraternity drinking life and, frankly, drinking life everywhere. At Colgate, we emulated and imitated the Delta house in several of the things we did. We had toga parties, pulled crazy pranks, drank competitively, and some of us were careless about grades (not me). We had a guy named Mongo. Did this behavior exist before *Animal House*? Probably, but *Animal House* supercharged it.

Likewise, *Beerfest* didn't invent binge drinking, though it did help organize it. Now we see videos of people who throw their own Beerfests, complete with organized teams and uniforms. And at the end of the night, when they're hurling in the bushes, is it because of the movie? Maybe partly. Hey, the Greeks drank until they vomited and we laud them for their culture. There's a joyous intensity that comes from drinking beer, wine, or liquor that is both irreplaceable and important to some people's lives. Okay, I'm one of those people. And the rest of you know who you are too.

Making a party movie has its benefits. Bouncers know *Beerfest*, which makes us royalty on the entrance line. Further, the film is popular with bartenders and waiters, so when Broken Lizard is there, the bar never closes. Or it closes, but they let us stay and they keep pouring. So, not bad.

At the end of *Beerfest*, there's a scene where we run into Willie Nelson in Amsterdam. Willie tells us that he's headed to a supersecret pot-smoking competition, but his teammates, Cheech and Chong, missed their flight. Willie asks us if we'll sub in for them in the competition. We agree and go into the door of Potfest. It was a joke and we never planned on making the film, but since then, we've been inundated with questions about the film. And we've actually written thirty pages of a draft, so . . . who knows?

CHAPTER 17

Television: Or, Models Talking Tough

In the years after *Super Troopers* came out, most of my focus was on getting more films made. But there was also something new in the mix: TV. In these creatively dark days when the major film studios have all but abandoned stories where the main characters are not wearing tights and capes, television has filled the void.

Television directing is a creatively different beast from film directing, in that in TV, the head writer is king. My goal when directing television shows is to give head writers the best goddamned episodes of their shows they've ever seen. And when I turn in my "director's cut," they get to see how *I* see their show. But after they've watched my cut, they're free to change whatever the hell they want to about it because *it's their fucking show.* If you can't make peace with that creative relationship, then TV directing is not for you.

TV is very satisfying because of the speed of work required. Unlike a film, which can take years from script to screen, television must often be written, shot, edited, and broadcast in only a matter of weeks.

I've directed a lot of television, but here are a few of the highlights:

UNDECLARED

In 1997, NBC executives attended a screening of *Puddle Cruiser* at Sundance and hired Broken Lizard to adapt the film for TV. Our half-hour pilot about funny, intellectual drunks and stoners at a northeastern school (Colgate) was called *Safety School*. NBC loved the script and green-lit the pilot. As we were casting, we made the decision not to act in it, both because we wanted to be available to make films and because we felt swearing was an integral part of who we were. I admit that that decision was probably dumb.

With a new cast in place, we shot the pilot, edited it, and presented it to NBC. The response was great. *Safety School* was an internal hit at NBC, particularly with the younger employees. We heard that the older execs were nervous about its edgy content but rattled enough by the youth-quake of support at NBC that they were having serious conversations about picking our show up. A meeting was scheduled for me with then NBC president Scott Sassa in his massive New York City office. It was a hot day in early May, but I decided to wear my lucky red flannel shirt to the meeting. The problem with this shirt was that there was a one-foot round hole in the back of it. When I walked into Scott's office, I made sure to never turn my back to him. Scott and I spoke about budget and about shooting the show in Toronto, a place I had already scouted. The conversation then moved on to whether we could fucking handle the enormous responsibility of delivering twenty-six episodes a year. When the meeting ended, I smiled and backed out of his long office like I was saying good-bye to a king. *He must have wondered what that was about.* In the end, my lucky shirt didn't come through, as NBC did not order our show.

Two years later, my agent called to tell me that Judd Apatow wanted to meet. I didn't know Judd, but I thought that *The Larry Sanders Show,* which he had been head writer of, was the funniest, most interesting show in comedy history, so I went. I met him on the set of a pilot he was shooting called *North Hollywood.* The show was about young actors and starred Kevin Hart, Amy Poehler, Jason Segel, and Judge Reinhold. Judd told me that he had seen and loved *Safety School* and thought we had gotten a raw deal. Then he asked me if I would direct an episode of *his* college comedy, *Undeclared.*

The set of *Undeclared* was fun and loose, and the cast was young. Seth Rogen was eighteen. Jay Baruchel and Charlie Hunnam weren't much older. The guys had a lot of energy, and they were constantly cracking tons of mostly excellent dirty jokes. At times, it was like herding hungover cats. But they were good too, and authentic. When you added in the writers, we had a set full of young, funny, talented people who were mostly newcomers to show business.

Judd once asked me to sit in on his "notes call" with the network. The network had read his draft and wanted to tell him their notes. He and I were on speakerphone, listening to the executive talk about her view of the episode's plotline. Judd interrupted her, loudly yelling, "No!"

Confused, she said, "What?"

"No! Bad note. Next!"

The call went on like that for ten minutes. After we hung up, I said, "You might want to at least pretend to respect their notes."

He smiled. "No. Fuck them. They're wrong!"

We had fun on that show, but Fox couldn't quite figure out how to corral an audience, so it was canceled after seventeen episodes.

ARRESTED DEVELOPMENT

In 2002, I met with the writer Mitch Hurwitz about his new show, *Arrested Development.* I watched the pilot and was intrigued. It was funny, and really smart, and weird, and Ron Howard was doing a voice-over. I was bold at the time, cocky from *Super Troopers,* and, frankly, unskilled in the ways of show business, so I told him what I really thought. I said that his show was great, but that it might be overcut. Had he considered a slightly slower pace of editing? Mitch seemed surprised by my candor, but he hired me anyway, saying, "Okay. Direct one and show me what you're talking about."

I directed four episodes in the first two seasons: "My Mother, the Car," "Beef Consommé," "Altar Egos," and "Justice Is Blind."

Working on that show was pure joy. Every actor was great, every writer was great, and the directors were all pretty good too. As Rob Lowe says about *The West Wing,* "It was a murderers' row of talent."

In addition to the amazing main cast of Jason Bateman, Will Arnett, Tony Hale, Jeffrey Tambor, David Cross, Michael Cera, Jessica Walter, Alia Shawkat, and Portia de Rossi, I also worked with the great Henry Winkler, Jane Lynch, Julia Louis-Dreyfus, and Liza Minnelli.

We thought we were making the funniest show on television. One day, when I was running a bit behind, the line producer approached to ask me if I was going to finish my work for the day. I looked at her and said, "This is art. We'll be done when we're done." If that makes me sound like an asshole, I swear I didn't mean it that way. What I meant was, *This is high art, and it can't be rushed. Who cares if we finish today's work on time? We can always come back tomorrow.*

In a film, you need anywhere from 20 days to 120 days of production. So falling one scene behind doesn't mean much, as you can always find a day to make it up. Television, on the other hand, works on a regimented schedule. For a half-hour show, each director has five days to shoot his or her episode. If I don't finish my day's work, I either have to make it up in the remaining four days or add a sixth day of shooting. If I need a sixth day, then the next director can't start his or her episode on time because I'm using the crew for the extra day. Adding a sixth day also means that the producer has to pay the crew for that extra, unbudgeted day. If every director goes over one day on their episode, the cost over a season would be enormous. But no one explained this to me.

A few years later, when a friendly line producer finally did, I said, "Oooooooooooh!" After that, I focused my attention on becoming a far more efficient director. Today, I almost never go over. That said, being on time at the expense of quality is silly and counterproductive. There's an old show business saying: "No one ever went to a movie because it was on time and under budget."

Today, my motto is, "I shoot as fast as quality will allow."

My biggest regret from *Arrested Development* was turning down the role of the veterinarian in the episode "Justice Is Blind." Julia Louis-Dreyfus plays a blind prosecutor with a guide dog. When Michael takes her dog to the vet, the vet tells him that the guide dog is, in fact, blind, which makes Michael realize that Julia Louis-Dreyfus is lying about *her* being blind. Mitch wanted me to play the part so much that he named the character "Dr. Jay." But I passed on the part, telling him that directing and acting was too hard, and I wanted to focus on making the scene great. That was cockamamie, considering I had directed and acted in two feature films already. The real reason I turned it down was because I wanted a bigger part. *What a fucking fool. If I had done a great job as the vet, who knows?* When actors do well in small parts, writers find reasons to bring them back. I could have been on-screen in *Arrested Development*. Sometimes I'm a fucking idiot.

As great as we all knew *Arrested* was, not enough people were watching, and the show died after three seasons.

ENTOURAGE

In 2003, New Line asked Broken Lizard to write a pitch for a new Cheech and Chong film, which was to be directed by Larry Charles, who, at the time, was most famous for being a writer on *Seinfeld*. New Line and Larry liked our pitch, but Larry wasn't sure how writing with the five of us would work, so he asked if New Line could buy the idea from us, so that he could write it himself. We said, "Sure," and sold it to them.

A few weeks later, my agent sent me the pilot for a new HBO show called *Entourage*. He said the producers were fans and wanted to talk to me about directing episodes. The show was about four young guys in Hollywood who were trying to make it in the film business. I had some real-life experience with the topic. I sat down to watch, and I hated it. While I wasn't quite as famous or successful as Vince, I had had a taste of it, and this pilot didn't feel accurate. Not even close. I called my agent to vent about how the show was neither funny nor good. "How could HBO pick this up?"

He didn't let me pass. "They really want to meet you. Will you just take the meeting?" Big mistake.

At HBO, I was directed to a meeting room. Already there were Doug Ellin, the creator of the show, and, I'm pretty sure, Rob Weiss, a producer. Also there was my Cheech and Chong buddy, Larry Charles, who was also writing on the show. I was happy to see Larry and spent the first forty-five minutes talking to him about Cheech and Chong. I barely even looked at Doug or Rob. Eventually, one of them broke in. "So what did you think about *Entourage?*"

I exhaled. "Okay, here's the thing. I didn't think much of it. This world is a lot funnier and more interesting than what you portrayed. I don't think I laughed once. Plus, it's miscast. If I were you, I would recast everyone except the guy who played E." With that rude and awkward statement, the meeting ended. I said good-bye to Larry and walked out. When I called my agent, I said, "Yeah, that show's not gonna end up working out."

When HBO launched *Entourage* the following year, I tuned in to laugh at it. But something had happened. The second episode was . . . good. And the third was better. The fourth topped the previous three. Wait, this show was actually good, really good. The show felt real and funny and authentic. Plus, the actors I previously didn't like were fucking great. By the end of the first season, *Entourage* was my favorite show. I watched every episode through all eight seasons. I even loved the Sasha Grey season.

Over the next few years, I met Kevin Connolly and told him the story and then asked him to apologize to Doug for me. When I worked with Perrey Reeves, who played Mrs. Ari Gold, I told *her* the story and asked her to apologize to Doug for me. When I worked with

Constance Zimmer, who played superagent Dana Gordon, I asked her to apologize to Doug for me. When I recently worked with Emmanuelle Chriqui on *Super Troopers 2,* I asked her to apologize for me.

So, I'm going to do it here: *Doug and Rob, I'm sorry. I was an asshole and I didn't know enough about television to have a little patience. You made a phenomenal show and I was 100 percent wrong about it. And I deeply regret not being nice to you and not being a part of your great show. I'm so sorry, guys.*

Here's the lesson: Pilots are often just okay. There's so much pressure on them to be great, and so many people giving notes, that the final result can feel watered down. Most shows need a few episodes to find their voice and become the great shows that their creators originally imagined. I didn't know that then. I know that now. *Dummy.*

COMMUNITY

Dan Harmon's brilliantly hilarious show about community college was challenging for directors in the best of ways. While *Community* seemed simple on its surface, it tackled complex themes, and it broke many storytelling conventions. The show required directors to think.

The other challenging element to *Community* was that the scripts tended to be delivered on the late side. In a typical show, the director has five days to prep a show and five days to shoot. Usually, you'd get the script on the first day of prep and then spend those five days casting guest actors, choosing locations, and picking wardrobe. *Community* was such a personal reflection of Dan Harmon, that most of the scripts had to be rewritten directly by him. *I get it. I might run a show that way too.* The problem is that, in addition to writing scripts, the show runner is also responsible for editing the episodes. The job requires being in many places at the same time. It's impossible and your work is never done. People put years on their lives running these shows, and Dan was no different.

I remember running into Dan in the hallway on Friday, the fifth day of prep. As we were chatting, he glanced toward the script in my hand. "What's that?" he asked.

"Uh, it's the script."

He grabbed the script and pretended to leaf through it, before throwing it over his shoulder. "Fuck that. It's junk. Total nothing. The real script is coming tonight!"

The next morning, I checked my email. No script. I checked again on Sunday night. Nothing.

On Monday at four A.M., my phone rang. It was the producer telling me that Dan's script was in my email. Did I need someone to drive over a hard copy?

I got out of bed and read the script. As usual, it was fucking brilliant. This guy really knows how to write. Mad genius. No doubt.

But it was four thirty in the morning, and I needed to prep what we were going to shoot in two and a half hours. So I called the producer back with a list of all the things that were needed for the day's work.

I might say, "I need six Hula-Hoops in every color because the script doesn't specify. I need top hats in three colors. Get small, medium, and large, as we're not sure who is playing the guy yet. I'm going to need a Steadicam. If you need names of operators, I have some," etcetera.

Was it a high-wire act? Sure, but if we didn't have what we needed to make the scene great, we waited for it to arrive. *I work as fast as quality will allow.*

Tone meetings with Dan were hilarious and unique. In a normal show's tone meeting, the director meets the head writer in his office for an hour to talk about the script, jokes, tone, and levels of performance.

In one tone meeting with Dan, we met at a restaurant (Little Dom's) on a Sunday afternoon. There was no script to discuss yet, so we talked about the history of the seven P.M. prime-time slot versus the eight P.M. slot. Dan asked about *Beerfest*, and then we went drink for drink during that three-hour "tone meeting," with him downing white Russians and me drinking vodka south sides. We both had to cab it after that.

The cast on the show was special. Joel McHale was edgy and hilarious and loved making fun of my shoes. Ken Jeong had a bizarre comic energy that was extremely original. Jim Rash as the preposterously flamboyant Dean Pelton was a Maserati of comedy. Alison Brie was a money player and nailed everything she attempted. I love Al. Gillian Jacobs played the knee-jerk college liberal so perfectly that I couldn't wait to hear her character speak. Danny Pudi and Donald Glover had such perfect timing that it felt like I only had to call "action" to see something comedically world-class. Yvette Nicole Brown had a million funny facial moves. And Chevy was, well, he was a comedic hero of mine. On some days, he was okay being directed, and on others, not. I'm going to leave it at that out of respect for what the man accomplished in his storied career.

Community was an entirely original show that came from an entirely original mind. Due to uneven ratings but a dedicated and vocal fan base, it was canceled and brought back from the dead three times. During the last incarnation, I made sure to savor my time with Dan and the cast, knowing deep down that that sixth season was likely the end. Unless, of course, Dan comes through on his frequent mantra: "Six seasons and a movie!" Dan, I'm available.

KNIGHT RIDER

When my producer friend called to ask me how I felt about *Knight Rider*, I laughed. "I felt great about it when I was a kid."

He told me he was producing the reboot and he wanted me to direct an episode. In TV, I take jobs for two reasons: either for art or because I'm friends with someone involved. In this case, I said yes for friendship.

On the first day of prep, I sat down to read the script and was surprised when Michael rolled down his car's (KITT's) window to talk to a hot girl. *Look, I'll admit it. I wasn't the hugest* Knight Rider *fan, but I was pretty sure that KITT's windows never rolled down.* When I brought this up with one of the senior writers, he laughed. "Don't worry about it. It's only *Knight Rider.*" It was then that I knew we were in trouble.

Though the original KITT was a Pontiac Trans Am, the 2008 KITT had become a Ford Shelby GT500KR. Ford was a sponsor of the show and also paid hefty fees to the network for product placement. Usually, with product placement, the company requests that its product be featured in the show in a complimentary way. Sometimes, actors will even say lines that are complimentary to the product, which can veer close to a commercial. I have no issues with any of that since the money the company is paying is very valuable to the budget of the show. Regardless, if the writers don't feel like they can work the product in, they don't. The story takes precedence. In the case of *Knight Rider,* the tail was wagging the dog.

When Ford wanted to show off the Explorer, they called the writers, and *bang!* KITT would morph into an Explorer. When Ford needed to sell vans, KITT turned into a van. When Ford wanted KITT to morph into a pink Mustang (in my episode), I almost walked. *Not on my watch.* Mercifully, they changed their minds and turned KITT into a pickup truck again—personal tragedy averted.

Though most of us were trying hard to make a great show, there was a feeling on set that we weren't making high art. I was shooting a scene in the Knight Industries control room, where there were lots of TV screens with generic diagrams, scrolling numbers, and spy blizz-blazz on them. In front of the screens, model-good-looking actors were arguing, spouting generic tough-guy lines about the fate of the Western world. As I watched, I laughed, and then leaned in to one of the funnier writers on staff. "This show should be called 'Models Talking Tough.'"

CHAPTER 18

Super Troopers 2: Bigger Mustaches and Hopefully
Funnier (or as Funny) Jokes

This won't be popular, but it's my book so I'm going to say it. We're living through what might be the least creative period in American film history. Yes, there are writers and directors who have managed to keep making movies their way: Quentin Tarantino, Martin Scorsese, Richard Linklater, Kathryn Bigelow, Judd Apatow, Catherine Hardwicke, Seth Rogen, Jodi Foster, Todd Phillips, Elizabeth Banks, and more—I know there are plenty more. But if you compare the list of the top ten movies of each of the last three years to the top ten for, say, any three years between 1970 and 1999, it's clear that the American film business has a creativity problem. This problem can be traced to something studio marketing departments consider to be the Holy Grail of modern film promotion, and it's called "unaided awareness."

When a film has "unaided awareness," it means that the audience is either already a fan of the title or is at least aware of the title before the studio has even spent a cent on advertising. *Mission Impossible* was a hit TV show in the sixties and seventies, so when Paramount announced the movie, audiences said, *Oh yeah, we love* Mission Impossible. *It's that spy show with the great theme song that opens with a self-destructing tape.* The movie has fans before the script has even been written. That is unaided awareness.

The other kind of film can only be described as being . . . original. I'm talking about films like *Reservoir Dogs, Lost in Translation, Napoleon Dynamite, Being John Malkovich, Slacker, Dazed and Confused, Kids, City of God, Children of Men, Do the Right Thing, Mo' Better Blues, The Hangover, Old School, Point Break, Rushmore, Bottle Rocket,* and *Super Troopers.* These films had no preexisting fan base to lean on, but they thrived all the same.

When Searchlight bought *Super Troopers,* no one knew what the film was about. Through a great marketing campaign, which included a cool trailer and poster, Fox Searchlight told the audience that our film was about unconventional cops who enforce the law in their own unique way. But audiences had to take a chance. If they chose wrong and the film sucked, they would be out $9. But if they chose right, they would be proud because they would be on the cultural vanguard of their friend group.

Because making and promoting films is so expensive, studios are always looking for ways to mitigate risk. In the nineties, this led to the industry-wide opinion that films with unaided awareness were less risky bets. But this financial strategy became a disease that infected the entire filmmaking organism. Unaided awareness took over and became almost a requirement for green-lighting a movie.

In the seventies and eighties, filmmakers used to complain about how TV writers copied their ideas, making watered-down versions of their films. *Smokey and the Bandit* became *The Dukes of Hazzard*, while *Ferris Bueller's Day Off* became a short-lived TV series. In fact, there's a famous saying that film people use to denigrate TV people: "Imitation is the sincerest form of television." That used to be true, but the film business's thirst for unaided awareness has flipped that equation. Now TV is the place to go for originality.

First the studios raided their TV departments, making movies like *The A-Team, 21 Jump Street, Batman, Starsky & Hutch, The Brady Bunch, Charlie's Angels, Mission Impossible, S.W.A.T.,* and yes, *The Dukes of Hazzard,* to name just a few. When they ran out of TV shows, the studios turned to classic film remakes, like *Dawn of the Dead, War of the Worlds, The Birdcage, The In-Laws, Ocean's Eleven, Charlie and the Chocolate Factory,* and more. I was once approached to remake *Caddyshack.* I told the producers that if I did that, comics in town would hang me from the Hollywood sign. (Frankly, I would pay for the rope.) *You don't repaint the* Mona Lisa. I suggested a new golf comedy, which I had been working on, but the producers demurred. They knew that the studio only wanted a golf comedy with unaided awareness.

Soon the studios turned to toys, with films like *The Lego Movie, Battleship, G.I. Joe, Mars Attacks, Transformers, Teenage Mutant Ninja Turtles,* and *Hot Wheels.* They went for video games, amusement park rides (*Pirates of the Caribbean*), and then, of course, superhero movies—more on that later.

You remember when we read in the financial pages about those major corporations that were buying up movie studios because they wanted a "media piece" for their portfolio? Well, this is the culture clash. As expensive as movies are, they are still inherently creative and artistic ventures. But aside from companies like Apple, which have deep creative streaks, most corporations aren't built to care about creativity or art. They exist to make a profit, and not just a reasonable profit, but the maximum profit. This lust for maximum profit has transformed the film business, which was once the most creatively vibrant moneymaking machine in the world, into what is now feels like just a moneymaking machine.

The problem with the film business is . . . the business.

I'm going to tell you a story about a conversation I had with a friend of mine who used to run one of the major studios. We were in his office talking about what movies we could make together, when my friend said he (his company) needed $100 million comedies, starring any two of the guys on a short list: Johnny Depp, Ben Stiller, Vince Vaughn, Will Ferrell, Mark Wahlberg. That was the *whole* list. They didn't want comedies with anybody else. To back this up, his company would pay the stars $20 million each, which would leave us with $60 million to make the movie. *Sounds like a good plan, right?* Here's the problem. The five guys on the list had stacks of $20 million offers from each of the major studios that were already sitting on their agents' desks. The wait for these actors to read a script ranged from three months to never. Worse still, often, the script would get pre-rejected by a manager or agent who had a financial interest in pushing their client toward a different film. Okay, but let's say a miracle happens, and one of these stars actually agrees to act in your film. Since these actors are booked for the next two years, you had better get ready to wait.

But since I was talking to the head of a studio, I swallowed my cynicism and said, "Great, let's do that. I'll write big-concept, two-hander comedies and we'll attempt to cast guys off of this list. However, while we're going down that road, why don't we make five $20 million comedies. We'll find big-concept, R-rated scripts, and we'll hire hip, young, funny comics to star in them." (I had my own list.) "That way, we'll take a couple of chances, we'll make some great movies, create some new stars, *and* we'll make some money."

My friend leaned back in his chair. "What's the most one of those movies can make?"

"A hundred million dollars," I said with reasonable confidence. They won't all make that, but I bet one or two out of five will. And the rest will make a decent profit or at least break even.

Then my friend shook his head and said six words that I think crystallize the problem with today's movie business: "A hundred million is a double."

I wasn't quite sure what I was hearing. "How can a hundred million be a double? With that huge profit, isn't it a home run?"

Then my friend explained the birds and the bees. "Look, *we* like the same kinds of movies. I would love to make smaller, more interesting films, but I have fifty people working in my marketing department. Whether they're working on a $100 million comedy with massive stars or a $20 million comedy with up-and-comers, they're working the same hours. As a company, we need to maximize the financial return on their effort. Your $20 million film that maxes out at $100 million is a double. I need grand slams. I need films that can gross $250 to $400 million. I need grosses that can move the stock price."

This need for maximum profit has made the $12 to $50 million movie a risk not worth taking. And $12 to $50 million is the exact budget level where most of the great movies are made. I'm talking about films like *Kramer vs. Kramer, Hoosiers, Breaking Away, The Godfather, Being John Malkovich, Dazed and Confused, Heathers, Flirting with Disaster, Clueless, On Golden Pond, This Is Spinal Tap, Stand by Me, When Harry Met Sally.* I'm not talking about art house. I'm talking about *The Player, 48 Hrs., Beverly Hills Cop, The Hangover, Beerfest, The Outsiders, Borat, Bridesmaids, Knocked Up, Old School, Animal House, The Blues Brothers, Trading Places, Midnight Run, Slap Shot* . . . I could keep going. The idea factory that was the American film business from the seventies through the late nineties can't function if the expectations on each film are that it make $250 to $400 million or be judged a financial failure. Corporations bought film companies, in part, because they were "fun investments." But when corporations took control of the studios, they took all the fun out of them by forcing film presidents to hit incredibly high profit targets. And if you're going to take the risk and the fun out of the movie business, you might as well put your money into something safer, like doorstops.

Now, to be clear, I'm not deluded. Studios need to make block-buster movies to survive. Marvel is making great movies that are fun, funny, and technologically groundbreaking, and they're making a financial killing. (I've interviewed for a couple of them, and I'm still interested.) There are a lot of great movies with unaided awareness that I love, including *Deadpool, Star Trek, Iron Man,* and *Pirates of the Caribbean.* Man, *Pirates* is a great movie, and it rivals *Raiders of the Lost Ark* in quality. But in the end, *Raiders* wins because it's based on an original idea, not a Disney ride.

The point is this: Blockbusters are great, but they can't be *the whole* film business. The old deal was that studios made money on blockbusters so that they could afford to take chances on high-minded dramas and envelope-pushing comedies. But the balance has shifted so brutally in favor of the blockbuster that the smaller films have mostly been abandoned. And I know what people in the business will say: *Hey, the audiences are speaking with their pocketbooks. They want splash, spectacle, and special effects if they're going to go to the theater. They don't want to go to midrange films anymore. Those films are for Fox Searchlight, Netflix, and Amazon to make. The audience has spoken and they just want superhero movies.*

Bullshit. We've conditioned the audience to be that way, and we can condition them back. If we make and promote these midlevel movies, people will go again. We need to decouple a film's box office gross from its perceived quality. We need to stop printing our grosses in the newspaper. How much money a movie makes is *our* business, not the audience's, and they shouldn't be judging a movie based on that. Humans love stories, both big and small. And there is no reason why we should give up the notion that audiences still want to see great, original, human films on big screens.

Today, if a movie makes a small profit, it's a failure. That's not us. That's not who we are. Obviously, we all want to make a profit, but everything doesn't need to be a grand slam.

So, my dear corporations, make your grand-slam profits on some movies, and also on computers, phones, cars, and insurance. But get back to making the $20 to $50 million theatrical film that makes enough of a profit. Do that, and there will be a creative rebirth that will propel a whole new generation of maverick filmmakers.

But I'm not naïve. Asking a drunk to give up booze is a waste of time. So maybe the bartender can help:

Dear Audience,

Aren't you tired of the same old slate of movies we're releasing? Stop rewarding us for only making classic film remakes and movies about toys, video games, and superheroes. Start rewarding us for making original, medium-size movies again. Only you can save the movie business.

Which brings me, finally, to *Super Troopers 2*. A little background: *Super Troopers 2* has unaided awareness thanks to the huge fan base devoted to the original film. *Super Troopers 2* feels like a good financial bet since the original film, which was made for $1.2 million, made Fox about $80 to $90 million in profit. So it's a no-brainer for Fox to fund the sequel, right? Not exactly.

I wasn't privy to their internal conversations, but maybe they went something like this:

"*Hmm, Super Troopers 2?* Do you think we could get Broken Lizard to transform the Super Troopers into superheroes? I'm thinking cops with capes. Hell, I'd love to see Farva in tights. We'd definitely make that movie."

Okay, to be totally honest, there were lengthy discussions. For a while, Fox was going to pay for the whole movie, then half, then none. Searchlight agreed to *release* the sequel, but they asked us to find the money, for both production and advertising. And, so we're clear, I'm not mad or bitter, because it's just business. Searchlight is the best small-film distributor in showbiz and they don't give up their distribution slots to just anyone. I love Searchlight because they took a chance on us and made *Super Troopers* a hit. They're exactly the kind of film company that needs our support because they are holding the line on the quality-film business. And to be clear, they believe in *Super Troopers 2*. They own the rights to the sequel and could have just buried the film if they wanted to. Giving us a distribution slot and letting us find the money was a huge give, considering the current state of film economics. They didn't pass on funding the film because they thought it wouldn't make a profit. They passed on funding the film because they were worried that it wouldn't make *enough of a profit*.

Knowing that we had to raise a lot of money, we went to our fans first. We partnered with the crowdfunding site Indiegogo and crowdfunding guru Ivan Askwith to craft just the right message. Then we grew some mustaches, pulled our uniforms out of storage, and shot some funny videos.

Now it was time to roll the dice on what was looking like an enormously risky bet. Because if our fans didn't respond to the campaign, it would be a message to both Hollywood and the investor community that no one actually wanted to see the sequel. As the time ticked down to launch our crowdfunding campaign, we were all noticeably worried. But when we finally pressed the button to launch, our fans responded, and big-time. The money raise got off to a fast start, and then took off like a rocket. Within twenty-four hours, our fans had "donated" more than $2 million. The remaining twenty-nine days felt like a political campaign. Every day, we launched new videos. Some were pretaped sketches and some were direct appeals to the audience. We gave away cool perks, like limited-edition T-shirts, posters, movie tickets to the sequel, and the right to play beer pong against us in a *Beerfest* tournament. There were also some crazier perks, like for $25 million, one of us would donate sperm to father your child. (No one bought that.) Every day was fun, and it was a thrill to sit by the computer and watch the love roll in. By the end of the month, we had raised more than $4.5 million from more than fifty thousand people, breaking the Indiegogo record for feature film campaigns.

As much as the money from the campaign was incredibly important to our production, the fan response was equally so, because it sent a message that there was an audience out there waiting for this movie. So when we went to the independent-film investor community to raise the substantial rest of the budget, the fact that fifty thousand people had already backed the film made that process just a little bit easier. The success of the campaign also gave Searchlight confidence that when it comes time to promote the film, there will be a rabid and ready audience.

Now, before you start screaming that *Super Troopers 2* isn't original (it's a sequel), I'll grant you that. But know this. *Super Troopers 2* is an independently financed film, so we had enormous creative control. We came up with a hilarious story, and we wrote thirty-three drafts of the script.

We just got back from Boston, where we finally finished the shoot. Man, it went well. We got great performances from Rob Lowe, Brian Cox, Will Sasso, Tyler Labine, Hayes MacArthur, Emmanuelle Chriqui, and a couple of secret others. I told all the Lizards that I would only make the movie if we all weighed the same as we did for the original. And we all did. So, folks, you may be able to say we're older, but you won't be able to say we're fatter and older. Ha! We're about to start the editing process, and I'm cautiously optimistic. *Very* optimistic. If we can match the tone and the jokes of the first film, I feel confident that we're going to make a movie that will merit being mentioned in the same breath as the original. Let's hope we're right.

One last thing: Please, go to the theaters and watch this movie.

Super Troopers 2 needs to do well, theatrically. Watching it on home video or Netflix is great, but studios don't respect it the same way. So, all you stoners, get in your car, drive to the theater, smoke your joint (safely) in the parking lot, buy a ticket, and go watch the film. If enough of you do that, I promise the wait for *Super Troopers 3: Civil War,* will be much, much shorter. (And yes, we'll fucking make *Pot-fest* too.)

ACKNOWLEDGMENTS

Thanks to my wife for sharpening my wit and for supporting me in this career that allows me to stay a kid.

And thanks to my kids, who are endless fountains of hilarity.

And thanks to my agent, Byrd Leavell, who has been a great ally throughout this new process.

And thanks to my editor, Jill Schwartzman, who was enormously helpful in making this into a coherent tale.